The Dutch Diaspora

The Dutch Diaspora

Growing Up Dutch in New Worlds and the Old

The Netherlands and Its Settlements in Africa, Asia, and the Americas

Howard J. Wiarda

LEXINGTON BOOKS

A division of
ROWMAN & LITTLEFIELD PUBLISHERS, INC.
Lanham • Boulder • New York • Toronto • Plymouth, UK

LEXINGTON BOOKS

A division of Rowman & Littlefield Publishers, Inc.
A wholly owned subsidary of The Rowman & Littlefield Publishing Group, Inc.
4501 Forbes Boulevard, Suite 200
Lanham, MD 20706

Estover Road
Plymouth PL6 7PY
United Kingdom

British Library Cataloguing in Publication Information Available

Library of Congress Cataloging-in-Publication Data

Wiarda, Howard J., 1939-
   The Dutch diaspora : the Netherlands and its settlements in Africa, Asia, and the
Americas / Howard J. Wiarda.
      p. cm.
   ISBN-13: 978-0-7391-2104-7 (cloth : alk. paper)
   ISBN-10: 0-7391-2104-9 (cloth : alk. paper)
   ISBN-13: 978-0-7391-2105-4 (pbk. : alk. paper)
   ISBN-10: 0-7391-2105-7 (pbk. : alk. paper)
   1. Netherlands—Colonies. 2. Dutch—Foreign countries. I. Title.
   JV2527.W53 2007
   325'.2492—dc22   2007016702

Printed in the United States of America

⊗™ The paper used in this publication meets the minimum requirements of
American National Standard for Information Sciences—Permanence of Paper
for Printed Library Materials, ANSI/NISO Z39.48-1992.

Table of Contents

Preface

My unusual name, Wiarda, is Dutch (though I've often been asked if it is Italian, Polish, or something else). I grew up in Grand Rapids, Michigan, a city that is referred to in those parts of the country as the Dutch "Zion," and in the bosom of the Dutch Reformed Church. All four of my grandparents were Dutch immigrants to Western Michigan in the 1880s, part of that great wave of immigration in the late nineteenth century that brought millions of Germans, Italians, Poles, Irish, as well as Dutch and others to America. I attended Dutch Reformed schools from kindergarten through high school, memorized the canons of Dordt and the Heidelberg Catechism as a young catechumen, and grew from boyhood into adolescence in an environment where all my friends were Dutch. I'm about as Dutch or Dutch-American as one can be. And I've always been interested in my Dutch roots.

But when I went off to university, I broke for a time with this strongly Dutch and Calvinist tradition. For a person of my background and upbringing, it was expected that I would go to Calvin College—the Dutch Reformed denomination's college, in Grand Rapids. Calvin is religiously affiliated; it is also a fine college and rates highly in the annual *U.S. News and World Report* survey of colleges. But I remember coming home one day my senior year in high school and announcing to my parents that, instead of Calvin, I wanted to attend the University of Michigan in Ann Arbor. I was not then a rebel against my church, my family, or my upbringing; I just thought that at the University of Michigan, which along with Berkeley is one of the great public universities in the United States, I would get a bet-ter education. Much to my surprise, and though I'm sure my parents had strong doubts about it, they acquiesced in the decision. And so, off to Ann Arbor I went, as a very young (seventeen), naive, and inexperienced kid, in the fall of 1957.

The University of Michigan was an eye-opener for me and it changed my life. It was so intellectual, the social life so strenuous, and the competition from the other students so intense that I almost got lost in the crowd. Fortu-nately I recovered, both my grades and my center of gravity, and went on to post an excellent academic record, worked as a writer for *The Michigan Daily*, a really good student newspaper, and learned and absorbed the culture, poli-tics, and sophistication of a major secular university community. I then went off to graduate school to earn an M.A. and Ph.D. and to begin an academic career dedicated to teaching and research. For a time in the secular world of American academic life, I forgot about, neglected, and at some levels even rejected my Dutch roots.

But it was precisely my academic and research interests that brought me back to things Dutch and the Dutch Diaspora. As a young scholar living in Europe in the early 1970s, my family and I visited The Netherlands for the first time, and then went back for several subsequent visits. I was fascinated by both the similarities and the differences between The Netherlands and my own Dutch (and Calvinist) background in Western Michigan. Later research projects brought me, rather fortuitously, to such former Dutch enclaves, colonies, or settlements as Curaçao, Suriname, South Africa, Japan, For-mosa, India, and Indonesia. I lived for a time in Geneva and Hungary, both at one time Calvinist centers and sanctuaries before the onset of the Counter-Reformation. And in the United States I explored such originally Dutch settlements as Lewes, Delaware; Paterson, New Jersey; and Pella, Iowa; to say nothing of New Amsterdam (New York City). In the process I rediscovered my history and my origins.

This book started off as a journey of discovery, research, and explo-ration. Quite frankly, I saw it as a way to get to a number of countries and areas—India, South Africa, Indonesia, Suriname, among others—that I'd not been to previously and in which I had little prior research interest. However, it ended not only as a fascinating exploration of new countries and new continents but also as a journey of self-discovery. The book is mainly about the Dutch countries and (mainly former) colonies I've been to but it's also about me as a Dutch kid growing up in a Dutch community and my efforts to understand my own culture, where I came from, why I am as I am, how my community and I differ from other ethnic communities. For, in my travels I found I was constantly comparing, contrasting, evaluating my upbringing in the Dutch community in Western Michigan with other Dutch communities throughout the world, and ultimately with The Netherlands itself. You will learn a lot in these pages about The Netherlands and its far-flung colonial empire, and how these colonial outposts have evolved, stayed the same, or changed over the centuries. For good or ill in these pages, you'll also see a process at work of rediscovery of my own history and origins.

This book tells the story of that history. It goes back into Dutch history to relate the chronicle of a proud people, never conquered by Roman legions, battling over the centuries against storms and the sea, struggling against much bigger powers for its independence, and eventually emerging as one of the most tolerant, prosperous, progressive, but also now troubled societies on earth. It tells the stories of the Dutch enclaves in those places already mentioned and what has happened to them sociologically, politically, culturally, and religiously over the centuries since the emergence of The Netherlands as a global power in the seventeenth century. And in the process, because this is also a personal book at some levels, it tells the story of what it means to be Dutch, or to grow up Dutch, or to be part of a Dutch heritage, in all its contemporary varieties, in these very different places in the world.

In all these Dutch communities, Calvinism was a powerful initial influence. But this is not a book about Calvinism per se as a body of religious beliefs, nor about the truthfulness or ongoing validity of those beliefs. Attentive readers will find that I have mixed feelings about my Calvinist past, even while recognizing I am indelibly shaped by that past whether I wish it or not. Rather, this book is about the impact of Calvinism and the Dutch tradition on society and politics, and about the countries and societies that were—like me—powerfully influenced by that tradition.

There is theory and social science here, however, as well as history and a personal story. For in my global meanderings among the Dutch "tribes" in various parts of the world, I came to a renewed appreciation of a thesis originally set forth by Harvard University historian Louis Hartz. In focusing on what he called "the founding of new societies," Hartz argued that colonies that the European powers (Spain, Portugal, Great Britain, France, The Netherlands) established in different parts of the world (Australia, Canada, Latin America, South Africa, the United States) tended to reflect the nature of the mother countries *at the time of the colonization.* Thereafter, colonies and mother countries went their separate ways, but the colonies, often existing in colonial isolation, tended to remain locked into the institutions and cultures of the founding period. Thus, Latin

America reflected—and continues to do so—fifteenth- and sixteenth-century Spain and Portugal, South Africa reflected—and under apartheid continued to do so—the Calvinist Netherlands of the seventeenth century, the United States reflected in significant part liberalizing Great Britain of the seventeenth and eighteenth centuries, and so on.

In other words, although they were born of a common colonial experience, colonies and mother countries immediately began to go their separate ways, to evolve in different directions. But while the European mother countries evolved in accord with the general directions of European culture, and civilization, their colonies throughout the world, existing often in not-so-splendid isolation, tended to remain locked into the sociology, culture, and religion in which they were born. Thus, Latin America continued with feudalism and as a product of the Middle Ages, South Africa (and this is an explanation for the apartheid regime) remained a fragment of primitive Dutch Calvinism of the seventeenth century, and my own Dutch enclave in Western Michigan reflected and reinforced the splits in the official Dutch Reformed Church of the nineteenth century.

This thesis is explained more fully and elaborated in chapter 1. For not only did these colonies continue to reflect the time period in which they were settled but, if we know the dates of their original and main settlement (feudal or modern, pre-French Revolution or post-French Revolution, sixteenth, seventeenth, eighteenth, nineteenth, or twentieth centuries), it already tells us a lot about their sociology and political culture. And about how they would evolve and adjust or fail to evolve and adjust.

Much of this travel, especially in the early years, was undertaken with my family. Three of my family members (wife Iêda and two of our children) were born abroad; all of us have grown up in an international, what we would now call a multicultural, diverse, and globalized world. While all of this travel was stimulating, not all of it was always comfortable or easy for the family. So many thanks to Iêda, Kristy, Howard E., and Jonathan. I know it was sometimes difficult to be away from home, friends, and school, but I hope we are all better people for the experiences we've had abroad. This book is dedicated to you; I also hope it helps you understand where we come from, who we are, and the life that we've led. For at one level this is a serious, scholarly account but at another it is also a personal and family journey.

Thanks also go to Doris Holden who has not only been my excellent typist, editor, and word processor for thirty years (the first book she did for me was *Corporatism and Development* in 1977), but also our good friend and collaborator on many projects. Iêda Siqueira Wiarda and our three children shared many of these journeys with me and were indispensable helpers. Perhaps my grandchildren—Kirk, Gabrielle, and Grant—will find something of their roots in this book as well.

H. J. W.
Bonita Hills
Athens, Georgia

CHAPTER ONE

Introduction: The Dutch and Their Colonial Fragments

Harvard historian and political scientist Louis Hartz wrote a famous book a half century ago titled *The Liberal Tradition in America*.[1] In it Hartz argued that the United States was unique among nations in that we had been "born free" (like the lion in Joy Adamson's book, *Born Free*); that is, liberal and without a feudal past.

Lacking a "feudal" past (except perhaps in the pre-Civil War South), the United States had begun life as a liberal, representative, democratic nation and had always maintained its affinity to liberal principles. By "liberal" Hartz meant an adherence to electoral politics and representative rule; in this sense, as distinct from its current ideological usage, the liberal label encompassed everyone from Jimmy Carter to Ronald Reagan, from Bill Clinton to George W. Bush. And because we had no feudalism or a traditionalist past, Hartz went on, we never had socialism either and, in contrast to Europe, never had a real tug-of-war between extreme left and extreme right. Instead, a "liberal tradition"—centrist, moderate, representative, and middle-of-the-road—remained in control for most of American history.[2]

I was particularly taken by Hartz's thesis, first, because it conformed to my own peaceful, happy, middle-of-the-road upbringing in Western Michigan and, second, because the area I initially studied as a young scholar, Latin America, was just the opposite of what Hartz portrayed. Discovered, settled, and colonized for almost a whole century—1492 to roughly 1570—before the North American colonies, Latin America, because of the historic legacy of Spanish and Portuguese influence, *did* have a feudal part. Latin America, in contrast to the United States, was feudal and medieval in terms of its founding principles of authoritarianism and hierarchy in the political sphere, had a two-class and caste society, mercantile economy, religious orthodoxy and monism, and a deductive system of reasoning based on revealed truth. Founded on a quasi-feudal basis, Latin America never developed the majority centrist liberal tradition as did the United States and, again in contrast to the United States, its politics have always been conflictual and driven by extremes.[3]

A few years after *The Liberal Tradition in America* Hartz published a second, edited book, *The Founding of New Societies*,[4] in which he expanded his analysis to new areas: Australia, Canada, Latin America, South Africa—all, or almost all, the areas reached by European settlement and colonization in earlier centuries. I found Hartz's analysis particularly useful in my efforts to try to understand the Dutch—and my own roots and history—and the various settlements or colonies they had set down in various parts of the world. These included, among others, Brazil, Suriname, Curaçao, New Amsterdam, South Africa, Indonesia, and, of course, Grand Rapids.

Hartz argued that all these and other enclaves—all the results of European colonialism and imperialism from the fifteenth century on—represented "fragments" of European civilization at different points in time. All of these fragments had been settled and colonized during a period when Europe was beginning, and then during various stages of its journeys toward modernization and into the modern world. All these fragments remained European in their core and essence, but they were reflections of Europe at different points in time: Latin America, a product of Spain and Portugal of the fifteenth and sixteenth centuries; South Africa, a product of Holland of the seventeenth century; the United States, a product of England of the seventeenth and eighteenth centuries; Canada, a product of both France and England; Australia, an offshoot of England of the early nineteenth century; and Western Michigan, a Dutch enclave of the mid-nineteenth century.

Once established, two things happened to these European fragments set down in new lands. First, they came in contact with and began to adapt to the new lands and peoples where they found themselves. That included adaptations to temperatures, rainfall, climate, terrain, location, and geography, as well as indigenous peoples. Life in the tropics (Brazil, Indonesia, Latin America), for example, would imply a different response and different socioeconomic conditions, than life in more temperate (North America, South Africa, Japan) regions. These adaptations would also imply miscegenation or mixing with the native or indigenous populations, again in different patterns: Latin America was viewed by Spain as a military conquest so families were not brought along and there was extensive miscegenation (and over time little racial prejudice), whereas North America was settled mainly by families; therefore, little miscegenation but much racial prejudice.

The other thing that happened in these European fragments is that, once colonized and settled, they became increasingly cast off from the main-streams of culture and civilization back in the European core. They reflected the European epochs in which they were founded, but then they failed to continue to evolve in the same ways as did Europe as a whole. They tended to become very conservative, seeking to preserve the foundations of Euro-pean civilization on which they were based but failing to move on. In part, this was a defensive action to maintain the sometimes-weak ties to Europe that the difficulties of distance and slow transportation in those centuries oc-casioned. In part, also, the conservatism of the colonies was a response to the threat, real or perceived, that came from the indigenous populations in these places who often far outnumbered the Europeans. Think of the Spanish in Latin America, the Dutch in South Africa or Indonesia, the British in India or Kenya. In each of these cases the Europeans were outnumbered by ratios of thousands or even hundreds of thousands to one. Small wonder that these often-frightened, sometimes-besieged "white tribes" would become so con-servative, often ultra-reactionary (as with the Dutch in South Africa) and would try to hang onto their increasingly fragile European cultures, politics, and sociology at all costs.

In the case of the Dutch in Western Michigan (my own "white tribe"), there was an added complication. For not only was there still the danger of hostile Indian attacks as well as extremely harsh local living conditions (leaky mud huts as homes, severe winters, disease, poor soils), but there was also a religious component. In part at least, the Dutch in Western Michigan had come to the New World fleeing religious persecution or the fear thereof back in The Netherlands. But in the New World they would face the in-credible pressures toward pluralism, Americanization, and secularism that is the United States. Thus, in trying to maintain the purity of their Dutch Calvinism in the face of pressures all around leading to assimilation, the Dutch colony became very conservative, indeed a bastion of Republican conservatism and even reaction in a state becoming increasingly liberal. And far more conservative and locked-in-place than either The Netherlands itself or the Reformed Church back in the mother country.

But Hartz had something more interesting in mind than just his notions of European fragments cast out and isolated in various colonial settings. He wanted to be able to predict, based on the century or period of their initial discovery and colonization, which, recall, locked them into that period and turned them quite conservative, what these different colonies founded in different historical eras would look like. Thus, he argued that Latin America and French Canada founded on an early sixteenth-century basis would retain many feudal characteristics into the modern era. South Africa, with its powerful Dutch Calvinism from the seventeenth century and outnumbered in such great ratios by blacks, would prove reactionary and self-destructive.

In contrast, the United States and British Canada, products of the seventeenth and eighteenth centuries, would be bourgeois—products of the Enlightenment, liberal, and progressive. Australia and British South Africa, strongly influenced by the proletarian upheavals of the Industrial Revolution, would be more radical than the earlier fragments. Whereas Indonesia of the mid-nineteenth century, born at the height of European colonialism in Asia and Africa, and my own settlement in Western Michigan, inspired by the desire for Calvinist purity apart from the mother country's increasing liberalism, would both be quite conservative. One more "fragment" that has been added to this story also forms part of the narrative related in this book: When a new wave of Dutch Reformed settlers from The Netherlands came to Western Michigan and Canada following World War II, they had by then been socialized in the mother country's policies of social democracy and tolerance for everything and everyone, and their politics would be very different from that of the earlier, still conservative Dutch Calvinist settlers who had been there for a hundred years.

The Hartz analysis is useful here in this book because it so closely fits my own research findings in the various Dutch "fragments" that I have visited and studied. Whereas Hartz focused on the several colonial powers (Spain, Portugal, Great Britain, France, The Netherlands) and the quite distinct settlements they established at different times in different parts of the world, our focus here is only on The Netherlands and its colonies. But the Hartz thesis continues to be useful in dealing only with a single country because its colonies or fragments were similarly set down at different times and in different historical epochs. Thus, the Dutch colony of New Amsterdam is very different from that of South Africa; the one of Indonesia, very different from that of Western Michigan.

It is not our purpose here to reify the Hartz thesis; it has its limitations just like most theories and it does not fit all our cases. Moreover, it does not explain everything: why, for example, Suriname became a plantation colony (rather like Indonesia), whereas Curaçao, Japan, and New Amsterdam became commercial or trading centers. All these variables and differences will have to be dealt with as we explore the various Dutch colonies, outposts, and "fragments." But the Hartz analysis gives me a set of good working hypotheses to begin our study and a body of theory and interpretation to both utilize initially to frame our exploration and, eventually, to challenge or modify as new facts and information are revealed. That is all that any theory is supposed to do.

The Book: A Look Ahead

This book generally follows a chronological history, modified somewhat by the fact it is also *my* chronological history and *my* own journey of discovery in and to these Dutch enclaves. Chapter 2 explores the historical and cultural background of The Netherlands—what is unique in that background and why that country is so singular in its accomplishments. Chapter 3 chronicles my own history—what it's like to "grow up Dutch" within a Dutch community and within the Dutch Reformed tradition. Chapter 4 then talks about the modern Netherlands and my encounter, as a Dutch kid from Grand Rapids, with what I thought were my roots and the various surprises I was in for as I traveled to The Netherlands for the first time.

In Chapter 5 we begin to explore the far-flung Dutch diaspora and its varying characteristics. We start off with treatment of the Dutch colonial experiences in Brazil, Suriname, and the Caribbean. Chapter 6 deals with the important role of Dutch New Amsterdam (Manhattan) in shaping the American experience and the evolution of what we in Western Michigan call the "East Coast" or "Hudson River" Dutch.

Chapter 7 reports on a remarkable trip that I took around East Asia and my discovery of the Dutch role in Japan, Formosa, and Ceylon. Chapter 8 continues that same trip but now in Indonesia, once the crown jewel of the Dutch colonial empire. Chapter 9 relates an equally remarkable trip I took to South Africa and my research into the Afrikaner community and what has happened to them since the end of apartheid.

Chapters 10 and 11 take a slightly different tack, focusing not on the Dutch per se but on two places where I have lived and worked and which, at one point, were hotbeds of Calvinist influence—as was The Netherlands itself. That is why I feel a special affinity for them and have included a treatment of them in this book. These are Geneva (treated in chapter 10), where Calvin took refuge, lived, worked, and emerged triumphant and where, four-and-a-half centuries later, I sought to discover how much Calvinist influence was still present and whether I had roots there as well. And the Austro-Hungarian empire (I lived in both Vienna and Budapest for a time), analyzed in chapter 11, which was once 80 percent Calvinist before the Catholic Counter-Reformation reversed that ratio and changed the history of all of Central Europe.

Chapter 12, the Conclusion, returns to the themes of this Introduction in an effort to assess the merits of the "fragments" thesis, analyzes comparatively the varied Dutch enclaves throughout the world and their separate futures, talks about the roots *and branches* of Dutch history, and maps out future journeys and research terrains.

It is a fascinating journey. I hope you will come along.

Notes

1. Louis Hartz, *The Liberal Tradition in America* (New York: Harcourt, Brace, 1957).

2. Hartz was criticized for understating conflict in American history, for ignoring the influence of progressive groups in pushing for change, and for downplaying such wrenching experiences as the Civil War. Nevertheless, his thesis still holds and has withstood the tests of time.

3. Howard J. Wiarda, *The Soul of Latin America: The Cultural and Political Tradition* (New Haven: Yale University Press, 2001).

4. Louis Hartz, ed., *The Founding of New Societies* (New York: Harcourt, Brace, 1964).

CHAPTER TWO

The Netherlands:
A Proud History and Culture

The Netherlands is one of the most affluent, contented, most progressive—but now also deeply troubled—nations on earth. Even though it is a small country of only sixteen million, its economy ranked fourteenth among the two-hundred-odd nations of the world in terms of GNP and at or near the top in per capita income. Its businessmen and political leaders are disproportionately way over-represented in global banking, trade, and international leadership positions; Rotterdam is the world's biggest port, a gateway to Europe. Dutch social programs on aging, drugs, AIDS, prostitution, multiculturalism, homosexuality, and euthanasia are among the most progressive in the world—some would say too progressive. The Netherlands prides itself on its tolerance and its global leadership; it is one of the world's most successful countries. The Dutch are very proud of their small but very intimate (12,883 square miles) and progressive country—some would say their pride sometimes verges on arrogance.

All this and much more has been accomplished in a country that has almost no resources except its people and their talents and, at least historically, hard work and a resolute Calvinist work ethic. After all, most of the country is below sea level; for *all* of their history the Dutch have been battling against the winds, ferocious storms, and salt water that blow in from the tempestuous North Sea and inundate their country, killing people and cattle and, because of the salt, ruining their agriculture.[1] It is a country whose history was forged in challenge and against all odds of success—against the elements and against its much larger and more powerful neighbors: Spain, Great Britain,

France, Germany. The Dutch are very proud of their accomplishments and of the fact they have not only survived but also thrived in this sometimes rough neighborhood by turning their disadvantages into advantages.

And yet, today The Netherlands is a deeply troubled country. It seems at various levels to have lost its way. It has largely abandoned its earlier Calvinism, but the very passion and enthusiasm with which it embraces secularism seems almost Calvinistic in their intensity. It prides itself on its tolerance, but it is intolerant of those less tolerant than itself and expresses this with an intensity that is almost Calvinistic. Similar is true with its progressive policies: the Dutch are very proud of these and embrace them with a sense of moral superiority and ethical calling that is positively Calvinistic in its fervor. More recently the Dutch have embraced multiculturalism and diversity with the same Calvinistic intensity that they embrace other progressive causes; but the recent ritual murder/assassination of anti-Muslim Dutch film maker Theo Van Gogh (a distant relative of the famous, one-eared painter—more Calvinist intensity?), killed by an Arab immigrant who spoke Dutch and *was* assimilated, has severely shaken the Dutch faith in this, its latest piety, as well.

In this chapter we trace the history of the Dutch nation and culture. Our goal is not to provide a complete and detailed history but to try to understand how the country became what it is today and its relevance for the story told here. The discussion is, perforce, brief, and interpretive.

The Dutch Background

Little is known of the prehistoric peoples of The Netherlands. Because so much of the country is low-lying, under water, or waterlogged, it has no early cave paintings as in Spain at Altamira or in France at Lascaux; nor is there much in the way of artifacts or archeological record. In the area where my ancestors came from, Friesland, in the far north of the country across the Zuider Zee, there are mounds called *terpen* built to hold back the sea from the houses built on them which doubled as burial grounds; and in Drenthe there are headstones over ancient tombs (*hunebeds*) stretching across a low ridge. But none of them tells much about the ancient peoples of the area.

The Netherlands is so wet and watery that in my family, in the absence of much in the way of written or archeological evidence, there are a lot of half-baked myths and stories about how we emerged from this landscape. Today, the Dutch countryside, drained and protected by earthen barriers and elaborate systems of water controls, looks quite dry and civilized, but in early times it was wet, wild, barren, and often under water. These wet areas are called *polders*; the fog and vapors that rise from them are referred to as the *pold-*

ergeist. The family stories have it that is how the Wiardas emerged as well, not carried by storks as in much of Europe but arising, in some primitive form (as in a Hollywood horror movie) directly out of the *poldergeist,* a vague and distant vision or apparition in the mist, or maybe like frogs emerging from pollywogs in the primordial slime. I cannot vouch for the accuracy of this Darwinian account of how we Fresians originated.

Once we get into the Roman period of two thousand years ago, the picture becomes a little clearer. As Caesar was conquering Gaul in approximately 50 BC, he found three main tribal groups living in the far northern fringes of the empire in what we often call the Low Countries. The southernmost of these were called the Belgae (after whom the country of Belgium would be named) and they were conquered by Rome and incorporated in the empire. But the other two groups, the Batavi in the southern Netherlands and the Fresians in the north, were never conquered by Rome. One of Rembrandt's great paintings shows the resistance of the so-called Batavian Republic to Rome;[2] the Fresians were considered so fierce and warlike and their swampy, riverine sanctuaries so difficult to penetrate that Rome was unable to conquer them as well. The family mythology has it that it was our fierce resistance that kept the Romans out, but an alternative explanation is that these waterlogged lands were so worthless that the Romans didn't want them.

Without Roman law, language, roads, or political organization, the land that is now The Netherlands remained a wild and uncivilized place. It was beyond the dividing line (the Rhine River) that separated civilization from barbarism. In 50 AD in a famous and oft-quoted characterization, the Roman historian Pliny wrote, "Here a *wretched race* is found, inhabiting either the more elevated spots or artificial mounds. . . . When the waves cover the surrounding area, they are like so many mariners on board a ship, and when again the tide recedes their condition is that of so many shipwrecked men."

Rome occupied Belgium for five hundred years and brought civilization there, but the situation in The Netherlands remained confused and disorganized. As the Roman order collapsed, German tribes, such as the Franks and Saxons, moved into the area of Belgium as well as the southern Netherlands. Meanwhile, my ancestors, the Fresians, living in the most remote area of the country, clung to the coast along the North Sea.

In the fifth century AD the Frankish King Clovis was converted to Christianity, and the Christian faith (and civilization) gradually spread north. But civilization did not yet extend as far north as Friesland. When the Catholic missionary St. Boniface finally ventured into Friesland in the 750s, he was killed by the Fresians in what turned out to be the last act of pagan independence and resistance. A family story has it that we ate him.

Within the next few decades, however, The Netherlands was largely pacified and Christianized under Charlemagne whose empire stretched all the way north to Denmark and who in 800 AD was also crowned Holy Roman Emperor. But whether under French kings or German emperors, their control over The Netherlands was largely nominal; real power still rested in the hands of local notables who largely operated autonomously and gradually brought a degree of stability, progress, and civilization to the area.

Dutch "feudalism," if it may be called that, was never so rigid or complete as it was in France and other areas. The nature of the Dutch landscape, the frequent floods, the small, often self-sufficient farms, and the "wild and wooly" interior ruled out the strict regimentation of society along feudal lines. Dutch citizens had to make do with the meager resources they had; here we may have the origins of the Dutch self-sufficiency and entrepreneurship that would be so prominent in later centuries. Meanwhile, from about the twelfth century AD, independent towns began to grow (Flanders, Ghent, Rotterdam, Amsterdam) which, based on trade and taking advantage of the Low Countries' location at the headwaters of some of Europe's main river systems, began to bring prosperity as well as art and culture to the area. These and other northern Netherlands' towns were incorporated at various levels into the Baltic-centered Hanseatic League which brought added prosperity.

The expansion of trade and commerce and the need for a settled and productive countryside to go with them helped provide the impetus for the Dutch to control their treacherous coasts and the devastating flooding that periodically inundated large areas of the national territory. This would prove to be a centuries-long project that is still going forward today, mainly in the effort to drain the Zuider Zee and turn it into productive farmland. Imagine how difficult and labor-intensive those efforts would be in the earlier centuries before the development of modern, earth-moving equipment. Everything had to be dug and filled by hand.

This massive national effort was multi-pronged, yet also coordinated; and it gave rise to some of the earliest stirrings of the Dutch work ethic, pride, and nationalism. It involved, among other things, the draining of swampy areas, efforts to control flooding along the main river systems, the erection of gigantic berms to keep out North Sea storms, desalinization of farm areas, and the building of dikes and canals throughout the country to control the water and at the time increase both agricultural and city (look at Amsterdam with its alternating streets and canals) land. These efforts gave rise to some of the great heroic epics of Dutch literature and storytelling, such as the little boy who sticks his finger in the dike to save his town from flooding.

I remember as a boy growing up in Michigan, far distant from The Netherlands, hearing these stories of Dutch heroism and accomplishment; somehow, by my parents this story was translated into the need to do well in school. I also recall on my first visit to The Netherlands driving along on a country road, looking up, and noticing a gigantic, ocean-going ship actually riding *above* us on the canal, separated from the below-sea-level road only by an earthen berm. What a shock to see a ship actually above our heads as we drove along.

Meanwhile, getting back to the history, the issue of local autonomy versus central control ebbed and flowed. In the fifteenth century Philip of Burgundy extended his control to the previously largely autonomous Dutch provinces of Holland and Zealand. His daughter Mary married a Hapsburg, Maximilian of Austria, which brought The Netherlands under Hapsburg dynastic control. When Maximilian was crowned Holy Roman Emperor, he gave the Low Countries to his son, Philip the Handsome, who then passed them on to his son Charles, who also inherited the Spanish throne as Carlos I and, shortly thereafter, became Charles V of the Holy Roman Empire. As an academic specialist on Spain and later a resident of Vienna, I know a lot about the Hapsburgs, both their Spanish and Austrian branches, and how their imperial and dynastic policies served to ruin The Netherlands—while also providing the energy and motivation for Dutch nationalism and independence.

It is precisely at the time that Carlos I assumed the reins in Spain that the Protestant Reformation occurred in Germany, Switzerland, and the Low Countries. The humanist Erasmus (of Rotterdam!) put *man* more than God at the center of the universe. Martin Luther emphasized *individual* salvation rather than intermediation through the at-that-time thoroughly corrupt Catholic Church; while John Calvin similarly emphasized individual conscience, the grace of God as providing for salvation rather than the Catholic Church, and the importance of hand work, striving and getting ahead ("the Protestant ethic"). In The Netherlands the messages of Erasmus, Luther, and Calvin found especially fertile grounds, aided by the invention of the printing press that the Dutch perfected and which vastly expanded the spread of the new Protestant ideas. The merchants and guilds of the newly prosperous Dutch towns also favored Protestantism, both in itself and as a way of eliminating the last vestiges of a feudal caste system that stood in the way of their profit-making.

The rise of Protestantism in The Netherlands in the mid-to-late sixteenth century was intimately tied in with the Dutch struggle for independence during this period. The Low Countries remained at this time under Hapsburg control, which meant Catholic, Spanish, papal, and inquisitional rule. Carlos I in Spain had been succeeded by his son Philip II who sought to restore

Catholic hegemony and orthodoxy in Europe, to snuff out the Protestant "heresy," and to eliminate the rising Dutch rebellion.

But the Dutch were clever and resourceful, employing guerrilla tactics against the bigger and more professional Spanish armies, using religion to rally their Protestant forces against the hated Catholics, and even breaking the dikes they had built with such effort to frustrate Spanish advances. Led by William the Silent of the House of Orange-Nassau (which would become the founding dynasty of The Netherlands), the Dutch succeeded in driving out the Spanish forces. In 1579 seven provinces (Holland, Zealand, Utrecht, Groningen, Friesland, Overijssel, and Gelderland) came together as the United Provinces, the first time these separate provinces had joined together as a more-or-less unified country. But the struggle against both external foes and internal divisions continued; it was not until the Peace of Westphalia in 1648 (which also ended the Thirty Years' War) that the full independence of The Netherlands was formally recognized.

The Netherlands during this period, which came to be called the "Golden Age" in Dutch history, became perhaps the wealthiest, most tolerant, most powerful nation in the world. The seventeenth century may be called "The Dutch Century" just as the sixteenth was the Spanish, the eighteenth the French, the nineteenth the British, and the twentieth the American. During this century the economy boomed; the Dutch became world leaders in trade; its ships and sailors were the envy of the world; and Dutch Calvinism and capitalism (the two were all but synonymous) vaulted the country to the forefront of nations. Dutch science and engineering (Kepler, Grotius, many others) were unrivaled; Dutch companies (the East and West India companies) and banking were innovative and among the world's first globalizers, and the Dutch navy roamed the seven seas on a par with, and often surpassing, the much larger British. Dutch art (van Eyck, van der Weyden, Hieronymous Bosch, Peter Bruegel, Van Dyck, Jordaens, Rembrandt, Jan Steen, Vermeer, Hals) became *by far* the best in the world. In the course of my many travels, I have now become something of an expert on Dutch art history.

But The Netherlands also had a reputation for tolerance, progressive thinking, and open-mindedness. To Holland in search of refuge came Spanish and Portuguese Sephardic Jews, the Puritans from England, and political and religious refugees from all over Europe. In turn, the Dutch reached out and established colonies during this period all over the world: Brazil, Suriname, various Caribbean islands, New York, South Africa, Mauritius, Ceylon, Indonesia, Japan, Formosa. The Dutch thus acquired a global empire, at the time the world's largest and richest. It is these colonies that form the subject matter of many of the subsequent chapters of this book.

The Netherlands: A Proud History and Culture   ✤   13

The eighteenth century in The Netherlands was not so much one of decline, as some have alleged, but of stagnation, consolidation, and increased
conservatism born of success. The economy remained dynamic but Dutch reserves were heavily depleted in fighting off French designs on the United
Provinces. The wealth born of the previous century now helped turn the social system static and conservative. Political squabbling among the country's
rival factions in the last decades of the century added to the woes. As its internal situation showed increasing signs of wear and tear, The Netherlands
lost or sacrificed a number of its important colonial possessions.

In 1795, in the aftermath of the French Revolution, French armies invaded the Low Countries, dissolved the United Provinces, and established
the Batavian Republic, a name not used officially since Roman times.
Reestablished as part of the Napoleonic empire, The Netherlands lost all its
sovereignty when Napoleon appointed his brother Louis to the Dutch
throne. French armies occupied the country, and the Dutch were forced to
pay heavy taxes to support Napoleon's war efforts. After Napoleon's defeat at
Waterloo, Dutch sovereignty was restored by the 1815 Treaty of Vienna.

Because of resentments generated by the Protestant north's efforts to dominate the Catholic south, animosities which had simmered for generations
now bubbled forcefully to the surface. The (Protestant) Netherlands and
(Catholic) Belgium went their separate ways in 1830 and became, permanently, two separate nations. Only half-jokingly the Dutch still refer to Belgium, or at least its northern Flemish, Protestant, Dutch-speaking provinces,
as part of "The Greater Netherlands."

The rest of the nineteenth century was less eventful: the country's trade
surpluses built up again; the political situation stabilized; and its borders were
firmed up. Although some advocates had wanted to try to resurrect the glory
years of the seventeenth century, more realistic voices argued that the country needed to adjust to the realities of being a small but still robust nation.
Without such a grandiose global ambition, the country was able during the
course of the nineteenth century, rather like Great Britain and the United
States, to expand liberty, literacy, democracy, and civil and political rights.

Three events during the nineteenth century had a special effect on my
family and my family history and, therefore, on me. The first involved a split
in the long-dominant Dutch Reformed Church. By the nineteenth century
the Dutch Reformed (Calvinist) Church of The Netherlands, rather like the
Anglican Church in England, was rich, staid, and set in its ways. It was also
the established or official church, close to the monarchy and to the wealthy
elites. But out in "the provinces" (Friesland) where my family came from, the
official church was often viewed as too rich, too established, too liberal, and

too out of touch with the mass of the population. In 1834 these groups (called "Remonstrants" because they wished to remonstrate against the established church) split from the state church and formed their own, more orthodox Calvinist denomination. It was this splinter group that, looking for both religious freedom and economic opportunity, emigrated to Western Michigan a generation later in 1857. And it was to this isolated, more orthodox Calvinist outpost in Western Michigan that my grandparents migrated in the 1880s—although in my family we had both established (Reformed) and remonstrant (Christian Reformed) factions.

The second event was growing poverty in these same rural areas. While Amsterdam, Rotterdam, and the southern Dutch cities had forged ahead and grown prosperous based on trade and commerce, the rural areas had lagged behind. Especially such isolated, cold, and storm-swept areas as Friesland. On top of other woes, a potato blight, like that which had earlier devastated Ireland and stimulated emigration to America from there, had destroyed the staple crop of these rural farmers and tipped them over the narrow margin from subsistence to starvation. Have you ever seen Van Gogh's famous painting "The Potato Eaters"?[2] Well, those gaunt, starving, emaciated peasants portrayed in that masterpiece are my ancestors! It has always been striking to me that the time and place Van Gogh painted in that haunting portrait—Friesland in the 1880s—is precisely the time and place in which my ancestors decided to leave.

The third event was the rising influence and eventual coming to power in The Netherlands of orthodox Calvinist philosopher, theologian, and, later, prime minister, Abraham Kuyper (1837–1920). Kuyper was an interesting leader in many ways. First, he came out of the Reformed Calvinist (Remonstrant) tradition and was serious about his religion at a time when much of the population was becoming less religious. Second, Kuyper was a kind of Protestant corporatist, a counterpart to the Catholic corporatism that was sweeping Southern Europe at this time (as exemplified in the papal encyclical *Rerum Novarum* of 1891) about which I have written extensively.[3] Briefly, corporatism in both its Catholic and Protestant varieties, calls for organic unity in society, class solidarity as distinct from Marxian class conflict, and the establishment of a sectoral or (in The Netherlands) "pillared" organization of society to represent its different branches (labor, employer, Protestant, Catholic).

Third, Kuyper believed and implemented into law the Remonstrant idea that the Christian life should encompass *all* aspects of existence; hence, he supported Christian schools, Christian labor unions, Christian businessmen's associations, a Christian (The Free) University, etc. At least, the first and third of these planks in his platform strongly influenced my Dutch community in Grand Rapids, although the second aspect, corporatism, never caught on much in liberal America the way it did in Europe and Latin America.

The Netherlands in the following decade grew both more democratic and, especially in the southern urban areas, more prosperous during the years leading up to World War I. It sought to remain neutral in the First World War but suffered privation and mass hunger as a result of the Allied blockade aimed at depriving Germany of needed goods. The Netherlands was spared the upheavals (fascism, communism, authoritarianism) that other European nations, East and West, experienced in the inter-war period, 1917–1939, but it did experience both political and economic tension mainly as a result of the Great Depression. In May 1940, despite Dutch efforts to stay neutral once again, German armies overran virtually the entire country in a matter of only four days.

The Nazi occupation was cruel and heartless. The Dutch suffered great privation. Hundreds of thousands, including virtually all of the country's sizable Jewish population, died of starvation, were shipped off to German concentration camps, or were killed by the occupation forces. The underground Dutch resistance was impressive as were the efforts of the Dutch to hide Jews at great personal peril to themselves—although in recent years the degree of Dutch complicity and collaboration in the occupation has become a matter of great national soul-searching. With the failure of the British plan to end the war quickly by means of a parachute drop on Arnhem (A *Bridge Too Far*), the allies had to resort to a more conventional strategy to defeat the Germans—a gradual and bloody process that dragged through the winter of 1944 into 1945. The German surrender came in April 1945.

Those last years of the war and the early years of the post-war period, while the country struggled to rebuild, were years of terrible hardship for the Dutch people, especially for those in the countryside. Many buildings had been destroyed; the country's infrastructure had been severely damaged; agriculture had been neglected or destroyed; and many areas had their dikes destroyed and had been flooded in an effort to slow and frustrate the German advances. One of my earliest memories as a small child during this period was of my father packing and sending box after box of food, clothing, and household necessities (soap, blankets, food, toilet paper) back to our cousins in The Netherlands. And I remember my mother, who never complained about anything, complaining to my father that he was sending so many things back to the Old Country that it was depriving our own family of its livelihood.

There was one other consequence of this ongoing poverty and deprivation back in The Netherlands: it stimulated a new, post-World War II wave of Dutch emigration to the United States as well as to Canada. Many came to

Western Michigan: I remember it was a bit of a scandal among my childhood friends that several of their fathers in the then-booming painting or construction business of the 1950s had sponsored and brought over Dutch workers on a kind of "indentured servant" basis and were growing wealthy by exploiting immigrant laborers.

By far the largest contingent of new Dutch emigrants during this period, however, went to Canada. Many of these were Reformed or Christian Reformed but as products of a post-war Dutch philosophy of social democracy— and in keeping with the "fragments theory" advanced in chapter 1—were much more liberal in their attitudes than the Dutch immigrants of the mid-nineteenth century or of my grandparents' generation of the 1880s. These differences would cause all manner of conflicts between the old immigrants and the new and between the Western Michigan and Canadian Reformed and Christian Reformed churches.

Meanwhile, as Dutch society in the 1950s recovered from the devastation of the war, it also partook of the rising general European prosperity of the post-war period. Indeed, by dint of skill, location, and hard work, it became one of the most successful and prosperous ("the polder model") of the European countries, resuming its seventeenth-century position as a leader among nations and one that "fights" way above its weight. Per capita income rose steadily; illiteracy and poverty were wiped out; an elaborate social welfare system was introduced that made The Netherlands like Sweden; and the economy hummed along at ever-higher levels that were the envy of Europe. The Dutch had found a way to blend welfare state policies with incentives for initiative, growth, and entrepreneurship into a combination that few countries could match.

I recall the first time my family and I visited The Netherlands, and particularly Friesland, in 1973. I knew Amsterdam and the cities were prosperous but, remembering my father's sending all those boxes of food and essentials to the Old Country in 1946–1947 and our own privation, I expected rural Friesland to be still poor. Instead, what I found were well-dressed people, nice farms, comfortable housing, an excellent road system, superb public facilities, and an elaborate welfare state that cared for the less fortunate. It was a bit of a shock. Knowing that my grandparents had emigrated from this desolate land because they were poor, starving, and saw no future there, the thought occurred to me: what if they had stayed and not emigrated? Would their grandchildren (my cousins and I) have become as prosperous, as successful, and with as many opportunities as those who found a new life in the New World? The unsettling answer was: it was a very close call. It was unsettling because we usually think of the United States as the land of opportunity, where children and grandchildren of immigrants have done very well. But over the generations those cousins who stayed behind in The Netherlands have also pros-pered and done well—as much or nearly so as we Americans have.

One other thread needs to be tied up here, and that involves the various colonies or "fragments" that the Dutch established back in the seventeenth century. The United States and South Africa had long ago achieved inde-pendence, but now in the general post-war era of decolonization, it also be-came the turn of Indonesia, Suriname, Curaçao, and other former colonies to go their separate ways. Decolonization proved to be an often-wrenching ex-perience both for the mother country and for the colonies;[4] it resulted in dif-ferent outcomes with some (Indonesia) achieving full independence while others (Suriname, Curaçao) maintained varying kinds of special relationship with the mother country. We will have much more to say about these vari-ous fragments of Dutch culture and society later in the book.

The Netherlands has a well-deserved reputation as one of the wealthiest, most successful, most tolerant, most progressive nations on earth. It has a heroic history first of resistance to Rome and then to a succession of larger, more powerful neighbors. It has succeeded and accomplished a great deal, overcoming great odds both of native and of foreign interlopers. Its Calvin-ism long made it an upright, honest, God-fearing nation. It is a land of gor-geous tulips, wonderful paintings, an incredible water- and flood-control sys-tem, and a happy, comfortable, prosperous people. That is its own and the outside world's overall impression.

Imagine my shock, therefore, upon first visiting the country, to discover that it was not at all in accord with what I imagined it to be. That it was not at all like my own Dutch background in Grand Rapids. That the fragment had diverged so far from the mother country (or was it that the mother coun-try had diverged so far from the fragment) that the two operated on com-pletely different wave lengths and were all but unrecognizable to each other. That is the theme of the next two chapters, in which we discuss the Dutch fragment in Western Michigan and then return to a discussion of The Netherlands in the contemporary period.

Notes

1. The most recent of these was in 1953 when a terrible storm overwhelmed the Dutch dikes and hydraulic controls and killed eighteen hundred people while also flooding much of the country.

2. The Batavian Republic and its ability to resist Rome became a major, semi-mythologized epic theme in Dutch history. When the Dutch conquered Java, they named their capital Batavia (now Jakarta, Indonesia).

3. Howard J. Wiarda, *Corporatism and Comparative Politics: The Other Great "Ism"* (New York: M.E. Sharpe, 1997).

4. It also produced a trauma within our family. My Aunt Julia Wiarda, a pioneering woman in the American foreign service, was stationed in Indonesia in the late 1940s when it was moving toward independence. Her beaux at that time was a pilot for KLM (Dutch) airlines. She favored independence in accord with the U.S. position; he favored keeping Indonesia under Dutch control. The family story is that the romance foundered over this issue.

CHAPTER THREE

The Dutch Community
in Western Michigan

Origins

Although my entire family was from Western Michigan, I was born in 1939 in Grosse Pointe (Grossey Pointey as we derisively mispronounced it) Farms, a wealthy suburb of Detroit on the eastern side of the state. The French name, Grosse Pointe, derived from the early French explorers who had come up the St. Lawrence River and then sailed down the Great Lakes (Ontario, Erie) until they reached Detroit where they established a flourishing trading post. Grosse Pointe is actually a strategically located island in the Detroit River separating Michigan from Canada.

Although the name Grosse Pointe conjures up images of great wealth (this is where the Fords of Ford Motor Company fame live), my family was poor. We did not live in Grosse Pointe or even Grosse Pointe Farms, but in Detroit, out near the intersection of Telegraph and Eight Mile Roads. I was born in the Grosse Pointe Hospital only because that was the nearest hospital to our house; it was the designated hospital for our neighborhood. But, depending on my audience, I've sometimes claimed the Grosse Pointe heritage.

Even our being in Detroit at that time was an accident of history and economics. My parents had married in 1927. In the 1920s my Dad, along with his father and brother, had been in the home-building business in Grand Rapids. During that decade of growth and prosperity, home construction in Western Michigan had boomed and my Dad had done well, buying a flashy car and wooing my mother in it. They had even sailed to Europe on their

19

honeymoon, among other reasons so my Dad could revisit the World War I battlefields where he had fought and been wounded.

But then came the Great Depression and the world market crash of 1929–1930. The housing business collapsed and for years and years my Dad could not find work. My mother had to take a secretarial job in the Kent County courthouse to support herself and her husband. All during the 1930s, I later learned, they postponed having a family because they didn't think it was responsible to bring a child into the world unless they could afford it. That explains why my father was thirty-nine and my mother thirty-five when I was born. Much later in life I learned that my mother, because of her age, had subsequently had several miscarriages during the early 1940s, with the result that I am an only child.

Finally, my Dad saw a notice that the Railway Mail Service, a small federal agency distinct from the Post Office that sorted the mail while it was being transported between cities by train (no interstate highway system in those days), was hiring. He took the exam and received the highest score in the state. But to get the job he would have to move to Detroit. That's why I was born there. The next year, 1940, he was given the opportunity by the Railway Mail to transfer back to Grand Rapids. Because all our roots and family were there, he immediately accepted. So I really grew up in Grand Rapids and not Detroit, and spent the first seventeen years of my life there.

The Dutch in Western Michigan

The Netherlands had been a thoroughly Calvinistic culture and society since the sixteenth century. Calvinism had been closely associated with Dutch nationalism in the struggle against Spain; it was part of Dutch national identity. Calvinism in The Netherlands was, therefore, not just religious; it was associated with the glorious art of the seventeenth century, with Dutch prosperity and entrepreneurship (The Netherlands was Max Weber's main case in *The Protestant Ethic and the Spirit of Capitalism*) and with the power and successes of "the Golden Age."[1] Calvinism and the Dutch Reformed Church had sunk deep roots into the social structure, the culture, the entire Dutch way of thinking.

Over the course of three centuries, success and prosperity had made the Dutch Reformed Church rich, proud, and puffy. It was associated with wealth and the urban power centers. It was close to the elites and the royal family, itself similarly rich and proud. It was the established church, the official church, with an abundance of wealth and perks. In its comforts, it had forgotten the early struggles against Spain, the elements, and poverty. It had also forgotten much of its religious orthodoxy. It no longer put God at the center of existence. It had its rituals but it had neglected its basics: the orthodox reformed faith of the Heidelberg Catechism, the Canons of Dordt, and the Belgic Confession. It had become, like the Church of England, too rich and comfortable for its own good.

People in the Dutch countryside, including the isolated Fresian area where my ancestors came from, tended to be considerably more conservative, traditionalist, and orthodox Calvinists than those in the cities of Amsterdam, Rotterdam, The Hague, and Utrecht. They resented the wealth of the official church, its closeness to the elite class, and its gradual abandonment of—not really abandonment but drifting away from—Calvinist precepts. They felt the state church had been corrupted by wealth and power, that it was arrogant and out of touch with its own people and congregations.

In 1834 a relatively small faction of the Dutch Reformed Church parted ways with the mother denomination and formed its own, more orthodox group. The center of this new splinter group was in the rural provinces of Friesland, Groningen, and Zealand, far from the urban centers. Many of its pastors (the painter Vincent Van Gogh's father was one of them) were quite fiery and inspirational orators who urged their congregants to return to their Calvinist roots. The separatists, or Remonstrants as they were called, accepted the sixteenth- and seventeenth-century Canons of Doubt and the Heidelberg Catechism as the basis of their religion and believed the local congregation, not the national or official state church, to be the independent, fundamental foundation of Christianity.

At first, the new church suffered persecution and was victimized, although—this is The Netherlands after all—not anywhere to the degree of the earlier, hated Spanish Inquisition. Some of its members lost their jobs; some of its pastors were coerced into silence or even thrown in jail; some of its churches and church properties were seized by the state. This new church was also quite conservative, maybe even traditionalist—not at all unusual in pre-1848 Europe. In response to the measures taken against it, the new church tended to withdraw into itself, isolating itself from the surrounding society and taking an appositional position toward modernization. Sometimes—and that is my ancestors' history—this isolation from encroaching modernization and fears of its accompanying secularization took the form of emigration all the way to America.

In the early 1840s some of the breakaway church pastors, in the face of both economic hardship in The Netherlands and continued religious discrimination against their members, began to talk of moving to the United

States. As with other emigrant groups, it was not an easy decision, moving away from country, friends, family, and community.

In 1846 the first group, numbering only fifty, under Albertus Van Raalte, set sail from Rotterdam. It was a rough voyage under extremely trying conditions that lasted seven weeks. Looking for cheap, available land, the group landed in New York, made their way to Detroit, and finally settled in Western Michigan in early 1947. Another somewhat wealthier group under Hendrik Scholte settled that same year in Pella, Iowa, a farm community that is still predominantly Dutch. If you have Pella windows in your house, you know they are Dutch made and high quality. Today Pella is a clean, quaint, nicely restored town whose Dutch origins are still visible in its architecture, windmill, baking shops, and tulip fields.[2]

Along the eastern shore of Lake Michigan, across from Milwaukee and northeast of Chicago, there is an inland lake, Black Lake or Lake Macatawa (the Indian name), connected to the Big Lake by a narrow passage. This is where the Dutch immigrants led by Van Raalte settled in 1847. A hundred years later this was the area where I grew up; we used to sail on Black Lake, fish and swim in Lake Michigan, and take our dates to beach parties in the sand dunes along the lake.

The early settlers didn't have it so easy. Most of the soil around their landing spot, which came to be called Holland after their country of origins, was sandy and of poor quality. There was no welcoming party, no housing available, bitterly cold winters, and fierce, biting black flies. The first few years people lived in leaky, dingy sod huts; they were always cold and always hungry. Like the Puritans and Pilgrims before them (or like the Old Testament Israelites, to whom they often compared themselves, similarly wandering in the wilderness and set down in an inhospitable land), they suffered hardship and privation; many died. Looking for better land, some of the early settlers fanned out to small farming communities a few miles inland that they called Harlem, Overissel, Drenth, Zutphen, Noordeloos, Graafschap, Zealand— after the towns and provinces in The Netherlands from which they had come. As a junior-high kid growing up, I played in a fast-pitch softball league against teams from all these small towns. About thirty miles inland, on the banks of the Grand River, was Grand Rapid—the only established community at that time, a trading and commercial center that would over time become the center of the Dutch community in Western Michigan.

In 1849, only two years after the settlement's founding, a pastor from the prosperous, established Dutch communities on the U.S. east coast (what I would call the "Upper Hudson Dutch," see chapter 4) rode out to Western Michigan. He invited the Dutch there to join with him in the Dutch Reformed Church of America, the congregation formed by the eastern Dutch communities. Joining an established church was attractive in many ways to the struggling settlers: it had pastors that the new communities in Michigan sorely needed, wealth, connections, and political influence (remember Commodore Cornelius *Vanderbilt*, recent President Martin *Van* Buren [emphasis added to stress their Dutch backgrounds] came out of this east-coast community). But the Reformed Church of America was closely tied to the official state church, the Reformed Church of The Netherlands, which had recently persecuted them and whose ranks the settlers had just left.

The issue was controversial and the argument went on for several years; finally, in 1857 the settlers in Western Michigan formed their own Calvinist denomination that they called the Christian Reformed Church. But that did not prevent the Reformed Church from also establishing itself in the area, especially in more cosmopolitan Grand Rapids. There the Reformed and the Christian Reformed, both Calvinist but the former somewhat more liberal than the latter, maintained an intense but usually good-natured rivalry over the years and even established their own separate colleges: Hope College for the Reformed Church and Calvin College for the Christian Reformed.

In my day, Hope College was similarly the more open-minded and liberal of the two, allowing its students to go to dances and the movies and, like the mother church in The Netherlands, not being so strict about Sunday ("the day of rest") observance, while Calvin College was stricter and more orthodox. My own family was split between these two congregations: when they came to America my grandfather on my father's side and his family joined and largely stayed with the established Reformed Church, whereas my father and mother joined the Christian Reformed. Quite frankly, as a kid growing up, I saw few differences between the two (how much attention do you pay to theology at that age?); they were both Dutch and part of the Dutch Reformed culture; and I had friends and schoolmates from both churches.

The Dutch community in Western Michigan was a true "fragment," in the Hartzian sense, of rural, orthodox-Calvinist, and mid-nineteenth-century Dutch culture and society, now transported to the New World. At least initially, its church services were in Dutch; Dutch was spoken in the home; and the first newspapers were in Dutch. Dutch theological debates were quickly carried across the ocean to America, and the debates and divisions in domestic Dutch politics had their reverberations in Western Michigan as well.

Because of its isolation and the "wilderness mentality" of the settlers, however, the ties between the mother country and the Dutch enclaves in America became gradually more strained. The two increasingly went their separate ways. The Netherlands became over time more progressive and liberal, whereas Western Michigan continued with its conservatism and orthodox Calvinism. It is not as though the Western Michigan Dutch communities were "locked in place," for they changed, too, under the impact of modernization, secularization, and Americanization; but the pace of change in this isolated fragment was far slower than that of The Netherlands. Today the two, fragment and mother country, are so far apart culturally and ideologically as to represent two very different societies with almost no connection except maybe nostalgia between them.

As Van Raalte and his small group settled in the forests and swamplands of Western Michigan, they discovered a terrain that was very different from the flat, cleared, open fields of The Netherlands. They had to cut forests, drain the swamps (the Dutch were good at that), clear the land, and build shelter. Gradually, the new communities of Holland and the others began to prosper. Word filtered back to The Netherlands that here was a country where you could not only practice your religion freely without fear of persecution but where land was abundant and cheap. America was the land of opportunity.

And so, more immigrants, most of them poor and from rural areas, came in the 1850s, 1860s, 1870s, and on into the twentieth century. They came by boat through the Great Lakes, by train to Detroit, by wagon, and even on foot. Many settled in the area; others, surprised by the harsh conditions, moved on to found other Dutch communities in Sheboygan (Wisconsin), South Holland (Illinois), Sioux Center (Iowa), and Lynden (Washington). Each of these Dutch communities had its own "fragment" experience; each retained its Dutch ways in many respects even while making its own accommodations with America. But all have this common Dutch culture and belief system (Calvinism) that persists to this day.

For a considerable time (let's say, about fifty years or a generation and a half) the mother country continued to be relevant; after that it rapidly lost influence as the fragments established their own independent existence. For example, in the 1880s and 1890s the Dutch theologian-turned-politician (and future prime minister), Abraham Kuyper, had a huge impact in both The Netherlands and among the Dutch communities in America. Kuyper, an orthodox Calvinist and a brilliant scholar and dynamic preacher, taught that God was sovereign over *all* areas of life. Christians must, therefore, bring their faith to work, school, and into politics. In The Netherlands Kuyper's message was instrumental in establishing Christian trade unions, Christian businessmen's associations, Christian schools, and Christian political parties. As indicated earlier, Kuyper's politics were those of a Protestant corporatist; his ideas spread throughout the world. In The Netherlands Kuyper led an orthodox Calvinist faction ("Kuyperians") that broke away from the state church, just as the separatist Remonstrants had done a half century earlier.

Kuyper's time of major influence, the last decades of the nineteenth century and the first decades of the twentieth, corresponded with a new wave of Dutch (and European more generally) immigration to the New World. In the case of the Dutch, the motives for emigration were both economic and religious: depressed economic conditions in The Netherlands, again especially in the rural areas, and the desire for greater religious liberty and freedom. Among the immigrants were now thousands of members of Kuyper's breakaway church—including a couple of my grandparents. They were told that they should go to Western Michigan. There, it was said, you will find not only jobs and opportunity but also groups of Dutch Calvinists who think like you do!

We have emphasized the religious motivation here (1) because it was important and (2) because it is interesting; but at this stage we need to pay more attention to the economic reasons for immigrating. This shift in focus corresponds to changes taking place in Western Michigan. For while the first generation of Dutch immigrants had been settlers and farmers, the second and third generations were attracted both to farming and to commercial and business activities in the only major urban center in the area, Grand Rapids. And, in fact, Grand Rapids during this period of the mid- to late-nineteenth century was undergoing an economic boom of unprecedented proportions.

In 1847 as the first Dutch settlers arrived on the shores of Lake Macatawa, Grand Rapids (as its name implies, Grand River was founded on the rapids) was still just a small trading settlement. By the 1880s, when my grandparents arrived there, it had turned into a boomtown. What had changed? First, there was a general increase in the U.S. population, from twenty-three million in 1850 to double that in1880. Second, the United States was expanding west, especially into the newly opened Northwest Territory that included Michigan. Third, the United States was changing from a rural agricultural society to an urban, business-manufacturing one. And fourth, there was a tremendous growth in the demands for new-and-updated housing, including furniture. All of these forces came to fruition in the phenomenal growth of Grand Rapids as "The Furniture Capital of the World."[3] And as "The Dutch Zion."

Grand Rapids was not initially a Dutch city; it had been founded several decades before the first Dutch settlers arrived. None of the town's early founders and leaders—John Ball, Louis Campau, George Pullman (the inventor of Pullman railway cars), George Widdicomb (of Widdicomb furniture fame), William Berkey (of Berkey Furniture), George Bissell (of the carpet sweeper Bissells) had Dutch names. They were all Yankees or the descendants of French fur traders. But Grand Rapids had a lot of advantages as a future growth hub: the river, proximity to the Great Lakes, abundant lumber and hardwood, cheap land, closeness to the big emerging growth hubs of Detroit and Chicago, and abundant, cheap labor consisting of all those Dutch immigrants. Soon the city as well as the small farming communities forming a triangle between Holland, Grand Rapids, and Grand Haven (also on Lake Michigan) were overflowing with Dutch immigrants.

At first, furniture was the key to Grand Rapids' prosperity. And this meant fine, quality furniture, the kind that (Dutch) skilled craftsmen would do. There was an interesting sociology at work here: for one thing, the fine furniture was in accord with the then-ascendant Victorian cultural values into which the Dutch with their Calvinism fitted well. For another, fine furniture was increasingly seen in post-Civil War America as evidence of gentility and God's just rewards, again a reflection of the Dutch Calvinist ethic. Third, as the slogan of the time put it, "Good furniture means good morals," another theme dear to the hearts of the Dutch. In ways that may seem strange to modern, secular Americans, in Grand Rapids, religion, furniture, and the Dutch all seemed to go together.[4]

While the Dutch began as a minority immigrant community within an initially Yankee-dominated city, over time they grew in numbers, wealth, and power to the point where *they* dominated the city. The Dutch eventually came to control the city council, the mayorship, representatives to the state legislature, and the two congressional seats in that area of Western Michigan. Many of the new businesses, law firms, and the civic clubs (Rotary, Lions, etc.) in Grand Rapids were heavily infused with Dutch money and members. The new and wealthy suburbs to the south and east of Grand Rapids were almost exclusively Dutch. And the Dutch were often able to enact citywide blue laws and Sunday-closing laws that were opposed by more secular residents.[5]

The industrialization of Grand Rapids (American Seating, Steelcase, Fisher Body, Hekman Biscuit were the biggies, along with the smaller furniture makers), when combined with the Kuyperian influence, produced some interesting dynamics that made it different from other cities. For one thing, the Dutch owners tended to hire their own countrymen whom they could trust and knew as honest, devout Christians, who for many decades effectively kept other ethnic and minority groups from getting jobs in the city or even kept them out entirely. Second, Grand Rapids, unlike Detroit, Flint, or other cities in the eastern part of the state, was a non-union city; many Christian Reformed people equated unions with Marx, class conflict, and (literally) sin. Third, in the few shops that were unionized, the unions that existed, in keeping with the Kuyperian injunctions, tended to be Christian unions and not associated with any of the big national and international unions. Grand Rapids also had few lodges because groups like the Masons were considered quasi-religious bodies whose beliefs were contrary to Christian (Calvinist) doctrine.

Grand Rapids had many aspects of culture, society, politics, and, of course, religion not found anywhere else in the United States. I was born into this society so I understand it and its underlying beliefs and how to operate within it; but to outsiders, Grand Rapids and the Dutch community there must seem strange indeed

When I now return to the city, I am amazed by its wealth, prosperity, and success. Furniture-making gradually faded as the industry moved to the U.S. South but, following the path of diversification, the city has continued as a thriving commercial, manufacturing, and business center. The Dutch have done very well in America and Western Michigan. On all sides of the city there are hundreds, maybe thousands, of small, family-owned manufacturing plants whose owners (my high school classmates!) have become multimillionaires. The suburbs along the Thornapple River in Ada, and all the way out to the shores of Lake Michigan, are dotted with wealthy, gated communities. There is a political dimension to this as well: when I grew up in the 1940s and 1950s, G. Mennen Williams, the United Auto Workers, and the Democratic Party machine in Detroit (Wayne County) largely dominated state politics. But now that power has shifted to Western Michigan: Dutch money and the fact the civic-minded Dutch vote in proportion of 80–90 percent (versus only 20–25 percent in Detroit) has evened out the odds and made Michigan a two-party state again, one of the swing states in every recent presidential as well as the statewide elections.

Success has also exacted its costs, however. And this, too, relates to our understanding of the "fragments" phenomenon and the evolution of diverse, European-based societies in different parts of the world. For while the Dutch in Western Michigan are still considerably more conservative and Calvinistic than their Dutch cousins back in The Netherlands, they have also changed over time. Few of them speak the Dutch language anymore. There are no more Dutch newspapers or radio stations. Whereas before, church services were regularly in Dutch, now there is only one, weekly Dutch-language service in all of Grand Rapids. Dutch schools now sponsor dances; almost everyone goes to the movies (without having to sneak in with a handkerchief over your face as my generation did); the Dutch high school and college (Calvin) now put on musical shows and theater that are quite *avant-garde*. Many of the younger-generation Dutch have abandoned the faith of their fathers (read

Peter De Vries's novels or see Paul Boscher's movies, such as *Taxi Driver*). The Christian Reformed Church (CRC) is losing members (currently three hundred thousand) at the rate of about 3 percent a year; meanwhile, the CRC and Grand Rapids as well have become more religiously and ethnically diverse as many more blacks, Hispanics, and others have moved into the community. In short, the Dutch community in Western Michigan has become Americanized even while retaining many of the core values, including religious values that make it unique.

Americanization has occurred within my own family as well. My father told me the story of how his father, the immigrant, one day at the dining-room table, announced in his heavily accented English, "Ve are now in America and in America ve vill speak English." And from that time on, no one in the family spoke Dutch, although my parents could still read, write, and speak it and some Fresian as well. By the time it gets to my generation, the third one in America, I learned only the Dutch that a mother would speak to a small baby—and then later in life wished that I had studied and learned it better. My children, who in their professional lives are scattered all around the country, feel no affinity to Western Michigan at all, speak no Dutch and are thoroughly Americanized; all traces of the Dutch past except their funny Dutch name have been long ago forgotten.[6]

Notes

1. Simon Schama, *The Embarrassment of Riches: An Interpretation of Dutch Culture in the Golden Age* (New York: Knopf, 1987).

2. We visited Pella in the summer of 2002.

3. Christian G. Carron, *Grand Rapids Furniture: The Story of America's Furniture City* (Grand Rapids: The Public Museum of Grand Rapids, 1998).

4. Grand Rapids also experienced significant Polish immigration during this period, but the Poles were generally less well-educated, less skilled, and less wealthy than the Dutch and lived on the West (or lower-class) Side (of the Grand River). At high school basketball games between my own Dutch Reformed high school and Catholic Central, the Dutch on one side (mostly the parents), remembering the Reformation, the Counter-Reformation, and those sixteenth-century religious wars, would shout, "Kill those dirty Catholics," while the Poles on the other side would yell, "Boil them in oil." Unlike today, however, I can't remember these taunts ever leading to violence.

5. It often happens that newcomers move to Grand Rapids unaware of the city's ethnic heritage and religious background and expecting it to be like any other American city. They are often surprised, therefore, when they cannot get liquor licenses, shop on Sunday, or open porno shops. Some of them end up resenting or even hat-

ing the Dutch and their influence; most adjust. Recently there have been challenges to these laws and many have been relaxed.

6. My daughter even told me once that, when she married a young man named Williams, she was so happy to have an English name that people could pronounce and spell instead of her old Dutch name that people couldn't spell, couldn't pronounce, and often made fun of.

CHAPTER FOUR

Growing Up Dutch:
Zion on the Prairies

I grew up within the bosom of the Dutch community in Western Michigan and of the Dutch (Christian) Reformed Church. As mentioned before, all four of my grandparents, were Dutch; I went to Dutch Reformed schools and catechism; all my friends were Dutch; all the girls I dated through high school (all but one; more on that below!) were Dutch. I grew up thinking everyone would be just like my community was: hard-working, Calvinistic, with high moral standards, no crime, no broken families, no drugs, no alcoholism. It was a comfortable cocoon to grow up in, and perhaps it reflected the conservative, *Leave It to Beaver, Ozzie and Harriet* America of the 1950s; but it was, definitely, a cocoon. I did not really discover other races, other religions, other ways of thinking, and a diverse, pluralistic culture and society until I went off to university.

Although I had been born in Grosse Pointe just outside Detroit, within the first year of my life a job transfer opportunity for my father had brought us back to Grand Rapids where both my father's and mother's families were located. Using the skills learned earlier in the home-building business, my Dad built a house on Godwin Avenue (2064) in the southeast section of town, near Garfield Park. It was a wonderful neighborhood of nice, upper-middle class houses, baseball fields in the empty lots that then still separated the houses, touch football and sledding in winter on our peaceful, tree-lined street, and the park nearby. There we flew kites, learned to ice skate (I won a few trophies in races as a kid), and transferred our baseball games after we had broken one-too-many windows in the houses surrounding the building lots where we had played initially. Since my Dad was the only carpenter among my friends' fathers, he was invariably the one called on to fix the windows we broke.

The house he built for his family in Grand Rapids in 1940 was a beautiful home. Some fifty years later it was a terribly wrenching experience for me to have to sell that house, but by then we were living nearly a thousand miles away and there was no way I could keep it up or oversee tenants in it from long distance. The house featured a graceful, centered, circular staircase that wound its way from the front entry to the second floor, where it emptied onto a beautiful curving balcony that matched the curve of the stairway and led to the one bath and three bedrooms upstairs. We were not a wealthy family (the only reason we lived in that nice neighborhood is that my Dad built the house himself, with his brother Roy), and usually it takes a much bigger house than we had to set off a circular stairway properly. But this one had just the right proportions; it had been lovingly constructed completely by hand (no factory-product circular stairway here); and it was my Dad's pride and joy. Everyone who came to that house always admired that staircase; sometimes visitors offered to buy the house on the spot just for that stairway.

So that is where I grew up. It was idyllic. I had great parents, good Christian friends, a wonderful and caring Christian school and teachers, a nice and peaceful neighborhood with no crime and plenty of space to play and stretch out. I don't recall ever seeing a crime committed,[1] hearing a gunshot in the neighborhood, or playing with a friend from a broken family. In Grand Rapids in those days in Calvinist circles, divorce was unheard of; marriage was for life—literally, "until death do us part."[2] Nor, once we had moved back to Grand Rapids, did we ever move again, providing another element of stability to this peaceful, idyllic picture. The incredible mobility of American society and our often-transient lives moving from one place to another, which my own family has experienced, did not affect me as a kid growing up.

Roots and Origins

The Wiarda family tree in The Netherlands can be traced back twenty-six generations to 1369.[3] The first Wiarda in recorded history was Sjoerd Wiarda.

The Wiardas originated in Friesland, that cold, wind-swept, storm-swept, isolated province across the Zuider Zee in far northern Holland. With our fair skins and blond hair (mine was white when I was young), the Fries are really Nordic, almost Scandinavian in background. My relatives came mainly from Goutum, a small farming village a few miles away from the Friesland provincial capital of Lieuwarden. There is a "Wiarda School" there, a plaque commemorating the Wiardas, and a Wiarda Street and a Wiarda bike path. In the municipal museum of Lieuwarden are pictures of contented Dutch burghers and local officials named Wiarda. Nearby are the ruins of a manor house that is said to be the "Wiarda castle." Part of the provincial (and family) lore is that the Wiarda owner of the castle was so stubborn and hardheaded (a particularly Dutch and especially Friesian characteristic) that, rather than pay taxes on it, he burned it to the ground!

I am very suspicious of these claims of a long family history, a castle, and a noble past. For one thing, before Napoleon, the Dutch had no last or family names, so I'm not sure it's possible to trace us all the way back to 1369. For another, there is a tendency among today's generations to exaggerate and thereby glorify the family's past, when the reality is almost certainly somewhat less glorious. I believe my family was poor, not noble; that is why they emigrated to America. It was not rich people who came here but poor, starving peasants.

Rather than being wealthy, my grandfather on my father's side was an orphan (I know less about my family tree on my mother's side, except that they were also poor and also came to America in the mid-1880s). He had been born into a large family that was not wealthy enough to feed them all. So he and his brother had been placed in an orphanage. When they were released from the orphanage at age sixteen, they had no jobs, no prospects, and no future; but they did know about farming and carpentry. So the two brothers determined to come to America. No one yet surviving in the family knows for certain if they came on their own (where would orphans get the money for an ocean passage?) or if they came in some kind of indentured capacity— probably the latter. Arriving in America, one of the brothers became a farmer in the small Dutch community of Coopersville in Western Michigan (I remember as a youth going out to the farm occasionally), while the other (my grandfather) settled in Grand Rapids and began to earn a good living as a carpenter and home-builder.

My grandfather built a number of the nice, now historic homes on the Fulton Street hill overlooking downtown Grand Rapids. I recall my father pointing out with pride the houses he, his brother, and his father (my grandfather) had worked on. My grandfather also built quite a number of somewhat more modest, middle-class homes about a mile east of Fulton Hill in what is the Houseman Field/Brickyard section of the city (so named because there was once a clay pit there for making bricks, later converted in my time into a farmers' market). At first, my grandfather and his family built and lived in a fairly modest, wood-frame, two-story but small house in the Brick-yard neighborhood; later they built a nicer and quite comfortable brick house on the corner of Diamond and Houseman Streets. In my youth, that was the family homestead.

My grandfather had married a Huyser; I was told by my aunts that their parents were actually of French Huguenot background. My grandparents had eight children—four boys and four girls: Mina (named after Wilhelmina, the queen), Roy (also a carpenter), John (my Dad), Julia (the foreign-service of-ficer), Cora (a housewife and the sole living family member), Cornelius (a prominent Grand Rapids attorney), Grace (a housewife), and Jerry (in auto-mobile parts). On my mother's side, the Droogers—again all Dutch—there were three children: Cornelia (my mother), Marjorie (a realty and stock dealer), and Lionel (who worked for Lever Brothers).

My grandmother on my Dad's side died about the time I was born; I never knew her. My grandfather lived through World War II; among my earliest memories are those of outracing my cousins in the Diamond Avenue house to fetch a match for him to light his pipe. I was closer to my grandparents on my mother's side because they lived only a mile away and, during the long years when my Dad had to travel on the trains or work nights, my mother and I walked up to their house several evenings a week.[4] My grandfather spent long hours with me playing chess, checkers, dominoes, and tiddly winks; his was also the first household in the family to have a television set. My grandmother on my mother's side developed nervous/mental problems that none of us ever completely understood; she was hospitalized several times and underwent electric shock therapy. My grandfather and mother were devastated by her sickness.

My Dad had been born in 1899; in 1916, at the youthful (and naive) age of sixteen, he had heeded President Woodrow Wilson's call to "make the world safe for democracy" by enlisting in the Army and going off to France to fight in World War I. He was badly wounded in the battle of Chateau-Thierry (I still have the shrapnel that the doctors dug out of his arm and skull) and eventually sent home. My Dad was a very intelligent man, but he now did a dumb thing. Because of his war experience, he was more experi-enced and two years older than his peers, and he thought it would be beneath him to enter college with persons younger than himself. So he never went to college or university, a decision he later came to deeply regret, even though he was always well-read, well-informed, and certainly well-qualified to do so. Instead he went into the home-building business with his father.

He did well as a home-builder in the 1920s, but then came the Depres-sion, unemployment, and eventually the job in the Railway Mail. After

World War II, as the housing boom took off and he saw many of his friends growing wealthy in the construction business, my Dad was urged to return to house-building. But the early experience of the Depression had been so searing that he refused to take the chance. He was absolutely convinced (and he was not alone in this) that, as after World War I, another severe depression was certain to follow the decline in wartime production after World War II (to offset that possibility is why the World Bank and International Monetary Fund were originally established). So he stayed with the Railway Mail Service and his guaranteed government job and salary rather than taking a chance on the private sector. It was his second big mistake in life. The Wiardas on Godwin Avenue thus remained poorer than most of their neighbors, even though, because of our nice house and my Dad doing part-time carpenter jobs to supplement his income, it never showed.

We had great neighbors on Godwin Avenue and these were my best friends growing up. Larry Allabin, the son of a prominent attorney who lived in back of us, was my best boyhood chum; but he moved away to an even more upper-class neighborhood in East Grand Rapids. Johnny Roossien down the street then became my best friend; his sister Nancy, a year younger than I, was the first girl with whom I went steady (I think my mother and her mother, who were best friends, conspired to advance this match). Johnny and I teamed up to play ping pong almost every night after school, and I went on to win the city table tennis championship in the sixteen-and-under group, beating Del Sweeris, then in the twelve-and-under group—I had longer arms—who went on to become a world champion and to defeat the Chinese in a championship match during President Richard Nixon's "ping pong diplomacy." I still proudly display the trophies from those table tennis days.

The larger neighborhood "gang" with whom we played baseball, football, and basketball included Bill London, Gordon Hondorp, and Pete and Stevie Patterson. The Pattersons had one of those extra lots (still empty today) between the houses where the entire neighborhood (boys and girls) gathered to play; Pete was a couple of years older than I, and when he was in junior high I began to notice that the girls who gathered there were not as interested in sports as they were mainly in Pete. Among the girls my age on Godwin Avenue was Evelyn Hollander, the daughter of our family physician, who represented another of my mother's efforts at matchmaking. Evie and I went to kindergarten, elementary school, junior high, and high school together; we dated a couple of times but it was never serious.

My elementary school, Seymour Christian, was about a mile away. It was part of the Christian Reformed Church's private school system, for which my parents had to pay tuition and with no tax credits. It was an excellent school with superb, dedicated teachers and excellent facilities. We walked to school every day, although sometimes in winter we would (dangerously) hook our sleds to the bumpers of passing cars (no salt was used on the streets in those days so the snow became hard-packed) and ride along that way. We often had snowball fights on the way home and I developed a pretty good and accurate pitching arm: one day I hit a neighbor girl, who was bigger than I, right on her teeth braces, and she chased me all the way home. I think it was in sixth grade that I got a three-speed, sky-blue Schwinn bike, my pride and joy, that facilitated the coming and going to school; I prided myself on being able to ride that bike all the way from school, through several lights and stop signs, and into our garage without once touching the handlebars.

My favorite subjects were math, history, and recess; through fourth grade I received all A's. The instructional curriculum at Seymour included a half-hour of Bible studies in the morning (our school ran about an hour longer than the public schools) as well as English, math, history, geography, and science. We had spelling contests in those days and I was usually one of the finalists along with Lois Albers and Kathy Van Der Wal; I also recall doing a semester-long geography report on South America in fourth grade that ran to fifty pages. Perhaps that was what initially kindled my interest in Latin America.

But something happened in fifth and sixth grades: was it testosterone or merely a brand-new, inexperienced teacher who couldn't keep order. It was nothing bad, by today's standards, but enough to get me sent out to the hall several times and once or twice to the principal's office. Several of us talked too much or were disruptive in the classroom; we had also discovered how to make bows and arrows out of bent-open hairpins and rubber bands and, when the teacher's back was turned, to shoot paper "bullets" or, worse, sharp toothpicks at the backs of other students' necks. And it was not just the boys; the girls, too, were disruptive and kept talking even when the teacher told us to be quiet. On several occasions we reduced this freshman teacher to tears when she failed to keep order in the classroom. She had completely lost all authority.

I am a product of the 1940s and 1950s, but I do not share journalist David Halberstam's critical view of that era. To me, the house, family, neighborhood, community, and city where I grew up were almost idyllic. We were patriotic (my Dad had served in World War I and was too old to serve in the 1940s but I remember the victory gardens of World War II), had a close and loving family, a wonderful neighborhood, good friends, a fine school, no crime; what could be better than that? My church (Christian Reformed) and school gave me a solid moral and religious foundation that, though I have somewhat strayed from it, has stayed with me and been a rock of support my entire life. True, we lived a sheltered life, were not exposed to other religious and ethnic minorities until later, and were not particularly critical of the American culture and society in which we grew up, including racism, segregation, and absence of civil rights for some groups. Those latter complications and controversies would be faced later in life; meantime, the environment in which we did grow up—conservative, religious, ethical, Republican, Eisenhower-ish—seems to me not all that bad in retrospect and certainly better than the often loud, garish, rude, amoral, and conflictual society in which we now live. I do not agree at all with Halberstam's view that the peaceful fifties were but a preview to the turbulent sixties; certainly in Western Michigan that was not the case.

When I was in fourth grade I started mowing, with a push mower, some of our neighbors' lawns: $1.00 per (quarter acre) lawn, $1.25 for harder or larger ones. By the time I was in seventh grade I had printed my own advertisements (with a small, removable-type, hand-cranked printer my parents had given me), broadened my business to include snow-shoveling, babysitting, house painting, and general lawn care, and was running a considerable business. Many of our neighbors had cottages at Lake Michigan or Lake Macatawa so I would often contract to care for their lawns (sprinkling as well as mowing) for the entire summer. I worked hard at this job, but I also had a system. With about twenty lawn-watering customers, I would hop on my bike every hour, make a complete round of changing the sprinkler location in the lawns of my customers in about fifteen minutes, and then return to my home to listen to the "Top Forty" for the rest of the hour. With that many customers, at 10 cents per hour each, I was making a good (for those days) hourly wage mostly for sitting around. That plus the lawn mowing, painting, and other enterprises enabled me to pull in up to $3,000 per summer for several years—enough to pay my way through the first two years of university.

Every summer my family would take a long vacation trip, and shorter rides almost every weekend. We went on separate occasions to Montreal and Quebec, Boston, New York (twice), Washington, D.C., Florida (twice), New Orleans, around Lake Michigan, and around Lake Huron. My mother usually went shopping in Detroit (Hudson's) and Chicago (a visit to Don McNeil's "Breakfast Club" was *de rigeur*) at least once a year; because they had lived there before I was born, they also had friends to visit in Detroit. Because of my Dad's work (and periodic re-exams) for the Railway Mail, he knew every crossroads in the state; it was fun taking trips with him because he knew so much about the local geography and history.

Every summer from about fifth grade on, my father would ship me out to a cousin's farm in Hudsonville (halfway between Holland and Grand Rapids) for about two weeks. The cousin, John (Jack) Brouwer, was no ordinary poor farmer; he was also a cattle dealer, businessman, dealer in land, and local political influential. My Dad thought it important that I, a city kid, be exposed to and learn about farming and the farm business. What a time we had out there! Uncle Jack (he was my Dad's cousin; hence, my second uncle) had a wonderful and large family including a son, Robert (now a doctor), my age. We played baseball, milked the cows, topped onions, picked pickles (the prickers stuck in my tender city hands), played in the barn, loaded hay bales, and ate my Aunt Jeanette's wonderful food (including chocolate milk and home-made doughnuts). I learned to hunt (foxes and pheasant) out there and also to drive, on the tractor, popping the clutch the first time I did it and plowing right through a barbed-wire fence before I could figure out how to stop. I also accompanied Uncle Jack on some of his cattle-buying excursions, marveling at his patience in talking to his fellow farmers endlessly about the weather, crops, their families, etc., all the while slowly edging the price down on the cows he was buying.[5]

What an education this was! Later on, when my own sons were old enough, I sent them out to the farm of some friends of ours in North Platte, Nebraska, where they had similarly great times, to the point that we had a hard time persuading them to return home.

In junior high, which was in the same complex but a building across the street from the elementary school, I continued my interest in math (I had already decided, based on a family trip out east where I saw the interstate highway system being built, that I wanted to be an engineer and design those cloverleafs) and history, and now added English and writing to my list of favorite subjects. I *loved* to diagram sentences; to me, breaking apart a sentence and being able to diagram it correctly was fun, like solving a crossword puzzle. I could write fast and easily, and I'm sure the journalism training I received here, then in high school, and later at the University of Michigan helps explain why, as an academic, my books were to number over seventy. I became sports editor of the junior high newspaper; the high point of my career was when I named the players "likely" to make the softball and basketball teams (on which I was also a member!) before the coach himself had made those decisions, thus angering the coach and forcing him to call me into his office for a dressing down. I think I learned something about both journalism and conflict of interest in the process.

In junior high I also discovered girls for the first time. How innocent we were in those days! There were about six boys in our "gang"—Bill Ryskamp, Jim Muller, Jimmy Van Den Berg, Eddie Mastenbroek, Jon Tanja, and myself—and the same number of girls: Evie Hollander, Kathy Van Der Wal, Donna Woldring, Laurie Bos, Lynn Hoeksema, and Barb Haveman. It's interesting that all of these were also the prettiest girls, came from the best and wealthiest families, and did the best in school; these same gangs would coalesce with other gangs from other junior highs when we got to high school to form an interlocking social elite, but more on that below.

Our "dates" in those innocent days consisted of gathering after school at the Garfield Park ice skating rink and, between games of tag and "skunk," occasionally holding hands as we circled around the rink. Later, we graduated to roller-skating (our parents had to drive us) at the Grand Rapids arena where we couldn't play tag so we almost *had* to skate around arm in arm with each other. Still later, on our ninth-grade trip (to Detroit and Dearborn) we "graduated" to a still higher level when some of the gang in the darkened bus on the ride home engaged in a little "necking" or kissing and got in trouble with school authorities. My recollection is that I was not one of them, but not for lack of wanting.

Within the family during this period my Uncle Neil, the lawyer, attempted to integrate me and my cousin Larry Butterworth into the power and political life of the community by inviting us to lunches at the Pantlind Hotel (now the Amway Grand) of the Rotary and Lions Clubs. All of us in my family were boosters of hometown boy and stalwart reform Republican (in 1948 he had beaten the local machine dominated by longtime boss Frank Welch) Jerry Ford; attending Ford's rallies and debates was my first introduction to politics.

All eight members of my Dad's family took turns hosting the Thanksgiving dinner. (Uncle Roy's wife Sadie failed to take her turn which caused a lot of tension.) Uncle Jerry had moved to Ann Arbor to pursue his business career, so when we visited him and his family, that was my first introduction to the life and spirit of the University of Michigan. A larger, extended-family gathering took place once a year in the summer when the Wiardas and Huysers from all over Western Michigan gathered for horseshoes, baseball, a picnic, and family gossip.

Aunt Julia was in the foreign service and had been posted to all the hot spots, then as now: China, Korea, Indonesia, Afghanistan. Since foreign travel was still relatively rare in those days (pre-jet), when she came home for a visit it was a major family event. I remember the whole family including all the cousins gathering at the airport to welcome her and then see her off. She brought exotic gifts: a kimono to use as a robe for my mother, an Afghan water pipe for my Dad, a Chinese dagger and sheath (both inlaid with precious stones) for my cousins and me. Aunt Julia was a gorgeous blond with translucent blue eyes (like Bo Derek); she never married but her several romances were the "stuff" of much family gossip.

In 1954 I moved up to Grand Rapids Christian High School (GRCHS), which like the other schools I attended was part of the Christian Reformed Church school system. My high school was one of seven in the city, the others being South, Central, Creston, Ottawa Hills, Union, and Catholic Central—against whom we competed in sports and other activities. GRCHS was *the* Christian high school with about a thousand students in three grades, tenth to twelfth, and bringing together students from all the five Christian Reformed junior high schools in the city: Seymour, Baxter, Creston, West Side, and Oakdale; plus Protestant Reformed, a breakaway church from the Christian Reformed which had its own elementary school and junior high but not its own high school. I've long ago forgotten, as have most people in our denomination, what the theological differences are between the two churches (there's an old Dutch saying: "When two people come together, there's a church; when they part, there are two more.").

The merging of the six junior high classes into one senior high class gave rise to one of the most interesting—in retrospect—social and sociological phenomena I've ever seen, but maybe this is true of all school systems. In junior high my friends and I, male and female, had been a part of a small social clique; now in high school I discovered the other junior highs also had small social elites. What was so interesting was that at the high school level these previously separate social elites now joined forces to form a larger, but still exclusive, social clique. At the junior high level this had consisted of about six boys and six girls in my class; now at the larger high school level, it consisted of about twenty-five to thirty of each.

In fact, because of its numbers and its sometimes exclusivity in keeping others out, this clique came to be called the "dirty thirty." Each previously junior high group kept its autonomy, its long-established friendships, and its car pools for transportation to school and sports events; but when the groups came together for parties, social gatherings, and beach bashes, we joined together in groups of about twenty-five to thirty boys and twenty-five to thirty girls. The girls in this elite group, as always, tended to be the prettiest, the smartest, and the wealthiest; the boys, only slightly more varied, included athletes, kids from good families, and class and school leaders. With this clique is how we sailed through high school. None of us ever asked what it was like for those not part of the "in" crowd.

Our group did everything together: went to sports events together, to the beach together, to parties together, and (mostly) into the National Honor Society together. We all took the same college-prep courses together, went out for the same sports teams together, and hung out in the hallways and at each other's homes together.[6] When our teams won the city championship in some sport, we all went down and did the bunny hop around the war memorial in Campau Square; when we started to drink beer, we went out to the distant fairways of one of the local country clubs where our late-night antics couldn't be heard. It was nice to be "in" with this clique and I'm sure it helped increase my self-confidence and my social graces (over time I must have dated two-thirds of the girls in the "dirty thirty"), but others even to this day resent the fact they were excluded and were not part of what we called the "with-it" group.

Because ours was a Christian high school, we were not supposed to do what other, more secular students did, including going to the movies. But I remember seeing some of the main movies that other people did, including the James Dean movie, *Rebel without a Cause*, and the moving (about drugs) Frank Sinatra movie, *Man with the Golden Arm*. Nor were we supposed to dance, but I remember seeing almost all the big bands then still touring out at the Fruitport pavilion on Lake Michigan: Les Elgart, Jimmy Dorsey, Glen Miller, Benny Goodman. Rock'n'roll was similarly *verboten* for good Christian kids like us but at the downtown Civic Auditorium in Grand Rapids I saw Bill Haley and his Comets, Fats Domino, Jerry Lee Lewis, Ray Charles, Carl Perkins ("Blue Suede Shoes"), and other groups. How harmless this all now seems!

In high school that first year I went out for the basketball team (my school didn't play football, although we did play sandlot; it was a violent sport and church authorities argued it was against God's wishes to harm our own or other people's bodies that way). I thought I was a cinch to make the team because I had been the second leading scorer on my junior high team and already knew from playing against them at that level who were the best players from the other city junior highs. But to my great shock and chagrin, I was cut after two weeks of tryouts. The coach's verdict was "Great shot [even today I can hit 80 percent of my free throws], but not fast enough to be a guard and not big enough to be a forward." I'm sorry to say he was correct, even though at the time I was completely devastated by the verdict. Everyone in my family is tall and thin and I do not have a large frame, so while other guys who were poorer shots but bigger than I made the team, I did not. It was *the absolute worst time* in my high school career.

In the spring I went out for the golf team and again got cut, despite beating some of the guys who made the team on the last day of tryouts. The coach said they had "more potential" than I. The next year I played with some of these same team members in a friendly match and beat them again—so much for their "potential" versus mine. Not only that but, in one of my smart-aleck phases, I went in after the latter match and told the coach à la the potential theme that I had just beaten, again, the persons who had made the team and for whom I had been cut. This did not exactly endear me to that particular teacher; fortunately, he taught accounting as well as coaching golf and I never had to take his class.

It turned out that tennis was my sport. I made the team my junior year and played on the no. 3 and then moved up to the no. 2 doubles team. I was slated to play no. 2 singles my senior year, but on the last day of practice the coach put me up against the no. 1-ranked player, Jon Tanja, in a winner-take-all match. I not only beat him but beat him badly, showing an aggressiveness and competitiveness that the coach (and maybe myself as well) didn't know I had. So I was elevated to the no. 1 position on a team that had a history of winning the city championship, and in my first several matches I, a complete unknown previously, continued undefeated knocking off two of the city's ranked players and winning notice and even headlines in the *Grand Rapids Press*.

All this did wonders for my ego and in terms of my standing among my fellow students and especially the girls of the dirty thirty. But then I ran into two of the city's best players, George Drasin and Larry Solomon, lost to both of them in tough, drag-out matches, and ended up being ranked third in the city. It was the high point of my athletic career.[7]

In high school I continued to favor English (still diagramming sentences), history, and math. My favorite subject was church history with Jimmy De-Borst who, unusual in a Christian school, offered a skeptical, even cynical view of church history. Jimmy went on to get a Ph.D. in political science from Michigan and later taught at Calvin College; our relationship grew into one of professional colleagues and friends rather than just teacher-student. As for the math, I did well in high school geometry, advanced algebra, and trigonometry; but when we got into calculus it threw me for a loop and I barely passed. That should have served as a warning signal that engineering should not be the field for me. But in those days, while the girls studied such "soft" subjects as languages, English, and social studies, it was thought to be manly and macho for boys to do math, physics, and chemistry. It would take my first, almost ruinous year at the University of Michigan for me to figure out that my interest in engineering and my talents didn't match up.

During tenth grade, and building on my writing and editorial experience at the junior high level, I joined the high school newspaper. I started as a sports reporter, then did general reporting, and eventually rose to be associate editor. But during that first year an event happened that was one of the decisive turning points in my life. I was chosen by the paper's faculty adviser and won a scholarship to attend a two-week summer program put on by Michigan State University's (MSU) journalism school, one of the best journalism schools in the country, for high school newspaper editors.

So off to East Lansing I went, a young, naive, fifteen-year-old, who had just completed his sophomore year, along with my classmate, fellow editor, and dirty-thirty member, Karen Helder, who had also been chosen to attend. There we were among a group of the smartest kids I'd ever met, from all over the state, all good writers and editors, and almost all of them older than we, going into their senior year whereas Karen and I were just going into our junior year. The atmosphere was electric; the classroom training, excellent; and the bull sessions incredible from the point-of-view of my experience as a kid growing up in a sheltered, conservative, Christian community. These were all bright, able students; they were more experienced and had "been around" more than I; and they represented a degree of pluralism and diversity that I had never experienced before in Calvinistic Grand Rapids. I think I learned and experienced more in those two weeks than at any previous time in my entire life—maybe more than my whole previous life cumulatively.

Two experiences particularly stand out. For the newspaper that we produced during our time there, I was assigned to interview Michigan State's legendary football coach, Duffy Dougherty. Dougherty had taken Michigan State from being an also-ran to a Big Ten and national championship team; the rise of the football team paralleled that of MSU itself, which, after being in the shadow of the great University of Michigan down the road in Ann Arbor for many decades, had now emerged as a first-rate university. I went over to the athletic department offices that were the largest and plushiest I'd ever seen. My interview with Dougherty, who was to that point the most famous person I'd ever met, consisted mostly of him talking nonstop in a profanity-filled monologue that was a total shock to my tender, Calvinistic (in Grand Rapids we never talked that way), fifteen-year-old ears. After the interview was over, Dougherty gave me a sheepish look as if even he recognized that he'd gone too far. I wrote up the interview, swear words and all, along with my description of the plush offices in which the athletic department was housed compared to the spare academic offices I'd seen, and we published the story. It caused quite a ripple on the MSU campus and our program received several tut-tut calls from University administrators. Fortunately, they were inclined to indulge us; perhaps the fact it was summer and few people would see the story also had something to do with the mild response.

The other experience was that I fell in love, really for the first time. Her name was Jane (Janie) Travis from St. Clair, Michigan, on the other side of the state. She was also a high school newspaper editor, very smart, quick, and a good writer. She was also pretty, with strawberry-blonde hair, quiet, a bit shy. I met her the first day in East Lansing; after that we did everything together, going to class, to the movies, canoeing on the Grand River that flows through the MSU campus. It's a beautiful campus, one of the nicest anywhere; I think I fell in love both with university life there and with Janie. We corresponded over the next year; I visited her the following summer in St. Clair; and when I was a student at Michigan and she at Eastern Michigan University, we dated once or twice. Janie was the first girl I'd ever dated who was not Dutch; I seem to remember it also got back to my high school via fellow editor Karen Helder that Howard had dated outside of the fold—that is, outside of the Dutch, Calvinist community. That was not forbidden, but it did raise some eyebrows.

Junior and senior years flowed along rapidly. I made the National Honors Society as well as the tennis team. I got my athletic letter; I was now a "jock." I joined the debate team with my good buddy David Fuller, the son of a prominent Grand Rapids Baptist minister; together, Dave and I had also won the Grand Rapids city table tennis championship in doubles. Being on the debate team taught me about the fun of doing research, sharpened my analytical skills, and provided valuable lessons in thinking quickly and on your feet and offering pointed rhetorical responses. I have to confess that Fuller and I were also sneaky: sometimes to bolster our position (the debate issue that year was "Resolved that federal aid to education will increase federal control of education"—how quaint that now sounds) we would *make up* quotes from prominent officials—and then hope neither the judges nor the other team tripped us up.

A big day was when I received my driver's license. I made my Dad get up at 6:00 A.M. on the day of my sixteenth birthday (you could get a learner's permit at fourteen, a license at sixteen) so we could go down to the police station and get the license before school started. That way I could take the car to school that day, a really big deal. You find you suddenly have many more friends when you can drive. Within two weeks, like many first-time teen-drivers, I had had my first accident while transporting my friends to a basketball game. It was a stupid, macho-driven accident when, urged on by my friends, I tried to beat another car at a red light, had to swerve in to avoid a parked car, and clipped the other car. My fault! No way around it. My father didn't say a lot and didn't ground me, but I knew he wasn't pleased. In the Dutch community that was usually punishment enough.

With my new driver's license I had lots of dates. Almost all were from the dirty thirty. I went steady for the first time, with Nancy Roossien, a romance that lasted for about a year. I also dated Marilyn Hekman, daughter of the cookie and biscuit Hekmans. She was older than I and not very pretty but she had a cottage on Lake Michigan with a tennis court. With my new tennis prowess and the glory that went with it, other members of the team and I hung out there a lot. One day her volatile father, who had a fierce temper, kicked us all off the court because we were monopolizing it so much that he was unable to use it himself.

The Hekmans, Hollanders, Hoeksemas, and other family friends and schoolmates all had cottages on the north side of "the channel," which ran between Lake Michigan and Lake Macatawa; this area, called Ottawa Beach, was all "Dutch country." But the southerly side, the towns of Douglas, Saugatuck (an artsy community and a gay hangout), and Macatawa just south of the channel, was "Yankee country." Here a lot of wealthy people from Chicago and St. Louis had cottages and kept their yachts.

One of my best high school friends in those days was Chris Van Den Berg whose father owned Klingman Furniture, one of Grand Rapids' biggest furniture stores, and had a gorgeous cottage at Macatawa, then as now an expensive, gated community. Chris and I hung out together at Macatawa and painted cottages during the summer. Chris's Dad had a big thirty-two-foot Chris Craft inboard cabin cruiser which he allowed Chris and me to take out. If you think having a car is a way to get girls, imagine what it's like having a cabin cruiser. One of the girls I dated that summer was Torrey Fritz, whose mother was an Anheiser from St. Louis, of Anheiser-Busch beer fame. Now, there was *real* money; Chris and I noted that Mr. Fritz, who had married into the Anheiser family, never worked a day in his life. Not exactly in accord with the Calvinist ethos but certainly a pretty soft life.

When it came time to apply to college, I let my folks know that I intended to go to the University of Michigan and not to Calvin College. As I said earlier, I was not a rebel against my church, my family, or any community. Instead I was convinced that Michigan had a better engineering school and that I could get through there faster than at Calvin, which only had a pre-engineering program. While this reasoning sounds perfectly rational, I'm sure there were other motives involved, perhaps unconscious ones only half understood at the time. These included Michigan's reputation as a truly great university, the prestige of its athletic teams that always seemed to win national championships, the excitement of the prospect of going away from home and conquering new mountain ranges, and doubtless also that summer experience at Michigan State University the year before where I experienced campus life for the first time.

So in the fall of 1957 we loaded up the car and off to Ann Arbor I went— a young (seventeen), naive, sheltered, Calvinist kid from Grand Rapids looking to make his mark in the larger world.[8]

Notes

1. I was once picked up by the police, ironically on my way home from a church youth meeting. Apparently a liquor store a few blocks from the church had been robbed and, walking home from the church, I was spotted by a police stakeout. It took the police about half a minute to figure out I did not fit the profile of the liquor store robber; they then drove me the rest of the way home.

2. My folks had occasional arguments just like everyone else, but they were never violent and divorce was out of the question. I recall after one of these arguments crying to my mother, "What will my friends say if you separate or get a divorce?" Apparently that—what would our friends and coreligionists say—was a powerful disincentive to even the thought of divorce.

3. Siegfried Wiarda, *Wiarda, 1369-1969* (Bolsward, The Netherlands: A. J. Osinga, 1970).

4. "Walked" means my mother walked and pulled, while I rode in a wagon or on a sled. One night in a heavy snowstorm, I rolled off the sled and into a large snow bank. My mother went several blocks ahead before discovering I was missing. Occasionally, we stopped off halfway for a special treat: an ice cream cone at Millers ("Real Cream") Ice Cream, then 5 cents.

5. I'm not sure if I should tell this story but, in the interest of truth in packaging, here it goes. One summer when I was out on the farm (it would have been 1953), the Rosenberg spy case was reaching its fateful conclusion; the Rosenbergs had been found guilty of passing nuclear secrets to the Soviet Union and were about to be executed. So cousin Robert and I devised a game that we called "Hang the Rosenbergs." We went way up into the highest beams of the barn, made a slipknot in the rope we carried, and managed to lasso one of the barn cats below. We almost (but not quite) killed that poor cat, managing to get the rope off just in time but leaving a rope-burn on the cat's neck. Unfortunately for us, Robert's older brother spotted the mark and reported us to his father. We both got a well-deserved bawling out for that one.

6. When my high school class had its thirty- and forty-year reunions, the self-same "dirty thirty," now accompanied by wives and husbands, still got together separately for pre- and post-reunion dinners and parties.

7. I actually got bigger headlines and my picture in the paper when in a practice match I killed a flying bird with my hard first serve. That was sufficiently dramatic and unprecedented (I've never done it since and wonder how many tennis players have) that I got more attention and notoriety from that one event than from any routine match victory.

8. The University of Michigan years, 1957-1961, are described in Howard J. Wiarda, *Universities, Think Tanks, and War Colleges: The Main Institutions of American Educational Life* (Philadelphia: Washington Center for International Politics, 1999), chapter 2.

CHAPTER FIVE

New Amsterdam
and the East Coast Dutch

By "East Coast Dutch" I mean the Stuyvesants, Van Burens, Van Cort-lands, Van Rensselaers, Van Leers, Vanderbilts, Roosevelts, and others who make up a kind of Dutch colonial elite in America. These Dutch pioneers and explorers came to America in the seventeenth century (as opposed to my ancestors who came in the nineteenth century), discovered the Hudson River (named for explorer Hendrik Hudson), settled in and around Man-hattan and the Tappan Zee (the Dutch word for sea), and were among the earliest colonists in America. Many of these families became incredibly wealthy and constituted an American aristocracy which is still making headlines today: witness the saga of Gloria ("poor little Gloria") Vander-bilt or the Vanderbilt estate (Biltmore) in Ashville, North Carolina, now a major tourist attraction.

Irreverently, I refer to these elite families as the "upper Hudson Dutch." For they were the founders of many of the cities around New York (Brooklyn is a Dutch name; so is Long Island), up and down the Hudson River (Peek-skill, Albany, and Schenectady were all founded by the Dutch), and across the river in New Jersey (Paterson, the Oranges, Passaic, Hackensack—all have significant Dutch populations). As the first settlers, they had the op-portunity to stake out claims to land and business opportunities (railroad, steamship lines, etc.) that later settlers lacked. Many of them became fabu-lously rich and took on aristocratic airs.

The original East Coast Dutch communities were, of course, supple-mented by later waves of Dutch settlers. Not all of these were wealthy, by any means, or became so—although they were all, doubtless, attracted by the wealth and opportunities that the earlier Dutch colonists accumulated. Many of these later settlers came in the nineteenth century as part of the same great wave of immigrants that settled Western Michigan. They got as far as the New York area, looked around, found fellow Dutchmen there, and decided not to go any farther west. After World War II another wave of Dutch immigrants: no longer very Calvinistic and, therefore, not enthused about settling in Grand Rapids, augmented the Dutch communities in New York and New Jersey.

Although my family and I always had a certain populist, recent-immigrant disdain for the older, more established East Coast Dutch whose main accomplishment seems to have been to inherit (as distinct from earning) wealth, recent historical interpretations have cast a new light on the early history of New Amsterdam (New York). In the work of Russell Shorto and others,[1] New Amsterdam has been portrayed as a bastion of liberty, tolerance, and freedom. New Amsterdam was patterned after old Amsterdam, even then Europe's most tolerant, pluralist, and freedom-loving (including free trade) city. Shorto argues that, while the Pilgrims and Puritans of New England were founding closed societies based on intolerance, in Manhattan and neighboring cities the Dutch were founding settlements based on free trade, liberty, and an upwardly mobile melting pot whose lasting influence was felt not just in New York but throughout America. Shorto is, in fact, arguing that it was the Dutch, not the Pilgrims, who, in their liberalism, open-mindedness, entrepreneurialism, commitment to freedom, and love of their new country, provided *the* model for America, with a lasting impact on U.S. history. This thesis is so important and so intriguing that it merits greater scrutiny.

Dutch Explorations

It was precisely at the time that The Netherlands finally succeeded in freeing itself from Spanish and Hapsburg oppression, around the turn of the seventeenth century, that the Dutch "Golden Age" began. We can date that period from roughly 1600 to 1680. It was a period of tremendous flowering of Dutch art and culture, as well as exploration.

When one looks at the map of Dutch conquests and explorations during this period, the extent of the Dutch empire is truly astounding. In the Americas, it included Brazil, the Guianas, the Caribbean islands of Aruba, Bonaire, Curaçao, Saba, St. Eustatius, and St. Maarten (shared with the French), as well as New York and its environs reaching all the way from New England to the Carolinas. In Africa it included South Africa, Mauritius, Delagoa Bay, even Ethiopia for a time. In the Middle East it included parts of Persia (Iran) as well as coastal islands off the Arabian Peninsula and the Gulf of Oman.

But it is in Asia that the primary Dutch colonial empire was established. The reach and strength of this seventeenth-century empire, for a time, was truly astounding. It matched in size the great empires of all time: the Roman Empire, the Spanish and Portuguese empires of the sixteenth century, and the British empire of the nineteenth century (upon which the sun never set!). That such a small country could conquer and sustain such a large empire, while at the same time taking on or holding at bay the other large powers of Europe, is quite remarkable. Even today there are "white tribes" of former Dutch colonialists in many of these non-Western areas.[2]

The Dutch colonies, settlements, or trading posts in Asia included the "spice islands" of the Moluccas, Amboyna, and Banda, much of Western New Guinea, Australia (explored by the Dutch long before the British arrived there), the Celebes Islands, Borneo, the big Indonesian islands of Sumatra and Java, Japan (from 1640 to 1854 the Dutch were the only Europeans in Japan, long before the American Commodore Perry got there), Formosa (controlled by the Dutch from 1624 to 1662, its capital called Zeelandia), The Philippines, various coastal enclaves around India, the key strategic port of Malacca on the Maylaysian coast, Ceylon (now Sri Lanka), as well as coastal areas of what are now Burma, Cambodia, and Vietnam. Indeed, one would be hard-pressed to find a place in Asia, or the world, which the Dutch did not explore and/or conquer in the seventeenth century. It is no wonder that the best maps of the world during this period were also produced by the Dutch.

We explore in later chapters quite a number of these colonial possessions and the theme of Dutch "fragments" in various parts of the world, but here our focus is on the Dutch in the eastern United States. The first thing to say is that this part of the New World was explored, settled, and colonized by the Dutch during precisely the same period, the early seventeenth century, as the other colonies listed above. Dutch explorers were apparently exploring the North American coast (Labrador, Newfoundland, Canada, New England) as early as the late sixteenth century, but it was not until 1604 when The Netherlands' Hendrik Hudson, sailing for the Dutch East India Company, began to lay claim to the area. The Dutch empire in North America, called New Netherlands, lasted until 1664 when they were defeated by a much larger British fleet, and New Amsterdam was renamed as New York.

Even in America the size of the Dutch empire in the early seventeenth century was astounding. We all know from our fourth-grade history courses that the Dutch settled initially in lower Manhattan and that Peter Minuit famously bought the entire island for twenty-four dollars and a few trinkets, but we are unaware of how large this early Dutch "New Netherland" colony was. Hudson had explored as far south as the mouth of the Chesapeake Bay, the entrance to the King's River where the English colony of John Smith was, and then continued south to Cape Hatteras, North Carolina. Turning around, he explored Delaware Bay that the Dutch later settled, and then sailed into the magnificent harbor that is New York and the Hudson River. Later, in looking for a northwest passage to Asia, he explored the entire east coast of Canada, the St. Lawrence River, and sailed into Hudson Bay. Manhattan was actually settled in 1624, fifteen years after Hudson's voyage of exploration, the same year the Dutch landed in and conquered Brazil.

Not wanting to frontally challenge the British in Virginia, the Dutch pulled back from establishing a colony that far south. Nevertheless, the "empire" that they did establish in America was extensive. It included Delaware as far south as Lewes, Delaware (more on this below), Delaware Bay, all of Pennsylvania as far west as the Ohio border, up along the Great Lakes (Erie and Ontario), the northern border (reaching to Canada) of what is now New York state and all of New York, much of Connecticut as far east as the Connecticut River (which the Dutch called the Fresh River), and much of the New England coast from New York, along Connecticut and Rhode Island, until it again began bumping up against the English colonies in Massachusetts. It would have been interesting for the future development of the country if all this area had remained Dutch instead of becoming British!

Shorto makes a compelling case for what the Dutch accomplished in their thirty-eight-year occupation of Manhattan and the surrounding area. First, they were committed to ethnic and social diversity and pluralism. To the New Amsterdam colony came all manner of men and women: traders, merchants, prostitutes, craftsmen, farmers, slaves and former slaves, sailors, riff-raff, trappers, explorers, the high and the low. To the Dutch colony came a mix of Germans, Italians, Swedes, Jews, Indians, and Africans that made New Amsterdam truly the first American melting pot. They all mingled together in an open, almost classless society that was much more egalitarian and democratic than the slavery-supporting Virginia Squirearchy or the exclusivist Puritanical New Englanders would ever be.

Second, they were free traders. That's what the Dutch did, whether in Curaçao, Malacca, Cape Town, Amsterdam, or New York. They believed, perhaps alone among Europeans at the time, in open markets, open competition, and free trade; those are the principles that were making the Dutch rich and enabled everyone to get ahead. The Netherlands was a trading nation;

as a small country, that was the only way it could survive. Of course, The Netherlands—and New Amsterdam—was also a Calvinist nation; but I am consistently amused as a student of Dutch history (and a lapsed Calvinist) that whenever these two, the Calvinism or the profit-making, came in conflict, it was always the profit-making that won out. Or else the Dutch in their clever way figure out a way to reinterpret their Calvinism to make it compatible with their profit-making efforts. *Never* does the Calvinism get in the way of the profit-making, although Calvinist preachers are constantly entreating entrepreneurs to recognize their Biblical obligations to share their wealth. And let us not forget those famous Max Weber findings about the intimate relations between Dutch Calvinism and its capitalism.[3]

Third, there is Dutch Calvinism. The Dutch brought their Calvinism to America. Calvinism can be a strict and unbending belief system, and at certain times and places in the Dutch empire it was. But in other, especially frontier areas of the empire—Jakarta, Malacca, Cape Town, Recife, New Amsterdam, and Amsterdam itself (where most of the Dutch settlers in the New World came from), it can be and often was quite tolerant. Not always because it wanted to be, but because often in these frontier areas with their polyglot peoples and belief systems, they had no other choice in the matter.

We have already seen in my own family history that the urban areas and cities of The Netherlands were much more liberal and tolerant (i.e., less Calvinist) than the rural areas, and it was indeed from the cities that the first New Amsterdamers came. Moreover, in the New World they found, or brought in, Lutherans, humanists, and free thinkers, atheists, Anglicans, Baptists, various types of Calvinists, and Jews, some from the Sephardic (Spanish, Portuguese) community of Amsterdam already living in freedom there, and some from the Jewish communities in Brazil, Suriname, and Curaçao recently transplanted to New Amsterdam. Remember this is the seventeenth century not exactly known for its religious tolerance, but within that context the New Amsterdam colony was about as free and tolerant as it could possibly be.

Fourth, New Amsterdam, following the lead of the United Provinces of The Netherlands, proved to be a cradle of political freedom and representative government as well, long before the Declaration of Independence or the Constitution. In my training as a political scientist, I had always looked to John Locke, the Mayflower Compact, Jonathan Edwards, and John Winthrop as the forefathers of American democracy. Probably that is true because the writings and documents they produced are all in English; plus, American history, except for the Revolutionary War and War of 1812, has always had an Anglophile bias. But the not-so-well-known history of the United Colonies in The Netherlands, and now the translation and release of the mammoth, heretofore largely untapped records of the Dutch New Netherland colony undertaken by Charles Gehring and the New Netherland project of the New York State Library in Albany, are revealing that the Dutch got to democracy and representative government long before the British did. And in Adriaen Van der Donck, whose writings about his beloved America are almost completely unknown mainly because he wrote in Dutch, Gehring, Shorto, and others have discovered a heroic figure who in the 1650s fashioned a proposal on democratic, representative, tolerant self-governance that may have been at least as important in the fashioning of a free and republican America as anything the Massachusetts, Philadelphia, or Virginia colony writers did.

So in New Amsterdam we have a very interesting situation in many ways. First, the Dutch empire in North America was much more extensive than anything I had ever been taught in my (British influenced?) history courses. Second, we have here a Dutch "fragment" but a very liberal, open, tolerant, free-wheeling, and democratic fragment that was a reflection of the free-wheeling Amsterdam of that time, and very different from the conservative, strict-Calvinist, rural-based Dutch fragment that would be set down in Western Michigan and other areas. And third, new research and documents are showing that New Amsterdam, not Boston, Plymouth, or Jamestown, was the cradle of our liberties, the foundation of our Bill of Rights, and the center of our open-market, globalized economy. It was the Dutch who spread the culture of the European Renaissance to America, and it was the Dutch who established a culture of pluralism, diversity, tolerance, and multiculturalism in a primitive and far-distant wilderness. It was the Dutch whose principles really founded America!

Roaming Around the Dutch East Coast

As a kid growing up in Western Michigan, I knew little of the extent of the Dutch colony on the east coast. Even in the (Dutch) Christian Reformed schools, which one would expect to be nationalistic and maybe even chauvinistic, when I took my first U.S. history course in fourth grade with Miss Hayes, we used a text that emphasized the British contributions to America, not the Dutch. I learned about Henry Hudson and the Hudson River, Peter Minuit and the twenty-four-dollar sale of Manhattan, and the peg-legged Peter Stuyvesant; but nothing more than that. Fifty-five years later I wonder if the Dutch schools in Grand Rapids have yet discovered *their own* national and ethnic history, as other ethnic groups have. Probably not; it would not be very Dutch for the nonchauvinistic and thoroughly Americanized Dutch to do so.

It was only after we moved to Washington, D.C., in 1981, bought a house in the Maryland suburbs, and began to explore the Delmarva

(Delaware-Maryland-Virginia) Peninsula that we began to discover this part of our roots.

Lewes, Delaware

Our first excursions to the Atlantic beaches with our kids were to Rehobeth Beach, a popular summer resort on the Delaware shore. But Rehobeth, though it had its roots as a Methodist town, was crowded, loud, and garish; we hoped to find another spot. Looking at the map, I discovered Lewes Beach, ten miles farther north, that looked more isolated and, therefore, hopefully less busy or loud. Examining my guidebook, I discovered a brief note that Lewes had a Dutch history.

So off we went; Lewes turned out to be as peaceful and as traffic-free as we'd imagined. It had a beautiful, uncrowded beach and several nice restaurants. But more than that, it had all this Dutch background! First of all, the name Lewes is a Dutch name, after one of the early explorers who landed on this point (Cape Henlopen, also a Dutch name). Henry Hudson had passed by just offshore on his way to the Chesapeake. Lewes had Dutch street names and even (a gem of a find for a builder-architect like me) some Dutch-style architecture. But most of all, it had a small gem of a Dutch museum, itself with an Amsterdam-like architectural building design.

Cape May, New Jersey

We didn't have the time to do it then, but on that first trip to Lewes we discovered there was a ferry that would take us up the coast to Cape May, New Jersey, at the mouth of the Delaware River. Hence, when we went to Lewes Beach the second time, we budgeted plenty of time for an all-day visit via the ferry to the Cape. Cape May is a pretty town, overlooking the water, with perhaps the best-preserved collection of Victorian-style homes and architecture in the United States. My father, who had once built houses like this in Grand Rapids, would have loved Cape May.

I had been aware of Cape May before but hadn't realized that it represented a misspelling, or an Americanized version of the Dutch name, Mey. And, in fact, Cornelius Mey was the Dutch sea captain who delivered the first boatload of settlers to New Amsterdam in 1624, later sailing down the New Jersey coast and rounding the point (Cape Mey, as it *should* be spelled) before entering Delaware Bay.

New Castle, Delaware

Just two miles from the (Delaware) Bay Bridge, tucked in between the ugly oil tanks and refineries, is the cute, quaint, historic, little town of New Castle,

Delaware. Who would have thought that a town named New Castle was once a Dutch settlement? It was originally called New Amstel—just like the beer.

New Castle was actually founded by Peter Minuit, the same Peter Minuit who bought Manhattan for twenty-four dollars, but this time in the service of the Swedish crown. So New Castle began in 1638 as a small Swedish colony, until Peter Stuyvesant—he of the one leg—defeated the Swedes and drove them out in 1655. Shortly thereafter, a group of some three hundred Dutchmen set sail from Amsterdam and reestablished the colony as New Amstel. It remained a Dutch settlement until the British defeat of the Dutch in 1662.

From this base on the Delaware River estuary, however, the Dutch dominated all the trade in the area: upriver in Pennsylvania (the Schuylkill River flowing through Philadelphia is a Dutch name), all of New Jersey, Northern Maryland, and Delaware down to Cape Henlopen, near Lewes. The main items of trade were furs, tobacco, and (of course, given the name of the settlement) beer. The Dutch, like the Spanish, Portuguese, English, and French during this time, were also involved in the slave trade, bringing slaves from Africa via the Caribbean directly into New Castle.

Rather like New Amsterdam itself, New Amstel was, above all else, a *commercial* enterprise. No effort, as far as anyone can tell, was made to Christianize, let alone Calvinize, the native population. Instead, the purpose here was trade and commerce; as in New Amsterdam, religious beliefs were never allowed to get in the way of profit-making. There were no attempts at religious conversion; few Calvinists were to be found among the Indians.

It's a beautiful little town, carefully and lovingly preserved and restored— like colonial Williamsburg, only nicer. We toured the Amstel House, the Straand, the Dutch House, and the Dutch Museum. The Dutch House, of sturdy brick and with red shutters, has real Delft pottery and tiles, Dutch cooking utensils and fireplace items, and original Dutch maps of the world. The Museum, embarrassingly and disgracedly, details the leading Dutch role in the slave trade. Lunch was on the green in the center of town in the Arsenal, which was actually an arsenal during the War of 1812, now converted into a fine restaurant. It was built long after the Dutch had been expelled, but it sure was a wonderful place to eat and catch our breath.

The Hudson River Valley Dutch

When I was a little kid, my father, who was very interested in Dutch history, took us on a tour of New York and the Hudson River Valley. We visited Peter Stuyvesant's grave at the church of St. Mark's in The Bowery; somehow my father knew that Stuyvesant was the son of a Calvinist minister and that he had originated in our own home territory of Friesland. My Dad insisted that I know that not only Manhattan but also Staten Island was bought by the Dutch, that Brooklyn was originally a Dutch name, that Bronx is a Dutch word, that Flatbush and Flushing were Dutch words, that Yonkers is also a Dutch name. He showed me all around the southern tip of Manhattan where the Dutch had first settled; he insisted that the Bowery, Canal Street, Broome Street, Wall Street, and Broadway, to say nothing of the Holland Tunnel—all had their origins as Dutch names or because of the Dutch historical background of the area.

After three days in New York, we set off up the Hudson Valley, with my father giving me a history lesson every step of the way. He insisted, correctly, that Hoboken in New Jersey, the Oranges, and Nassau County were all Dutch names. He told me that Princeton University (one of the places I was then thinking of applying to for college) was founded as a Dutch Reformed theological seminary, that Hofstra University (of course, "The Flying Dutchmen") on Long Island had also been founded as a Dutch college. While Tappan was the name of one of the Indian tribes in the area, the Tappan Zee and Tappan Zee Bridge were Dutch names. Although we did not visit them at the time, my Dad told me that Paterson, Passaic, Newark, Hackensack, and Montclair in New Jersey had all at one time been "Dutch cities" and still had strong Reformed or Christian Reformed churches.

Continuing upriver we went through Sleepy Hollow, deep in Dutch country, where Washington Irving had penned his famous stories about Ichabod Crane, the headless horseman, and the upper Hudson Dutch. On the way to West Point, we passed through Ossining, Verplanck, and Peekskill—all towns with Dutch origins. Farther upriver are Hyde Park, the estate of the (Dutch) Roosevelts, the Vanderbilt mansion, and the Martin Van Buren National Historic Site. The towns that dot the riverbank—Staatsburg, Kinderhook, Schodack and Schodack Center, Brookview, Nassau and East Nassau, Poestenkill, Defreesville, Rensselaer, and, of course, Stuyvesant—are named or formed from the Dutch settlements founded on the Hudson.

Much of this was, and in some places still is, apple country; the Cortland (originally Cortlandt) apple comes from here. This is where the Dutch colonial elite grew up—the Van Rensselaers, Vanderbilts, Van Burens, Schuylers, Van Leers, Van Cortlandts, and Roosevelts—names that are so famous they are now frequently caricatured on American television comedies as symbols of wealth, aristocratic status, and do-nothingness. Even as a child my Dad had warned me that the wealthy Dutch families in this area were different from the Dutch in Grand Rapids, that they had abandoned their Calvinism and were "too rich."

Albany, the capital of New York, was founded as a Dutch city by Peter Stuyvesant; there are still traces of this heritage left, and the rich Dutch archives of the New York State Library are located here. The original settlement was called Beverwyck (a Dutch name), later it became Fort Orange (after the Dutch royal family), and eventually was rechristened as Albany in 1686. A controversy exists now because archeological evidence of the original Dutch settlement has recently been found, but the State of New York wants to put an office building there.

Now traveling west on Interstate 90, the old Mohawk Trail, we come to Schenectady, Rotterdam, Amsterdam, Sprakers, West Schuyler, and Utica—all Dutch names. And then to Syracuse, not a Dutch name but a Greek one, although named by the Dutch; and don't forget the Syracuse University sports teams are the "Orangemen," named, like Fort Orange, after the House of Orange, the Dutch royal family.

Many years later I went back to the New York area to explore my roots. I attended Dutch Reformed and Christian Reformed churches in New York, Paterson, Paramus, Passaic, and Nyack. Congressman Marge Rokema, whom we got to know during our policy work in Washington, D.C., was the representative from this northern New Jersey district, a liberal Republican like me, and who, like me, came out of the Dutch Reformed tradition. Quite a number of these churches, however, were in bad shape with dwindling congregations, few young people, and an absence of pastors. Quite a few of the Reformed churches in this area had had to be closed down and the buildings sold for other purposes.

Out of this experience I learned quite a few important lessons. First, the historic Dutch families in the New York and upper Hudson areas had largely abandoned their Calvinist and Reformed religious roots. They had become too rich, too spoiled, too Americanized, too secularized. It was sad to me that they either had forgotten over time or abandoned their roots and origins. Great wealth, power, connections, and assimilation had caused them to lose touch with who they were. They reminded me of some of the Dutch in The Netherlands whom we met who had similarly abandoned their roots and origins, and who, ironically, struck me as almost Calvinistic in their degree of anti-Calvinism.

But not all the Dutch in the New York region were wealthy, well-connected, or social climbers. Some of these could also trace their origins back to colonial times; they often had Dutch names but had been so assimilated into modern, secular, American culture that they no longer felt any identity whatsoever as "Dutch-Americans."

A second group had come to America, like my forbears, as immigrants in the nineteenth century. But instead of going on to the by-then-established

Dutch communities in Western Michigan, Iowa, or Wisconsin, they chose to stay in the New York–New Jersey area. Many of them joined Reformed or Christian Reformed churches—at least for a time. But now, by the third or fourth generation, many of them or their children have drifted apart from the church. They no longer attend or attend regularly, do not support the church adequately financially, no longer send their children to Christian schools, etc. All this helps explain why so many of the Dutch Reformed churches in this area are in trouble, cannot attract pastors, or are being closed.

At one point, the Reformed Church of America was the dominant church in this area, whereas the Christian Reformed represented a small, more orthodox splinter group. But now the proportions have been reversed: the Reformed Church, not just in the east but nationwide, has become the smaller of the two. The Reformed Church has a total of about 200,000 members nationwide, while the Christian Reformed has a membership of 300,000—this in an American population in which about 2,700,000 persons self-identify as being of Dutch descent. Both churches are in decline but, whereas the Christian Reformed is declining by about 3 percent per year, the Reformed Church is declining much more precipitously.

I attribute this to two factors. First, the Christian Reformed Church, though it now has quite a number of churches in the east, is still mainly concentrated in "frontier" areas, in the Midwestern heartland, in relatively isolated areas like Grand Rapids, Pella, Sioux Center, Oostburg, or Lynden. As such, it has been more immune from, or able greater to resist, the Americanizing, secularizing, and overall decline of religion trends in which the more heavily East Coast Reformed Church finds itself. Second, of the two, the Reformed Church is more liberal. As such, it has been a victim of the general decline of the liberal, mainline denominations in America in recent decades, an affliction that has affected such other liberal groups as Unitarians, Presbyterians, Methodists, Friends, Congregationalists, and Anglicans. In contrast, we know that more evangelical, conservative, and orthodox churches (including the Christian Reformed) are thriving or at least holding their own.

Terra Ceia, North Carolina

Terra Ceia is an anomaly in this discussion: located on the East Coast, it is nevertheless an isolated, frontier, farming community, more akin to the strict, Calvinist Dutch communities of the Midwest than to those of the upper Hudson.

Terra Ceia is thirty miles east of Washington, North Carolina, twenty miles north of the Neuse River that empties into Pamlico Sound, and about eighty miles inland from the Outer Banks. Nearby is the town of Pamtego where a number of the Dutch families live; fifty miles to the east on Lake Mattamuskeet is New Holland, North Carolina. But what is New Holland without Hollanders?

Much of this area is swampy and wet, not far from Alligator Lake and the Alligator-Pungo Canal, which should tell you a lot about Terra Ceia, Pantego, and New Holland. Once it had been drained of water—something the Dutch are good at—what remained was a fertile, spongy soil with layers of peat moss underneath that sometimes caught fire from lightning strikes and proceeded to burn from underground, sometimes for weeks. The biting insects are vicious and travel in clouds; there are no urban entertainments anywhere nearby. I only discovered Terra Ceia by accident because my daughter lives in Havelock, back across the Neuse River, with the Marine Air Station base nearby, and happened to see an ad for Terra Ceia's Christian Reformed Church's Sunday service in her local newspaper.

Terra Ceia is a rural, farm community. By now, large agri-industrial farms are replacing the smaller family farms of the past. There are a few business or commercial establishments in town, but there are two churches, a parsonage, a thriving Christian school, and an old, run-down cotton gin next to a similarly unused and rusting railroad spur. The area once produced cotton and tobacco; now it is corn, vegetables, and flowers.

The Terra Ceia community is a very small and close-knit community; everyone knows everyone else and everyone else's business, family, and family history. It is also inbred and therein lies a potential genetic danger. Almost all the current residents are descendants of the early settler families—all inter-married. Everyone is a cousin of everyone else.

Terra Ceia (which is Spanish or Portuguese, not Dutch; it can be translated variously as Heaven's Land, Land of the Sky, or, more loosely, Where Earth Meets Heaven) was founded in 1925 when Hendrik Van Dorp, a Dutch farmer and farm manager, was persuaded to come to the area to manage a large, undeveloped ranch owned by an absentee New York lawyer, who saw future financial profitability in Beaufort and Hyde Counties. Van Dorp was the founding father; by placing ads in newspapers extolling the virtues of the area (warm climates, good and cheap land), he attracted a number of Dutch families to the area. Interestingly, those he attracted were not Hollanders from Holland but Dutchmen already in the United States who migrated to Terra Ceia from the Midwest, New York, and Canada.

The times were tough; it was the middle of the Depression. Some families moved away only to discover it was just as hard elsewhere; quite a number moved back. For a long time they struggled; even today the houses and the area seem to me quite poor and primitive compared to the relative affluence

I grew up within Grand Rapids. It is still a farming community; unlike far wealthier Grand Rapids, Terra Ceia has not diversified into a major business, commercial, and manufacturing center.

Terra Ceia is a Christian Reformed community, but in 1999 the community split. Dissident elements formed the United Reformed Church, a more conservative offshoot (if you believe that's possible) from the Christian Reformed Church. It's a familiar pattern in the Calvinist tradition: the main church adjusts to changing times, is accused of becoming too "liberal" by the more orthodox members, who then separate and form their own church. That is how the Christian Reformed separated from the Reformed and, in Grand Rapids, how the Protestant Reformed separated from the Christian Reformed. In Terra Ceia the split was caused by the old issues of women's roles in the church, the liberalizing trend within the CRC, and the fear the CRC was abandoning its roots. The Church lost its pastor in the process; the split divided friends and family; and the Terra Ceia Dutch Reformed community remains at odds, struggling, and still isolated.

Conclusion

It is estimated that there are about seven or eight million persons of Dutch descent in the United States. That is about half the population of The Netherlands itself. It is also far below the number of persons of German, British, Irish, Italian, African, and Hispanic origin in the United States. But of this seven or eight million, only about one-third of them self-identify as being of Dutch background; they have been thoroughly assimilated and are no longer "Dutch-Americans," just Americans. Also, of the seven to eight million, the vast majority are by now intermarried, of mixed ethnic backgrounds, and only partly Dutch.

The facts are that the Dutch are among the most successful and the most assimilated of all the immigrant communities in America. The Dutch have done very well here; they have been thoroughly integrated into the American melting pot. Almost no one calls himself or herself a Dutch-American anymore; that kind of ethnic identify has gone the way of the Model T. Dutch immigrant kids are quickly taught to learn English, dress like Americans, behave like Americans; they don't want to be "different." The Dutch are as American as apple pie (provided it is made out of Cortlandts!). That is true of both the East Coast and the Western Michigan Dutch.

Yet, I am fascinated by the differences between these two important Dutch communities. The Dutch in Western Michigan (and Pella, Sioux Center, Oostburg, and Lynden) tend to be conservative, Republican, self-reliant, independent, and strongly Calvinist in their ways. The East Coast Dutch, in contrast, tend to be more liberal, more diverse politically, more assimilated to the point of losing their identity as a separate ethnic group, and less Calvinist. They have joined the mainstreams, whereas the Western Michigan Dutch, while also doing well, still resist the pull of modern, secular culture.

But that is probably because the Western Michigan Dutch have only been here for a century-and-a-half, or six generations, while the East Coast Dutch have been here for four centuries. Driving into an East Coast Dutch community differs hardly at all from dropping into any other place on the East Coast, whereas spending only a few hours in Holland, Grand Rapids, or Pella you know quickly that you're in a town with a difference. So are the Western Michigan Dutch, as they're here longer, fated to become as assimilated and, therefore, as invisible culturally and religiously as the East Coast Dutch? Probably. But in the warp and woof of that transformation, let us hope that the Dutch are able to keep at least some elements of their culture, religion, identity, and distinctiveness intact.

Notes

1. Russell Shorto, *The Island at the Center of the World: The Epic Story of Dutch Manhattan and the Forgotten Colony That Shaped America* (New York: Doubleday, 2004).

2. Riccardo Orizio, *Lost White Tribes: The End of Privilege and the Last Colonials* (New York: The Free Press, 2001).

3. Max Weber, *The Protestant Ethic and the Spirit of Capitalism*

CHAPTER SIX

The Modern Netherlands: Community in Crisis

In his theory of the "fragments" of Western civilization—"islands" cast off from the "mainland" at different points sociologically and in history—Louis Hartz seems to suggest that it is the fragments that go astray because they are locked into or fixed (maybe even fixated) within the confining time period of their founding; whereas the mother countries remain in the mainstream of Western culture, progress, reform, and evolution.

But maybe the issue should also be looked at from the point-of-view that the fragments represent the true and authentic culture and civilization, that they also adapt and modernize, and that it is the mother countries that go astray by becoming too progressive, too advanced, and losing touch with their own traditions and culture. That is, in fact, how the Dutch in Western Michigan now view their compatriots back in The Netherlands: that we in America are the "true" Dutch, the repository of the historic values and culture as well as the incubation of the future, and that it is the Old Country that has lost its way, become secularized and maybe even decadent, torn itself away from its own history and moorings. I suspect that many Americans of European descent feel that way—particularly now that the Europeans have been less than faithful allies in the war on terrorism—about "Old Europe," their former home countries.

The Modern Netherlands

The Netherlands has always been a progressive country, going back to the Golden Age of the seventeenth century when, though a small country without abundant resources, it became one of the, if not *the*, leading countries in Europe. The Dutch pioneered in business, trade, exploration, capitalism, banking, mapmaking, sailing, the modern joint-stock company (the Dutch West and East India companies), finance, international law, and stock exchanges. Though the country went through its political ups and downs in the eighteenth and nineteenth centuries, it has always maintained its special edge in the economic marketplace. Today it is one of the richest, most progressive, most cosmopolitan, most dynamic countries in the world.

The Netherlands punches way above its weight in economics, business, and politics. It has only sixteen million people and no coal, no iron ore, no petroleum, no precious metals, few natural resources of any kind. Yet Holland is one of the most productive countries in the world; and the Dutch economy is one of the world's top fifteen in gross national product, way ahead of other countries that are far more populous. Think of a list of the leading companies in the world: Philips, Unilever, Royal Ahold,[1] Royal Dutch Shell, Elsevier Publishers, ABN Amro, De Beers, etc.—all of them are Dutch.

Now think of some of the world's leading politicians, especially at the international level: Rund Lubbers, head of the United Nations Refugee Agency; Willem Kok, the former Dutch Prime Minister and EU leader; Wim Duisenberg, head of the Central Bank; NATO Secretary General Jaap de Hoop Scheffer; and—not least—Gerardus Wiarda, President of the European Court of Justice. *All* of them are Dutch! The explanation is: (1) as a leading trading nation, the Dutch always think internationally; (2) as a small nation sandwiched between great powers, they give special emphasis to international law and institutions as a form of protection; (3) to survive and excel in a competitive world, the Dutch master at least three languages besides their own: English, German, and French; (4) they are viewed as moderates and political pragmatists, not hung up on ideology; (5) they are close to Brussels and the main capitals of Europe; and (6) it is often unacceptable to have representatives of the big powers (France, Germany, Great Britain) dominate international agencies so the Dutch are often turned to instead as acceptable to all and unacceptable to none.

The Dutch are progressive in their politics and society as well as their economics. In 2001 The Netherlands was the first country in the world to legalize same-sex marriages—seemingly flying in the face of its long Biblical and Calvinistic tradition. But then—again the fragment theme—The Netherlands is not the same country anymore that it was in the 1880s when my grandparents emigrated and carried their Calvinist religion with them. Today only about 4 percent of the population attend church regularly; the Dutch seem to be abandoning their Calvinist heritage as quickly as they can.

In addition to pioneering in gay marriage, The Netherlands seems eager to be the first also in gay divorce.

The Dutch similarly pioneered in the legalization of euthanasia. Over the last thirty years, the Dutch have become tolerant of euthanasia; they formally legalized it in 2001 (the same year as the legalization of gay marriage). At first, almost like a craze, there was a certain rush to voluntary death (in a few cases it was probably murder); more recently, the incidence of deaths by euthanasia has dropped off to hover around 3.5 percent of all deaths. It almost seems the Dutch were eager to embrace this progressive legislation just because it was progressive, but when it comes to actual implementation, the Dutch are still reluctant to defy their Calvinistic and Biblical ("Thou Shall Not Kill") precepts.

A pattern begins to emerge here. Back in the 1960s, The Netherlands was one of the first countries in the world to legalize abortion. It did so with great enthusiasm, defying religious authorities and wanting to demonstrate it was on the leading cutting edge of advanced social change. But along with legalizing abortion that made the country look progressive, it also sought to discourage it. That was the (residual) Calvinist side coming out. The Dutch simultaneously introduced a widespread, multipronged program of sex education for minors. The result is (rather like euthanasia) that, while The Netherlands seems very advanced on the side of abortion legislation, in practice the actual Dutch abortion rate is the lowest in the world.

Similarly with drugs. They are seemingly everywhere in Holland, especially in the big cities of Amsterdam and Rotterdam. The popular impression is that The Netherlands has legalized drugs, and for that it has been strongly criticized by a succession of U.S. drug czars; but the policy is actually more complex and sophisticated than that. There are, for example, in Amsterdam alone, some 250 "coffee shops" that offer a cornucopia of drugs with a menu that looks like the wine list in a five-star restaurant; it *appears* that drugs have been legalized.

But three other things are operating here: (1) drugs in The Netherlands are seen as a health and not a criminal issue, and, therefore, consumption of drugs is not illegal even while the authorities seek to reduce its use. And (2) the "coffee shops" are tightly regulated in terms of the amounts and age of the consumers, with the aim being to keep marijuana use from leading to the use of harder drugs. Finally (3), the Dutch system brings drug use out into the open instead of behind closed doors as in the United States so it can be carefully monitored and controlled rather than operating underground. The policy seems reasonable and maybe even Calvinistic—except that to visiting, sheltered Americans like me, it comes as a shock to see such an open exhibition of drug use. It is difficult to believe that the United States, with its own religious and pietistic traditions, could ever follow the Dutch example.

Prostitution is also legal in The Netherlands; in 2000 brothels were legalized. The again progressive Dutch idea was to turn prostitutes into "sex workers" and provide them with legal rights, social welfare benefits, and even their own union. But the prostitutes themselves were less enthused about the new policies because they included regulation, state inspections, and the requirement of paying income taxes! They also brought "sex tourism" to The Netherlands—planeloads of often drunk, rowdy foreign tourists looking for a good time. On the positive side, the Dutch program does seem to have succeeded in separating sex work from downright criminal activities.

All this modern Dutch progressivism dates from the 1960s. Perhaps no country in the world—not France, Germany, or the United States—was more affected by 1960s radicalism than The Netherlands. Religion, traditional authority, and the historic bases of societal consensus were all undermined. Young people, especially, abandoned the values of their parents; political power and decision-making passed to the streets in a series of "happenings." What was called "civil disobedience"—sometimes violent and anarchic protest movements—became the way to change society, not through the formal government institutions. Perhaps the "high point" of this era came with the coronation of Queen Beatrix in 1980 when the ceremony was drowned out in a haze of rioters, marijuana, and tear gas.[2]

From this period dates our perception of Dutch decadence—and, in the view of many, it has only gotten worse since! The trouble for The Netherlands is that this period of extreme tolerance for many forms of anti-social behavior came at the same time as extremely liberal and tolerant attitudes toward immigration. It is from this period that the flow of Muslim, mostly North African, immigrants into the country began, with virtually no background checks, extremely generous welfare payments for the immigrants, and open borders for "political refugees." The Dutch thought their assimilationist policies would work, that all these Muslims would want to become just like them, "little Dutchmen." But we now know that has not worked and, therefore, The Netherlands has a major potential terrorism problem on its hands. I believe the problems of terrorism and the problems of antisocial behavior in Holland are linked; that both stem from the abandonment of traditional moral beliefs (not just Calvinism but the emphasis on hard work, prudence, and discipline) and the acceptance of such an extreme sense of tolerance and political correctness that "anything goes," including both aberrant behavior and terrorism.

We have focused here on some of the seamier sides of "advanced" Dutch social programs, but it is also important to emphasize that The Netherlands has one of the most effective social welfare programs in the world. You never (well, almost never) see endemic poverty, malnutrition, bloated bellies, illiteracy, slum housing, or lost, hopeless street people in Holland. You see a lot of spaced-out kids—see the discussion to follow on the drug culture—but they all look six-feet-two and, as in Kansas, corn-fed. Meanwhile, in such social areas as education, housing, health care, old-age pensions, working conditions and hours, etc., the Dutch facilities and programs are superb.

There are some common threads here. First, the Dutch no longer believe in just condemning and suppressing "sin" but in bringing it out into the open and even treating it. Second, there is still a strong Calvinist streak in all of this: tolerance, yes, up to a point, but also a sense that many of these behaviors are wrong; good people (Calvin's "elect") do not engage in them; and they need to be corrected. After all, there is still a strong "Bible Belt" in both the South and North (away from the cities) of The Netherlands and, below the surface, a Calvinist ethic, if not any longer such strict religious beliefs. Third, the Dutch strategy is above all else pragmatic, aimed at solving problems rather than just condemning them moralistically but doing little about them. There is quite a distance here between the Grand Rapids and The Netherlands approaches to these issues, but below the surface common elements of that old Calvinist heritage still operate in both places,

Dutch Travels, 1973

In 1972–1973 we were living in Portugal but traveling extensively throughout Europe.[3] For a period in the spring, we were residing in the apartment of a friend of ours in Paris; from there my wife and I and our two children, Kristy and Howard, took the train up to Amsterdam. It was our first visit to The Netherlands.

Arriving at the Central Station, I almost went into culture shock. Instead of the clean, pristine, washed-daily streets of Dutch lore and my imagination, or of my own background in Dutch-clean Grand Rapids, Amsterdam was filthy. Or at least the area around the train station was; we later learned the rest of the country, even the Amsterdam suburbs, were as clean as we'd been led to believe. But central Amsterdam was dirty, grimy, and polluted: wastepaper, wrappings, cigarette butts, garbage. What you expect to see in a Third World capital but not in Holland. That was the first of several shocks.

Second, coming from a rather strict Calvinist background and expecting to see the same in The Netherlands, I was surprised to find how non-religious the country was. Almost no one went to church anymore. Only 40 percent believed in God—half that of the U.S. population. It was a thoroughly secular society—even though old Calvinist Sunday closing laws were still in force. Many churches had been sold to private investors to be turned into private homes, businesses, drug rehab centers, or for use—God forbid—as mosques. Visiting the Reformed churches on a Sunday morning and expecting them to be full as they would be in Grand Rapids, I was stunned to find even Rembrandt's church in the city center to be nearly empty—except for a few other Dutch-descent tourists like us from America.

As Iêda, the children, and I roamed around Amsterdam in the early evening, we were again stunned by the flagrant prostitution and open solicitation that we saw. I knew about Amsterdam's famous red-light (*Rosse Buurt*) district, but we had stumbled into it by accident and it was quite shocking to see it up close, especially with the kids along. At one house just as my nine-year-old daughter was going by, the shade flew open with a loud pop that, of course, attracted our attention. There in the window was this plump lady-of-the-night sitting in a chair completely in the nude. I had read about the liberal Dutch attitudes toward prostitution, but a blatant scene like this was too much. We hurried our children out of there as soon as possible.

I was similarly shocked by the open acceptance of homosexuality in The Netherlands (this was still the early 1970s), the tolerance of extreme kinds of deviant behavior, the embrace of left-wing, street politics, and the extent of the welfare state. What kind of a rock-ribbed Calvinistic, capitalistic country is this, I wondered, thinking of my own Dutch background in Western Michigan? The answer is: It isn't, or it isn't anymore. The mother country was now so different from the fragment that it was all but unrecognizable. Did we still have anything in common, I wondered? Not very much.

But what really shocked us more than anything else in Amsterdam was the pervasiveness of the drug culture. This was especially true for us coming from an earlier visit the previous fall to Latin America and now living in Portugal. There, people are poor, often malnourished, undersized, and often with malformed bodies; but at least they strive for self-improvement and work hard at it. In The Netherlands, however, what we have are otherwise healthy, well-fed, strapping young people throwing their lives away on drugs. These were not malnourished peasants but otherwise healthy kids frittering away their lives on the sidewalks of Amsterdam. What a waste! In walking around the city, we must have seen hundreds of these sorry, wasted youths whose ruination was, through readily available drugs, aided and abetted by the Dutch government. A disgrace! Shameful!

After only a few days in Amsterdam, I had begun to figure out what the country—"my" country—was all about. The Dutch, in order to appear more "progressive," had largely abandoned their religion and their Calvinism at the public level, but in many respects The Netherlands remained a Calvinist culture and society underneath. And, in some ways, a not very attractive one. For example, our daughter was balled out by some fastidious groundskeeper for playing on the grass in one of Amsterdam's parks, but what is a park for, I ask, if not for children to play? Our four-year-old son was screamed at by our hotel manager for pushing on the glass door with his fingers (thus leaving fingerprints!) instead of using the handle. I was, as a tourist unfamiliar with Dutch rules, yelled at on three occasions in two days, for inadvertently walking in a bicycle lane, walking across the street outside of a crosswalk, and crossing on a red light even if there was no traffic. Balled out in public by complete strangers! Only a Calvinist society would react in these ways, which were rude besides. I cannot imagine the same thing happening in similarly Calvinist, but much more polite and considerate, and much less uptight, Grand Rapids. At least there they're forthright about their Calvinism and don't have to be hypocritical about it.

Of course, our visit to Amsterdam was not all sour. In between these bad experiences, we had the opportunity to take in the Rijkmuseum, the Rembrandt Museum, Dam Square (where all the druggies hang out), the Anne Frank House, the Old and New (Reformed) Church, the Concertgebouw, the offices of the famous Dutch West and East Indies Companies. We took a guided boat tour up and down the canals, learning about Dutch architecture, construction, and the layout of the city. As usual on our trips, while Iêda and the kids napped in the early afternoon, I took the opportunity to take long walks farther and farther out into the suburbs. Out here, away from the tourists, the dirty canals, and the druggies, Amsterdam became a very attractive city.

On our last day we rented a car to go visit the area where the Wiardas came from in Friesland. We drove north from Amsterdam, across the mouth of the Zuider Zee, and into the Friesland provincial capital of Leeuwarden. This had always been a farming area, and it is still dotted with black-and-white cows, poorer than the southern Netherlands, a cold and windswept barrier against the North Sea where people had to build their houses on mounds (terpen) to keep out the rampaging waters. I could see why someone would want to emigrate from here. Mata Hari, the famous femme fatale and World War I spy was from here in Leeuwarden.

Until the completion of the Afsluitdijk in 1932, which seals off the mouth of the Zuider Zee from the North Sea and has a highway running across its top, the far northeast of The Netherlands, where the provinces of Friesland, Drenthe, and Groningen are located, was a distant, remote, and all-but-inaccessible area. It consisted of small towns and rural villages and farms isolated from the mainstreams of (richer) Dutch culture and society in the South. Its people have a reputation for being hard headed, independent, and stubborn (*friese stÿfkop*). This is where my grandparents emigrated from in the 1880s.

With the dike and its highway completed, the gap between northeast Holland and the rest of the country began to narrow. Friesland is now almost as rich as the more prosperous areas, the differences in culture and social norms are also less distinct. The main difference may still be language, and even that is starting to fade. Friesland has its own language, Fries, which is closer to low German than to the Dutch of Amsterdam. Fries is an Anglo-Saxon language and, therefore, with relations to English, Iêda tells me that, because of that, she can understand Fresian better than she can Dutch.

The Frieslanders have long been fiercely independent and proud of their separateness. Remember, it was the Fries who held out against the Romans and, in 754, martyred St. Boniface when he attempted to Christianize them. During the Middle Ages, Friesland maintained its independence from the rest of the country, until Charles V, the Holy Roman Emperor, absorbed it into the larger Hapsburg Empire. Even now, though the gaps have narrowed, Frieslanders are proud of their history and distinctiveness.

We didn't have much time on this trip, but we did manage a quick look in at the Fries Museum where my kids were impressed to find the pictures of several Wiardas as former town officials and local burghers on the walls (for all we knew at that stage, our ancestors could have been jailbirds). The museum has some fine exhibits of Friesian history, the Friesian resistance during World War II, and, of course, Mata Hari.

We then got directions and drove out to the small town of Goutom, now almost a suburb of Leeuwarden, where my family had come from. To our surprise, we actually found what we were looking for. There is out here a "Wiarda School" (the kids were really impressed to see a school named after their ancestors), a Wiarda street nearby, and a plaque celebrating the Wiarda contributions to the town. Much more than we expected. We roamed around the village and the countryside for a time, soaking up the ambience, then had to hurry back to Amsterdam. On this first and brief trip, we didn't have a chance to visit with any living Wiarda family representatives or to explore the area more than superficially. That would have to wait for a later visit.

For me, being in this ancestral homeland evoked a variety of sentiments. It was nice to know that at least some of the Wiardas had been successful. In driving around the barren countryside of Friesland, I was reminded of all the stories and legends I had grown up with: of Vikings and Norsemen, of evil Germans next door, of ice skating on the canals, of wooden shoes and tulips, of long poles used for dike-jumping, of heroic little boys with their finger in the dike holding back the often rampaging North Sea waters.

I was also reminded in this mainly empty, fog-ridden, and often spooky countryside of the primal *poldergeist* (it's funny, what you remember at times like these) out of which the Dutch Friesians are supposed to have emerged. Finally, on this and other trips, I was struck by how affluent this area had become, as compared with the poverty-ridden, potato-blighted, God-forsaken land of a century before which my ancestors had fled.

Dutch Travels, 1979

In 1979–1980 we were again in Europe on another extended sabbatical leave from my university, traveling throughout the continent and doing research on Northern versus Southern European democracy, political culture, and development.[4] We had started out in Great Britain, then took the ferry across the North Sea to Rotterdam.

Rotterdam was spic'n'span, amazing for a port city, indeed the world's busiest. But we didn't linger long, taking the train up to The Hague, the capital. Arriving near midnight with three very tired children, we discovered the hotel where we'd made reservations, the "Zuider Zee," had recently burned to the ground. Relying on our taxi driver, we eventually found "the only room available," the presidential suite in the Corena Hotel. It was outrageously expensive, plus ten guilders more for hot water! I told the manager how outrageous this was, whereupon he rudely invited us to look elsewhere, knowing full well there were no other rooms available in the entire city. Barely containing my anger but only because it was now past midnight and my children were already beyond the exhaustion phase, we took the room, meanwhile sputtering to myself all the stereotypes I'd learned as a kid about the cold-hearted, money-grubbing Dutch. You're not allowed to use stereotypes about other ethnicities and peoples, but when it's your own it's okay.

We had other bad experiences on this trip, nothing disastrous but certainly annoying. At one point someone yelled—the second time this had happened—at my kids for playing in a children's playground without paying, when there was no sign or other indication we were supposed to pay. At another point, my small, five-year-old son was reprimanded by a complete stranger for touching his nose to a glass mirror—not exactly a mortal sin in my view. But what most bothered us about the Dutch was the constant money grubbing and the fees for everything: the hot water, use of the WC, admission charges to public parks and playgrounds. The Dutch have this annoying tendency to be sanctimonious, to view themselves (perhaps because of the success of their economy and welfare state) as better than others, and to lecture others on proper behavior. I view this as a legacy of their Calvinist past, now expressed in a secular idiom.

The same with the money grubbing. The Dutch are known as shrewd businessmen, always exacting a price or commission, which helps explain why they are so successful as bankers, investors, and global businessmen. But we were coming to think of them as hard, cold, heartless, and unyielding. I had grown up in my church in Western Michigan to think that hard-hearted capitalism needed to be tempered by Calvinist-inspired justice, mercy, and charity. But not apparently in the Dutch case. Or maybe because, in no longer going to church and abandoning the Calvinist ethic, the Dutch had forgotten the mercy and charity side of the equation. Whatever it was, we didn't like it.

I suppose what bothered me most about the repeated instances of Dutch rudeness and extracting every last guilder from a poor tourist with kids like me was that I remembered the period after World War II, when The Netherlands was still devastated by war, especially frigid winters and food shortages, my family in Michigan had shipped box after box of food, clothing, and blankets back to the "Old Country." My family had, in fact, sacrificed its own well-being for the sake of our Dutch cousins. But were any of the Dutch we had met grateful for this? Did they even know or care? Shouldn't they? We don't expect anything overly much, but a simple "thank you" and something less than rude treatment would have been nice.

The next day, after a quick tour of The Hague including City Hall, the Grote Church, the Historical Museum, and the wonderful Mauritshuis Museum (Rubens, Vermeer, Rembrandt, and others), we headed for Amsterdam. But not before another rude encounter in the train station. I asked a fellow passenger, "Could you please tell me where the currency exchange is?" Answer: "Around the corner to the left." Me: "And is it open today?" Answer, rudely: "If it were not, I wouldn't have told you where to find it." The moral, at least to the Dutch, is, "Don't ask stupid follow-up questions." But does the response need to be so nasty?

The Dutch, I observe, are usually polite in a quite stiff and formal way, but not friendly or *simpático* in the Latin sense, and often so direct as to give offense. It is directness to the point of rudeness, again perhaps a carryover from the Calvinist past. My Latin friends are frequently just the opposite: so indirect and elliptical as to never give offense, but never answering a question directly. At the same time, in Michigan where I grew up, the Dutch are both profit maximizers in a capitalistic sense but also, as Midwesterners, relaxed, friendly, and not so uptight about it. I prefer the Midwestern variety.

We once again arrived in Amsterdam on a Saturday evening. As compared with The Hague, more sedate and conservative where everyone goes to bed at

10:00 P.M., Amsterdam is a lively city—too lively for my tastes—until the wee hours. Obviously, this is a wealthy country with money to spend; not just the tourists but the Dutch are out on the town on Saturday night. Yet once more we notice how many poor, pathetic Dutch kids are on drugs, spaced out on the streets, throwing their lives away. The litter on the streets includes discarded condoms and syringes as well as the more common trash and cigarette butts. The kids look so healthy—tall and well-fed—but also pale, devoid of ambition or even a reason to live, resentful, and often suicidal. My own kids observed these lost, sad, pitiful street people and, if my kids ever might have had some inclination to use drugs, our travel in The Netherlands knocked it out of them.

On Sunday morning, after a hearty Dutch breakfast, including rusk buns which my mother in Michigan used to serve, we went to church. Since The Netherlands is now a mainly secular society and often positively anti-Calvinist, no one at our hotel knew the time of church services. More and more churches had become tourist information booths, drug centers, private homes, and businesses. We attended the main Westerkerk and were pleased to see at least this church still thriving with about five hundred people in attendance. The singing is even spirited and Rev. Linden is very good. He is serious, scholarly, clever, and witty, not producing belly laughs (out of character for the somber Dutch) but gentle smiles. The congregation is prosperous and well-dressed. The collection plates are deep, so deep you can't tell how much your neighbor is giving—not good by the standards of modern fund-raising. Nevertheless, I'm happy to see the Dutch Reformed Church (my tradition) alive and more-or-less well in central Amsterdam.

After church we searched for a place to eat but were frustrated by the Dutch "blue laws," a carryover from the Calvinist past, which prohibit most bars and restaurants from Sunday opening. Dutch-owned restaurants required a special permit to open on Sunday; during our visit there was much debate over this issue, with local merchants pushing hard for the revocation of Sunday-closing laws. But multinationals were already exempt, so you can probably guess where we ended up with our children: McDonald's.

Our hotel was in the Concertgebouw area and within easy walking distance of the Rijksmuseum. What a marvelous collection: Vermeer, Hals, Rembrandt, and many others. On this, our second visit to the Rijksmuseum, I was struck that Rembrandt's masterpiece of "The Holy Family" was painted as a *Dutch* family; there were also scenes of Friesland and of Dutch conquests in "my" countries of Spain, Latin America, Suriname, and Indonesia. Taking our leisurely time going through the collection, I noticed numerous scenes of ice skating on the canals, struggles against the encroaching water, and heroic efforts to build and hold the dikes—all bringing back stories from my childhood.

Just down the street from the Rijksmuseum was the newly opened Van Gogh Museum. There I had a chance to see the painter's early masterpiece, "The Potato Eaters," for the first time. I had previously seen the painting only in my art history textbook; now, seeing the original, I realized just how close those gaunt, emaciated, starving peasants whom Van Gogh painted were to my ancestors. Van Gogh had, in fact, painted this picture in Friesland in 1885, the same decade that my grandparents had emigrated from there to Michigan. Because Friesland was still very poor in the nineteenth century, they ate (like the Irish) mainly potatoes. And then a blight struck the potato crop which pushed many of these poor farmers over the edge into hunger and starvation, just like Van Gogh's skinny figures. To many, it seemed, the only option was to leave, as my grandparents did. In the whole of art history, there is no painting that captures my family history better than this one.

After the museums we gave the kids a break and let them play in the Vendel Park. My kids, who are very polite and would never talk back to adults, were threatened by the manager and told to leave a kiddie playground because they had not purchased an ice cream cone as the price of admission. If those were the rules, fine, tell us or post a sign, and we'll happily pay; but do not threaten and harass my kids. I told the manager we would have been happy to buy his ice cream cones but, because of his rudeness, we would now not do so. He understood my English perfectly well, sputtered, turned red with anger, and slammed the park gate behind us.

Why are the Dutch so rude? Are they so uptight? Is it such a strict, rule-bound society? Is it a legacy of the Calvinism many Hollanders would now rather forget? Or the historic threat from the sea that left little room for margin and obliged everyone to live strictly by the rules? What was striking was that people seemingly went out of their way to be rude, or so direct and confrontational it amounted to the same thing. Mostly those who responded in this way were older people. Were they overreacting to some slight breaking of the rules by a younger generation? Is there bottled-up anger that explodes at the least infraction? What is going on here? I had always known some Dutch to be hard, aloof, cold-hearted, lacking *simpatía* in the Latin sense; but outright coarseness and rudeness are another matter.

The next morning we took, as we had done on an earlier visit, a canal tour of Amsterdam. It is good to do this to remind ourselves of what a hydraulic marvel this city is. We have already seen that the struggle against the sea is one of the great themes of Dutch history. This history of struggle helps explain the strong sense of distinctiveness and nationalism of the Dutch, and perhaps also their sense of superiority. Like the Old Testament (which they *used* to believe in) Israelites, they have often struggled in the "desert," against strong odds, resisting and often defeating more powerful neighbors (the Romans, Spain, Great Britain, France, Germany) and emerging as one of the most successful nations on earth. We cruised down to the main dam, to the Counting House, then down the Amstel River to the harbor, and around back to the train station. Where else (I had yet to visit Venice and Stockholm) in the world can you take a city tour entirely by boat?

Then a steak lunch to revive our sagging energies and off in the afternoon to the Van Mappes diamond factory. The diamonds came from South Africa (a former Dutch colony) via De Beers (another Dutch name) to London, and then to Amsterdam, a vertically integrated, monopolistic structure that is almost entirely Dutch. In other economic areas, too—petroleum, insurance, electronics, travel, real estate, banking, groceries—the Dutch have established integrated and tightly managed companies, usually highly leveraged, that have enabled them to compete successfully with the world's biggest firms and to become one of the most efficient and richest countries in the world. I have long been intrigued by how the Dutch, occupying a small country with only limited resources, were able to do this. The answer: hard work, the Protestant-Calvinist ethic, skill at foreign languages, an internationalist outlook, organizational abilities, innovations in banking and finance, and again leverage.

We stayed one more day in Amsterdam, then rented a car to make another pilgrimage to the Wiarda homeland in Friesland. We revisited the museum in Leeuwarden, the new Wiarda School (the old one had been converted into a school for the retarded) in Goutom, and the neighboring Reformed Church that once served as the family's "home" church. We noted that the Wiarda family crest, a Dutch swan with a ring around its neck, adorns the entrance to the new school. As compared with our earlier visit only six years before, we note that both Goutom and Leeuwarden are more prosperous with more people, more cars, and new housing. Van Gogh, his "potato eaters," and my grandparents who emigrated from here would not recognize the place.

We proceeded back to Leeuwarden for a meeting, at Marssumerstraat #6, with Mr. H. A. Jorritsma, secretary of the Wiarda family association, whose mother had been a Wiarda. Since our first visit in 1973, I had gotten more interested in the family history and joined the association as a dues-paying member. I was now on the association's mailing list and received (irregularly) the family newsletter, announcements, and information on family genealogy. The newsletter had published our daughter Kristy's high school term paper on the history and sociology of the Wiardas in America.

Jorritsma was big and gruff in the Fresian mode, but he and his wife were warmly hospitable to us and our children. They lived in a small but comfortable and immaculate single-family house in the outskirts of Leeuwarden. It had a nice garden, garage, entry, kitchen, living-dining area, bath, and two bedrooms—just right for a retired couple. He received a generous pension and had free medical and dental care.

I thought to myself, "Wow! My ancestors emigrated from here because they were poor and starving. But now the overall affluence of The Netherlands had reached even these remote rural areas; the prosperity, housing, and standard of living in once-poor Friesland were now as good as they were in the place they emigrated to, Grand Rapids."   ¦

We learned from Mr. Jorritsma that the Wiarda clan now gathered periodically for a family reunion. The Groningen (the next province) and German branches (von Wiardas) also came, even though, because of the German occupation of the country during World War II, there is still bitter resentment at Germany in Holland. The reunions go on for three days of tourism and beer-drinking. We were invited to attend, but I thought one day is probably plenty to spend with relations who are complete strangers. And, at age forty, three days of beer-drinking is no longer my cup of tea. At twenty, maybe, but not at forty.

We met with some of the other Wiardas: distant cousins. The younger generation were all nice, pleasant, professional, and with-it; they could not have been more hospitable. They were the postwar generation, whereas Jorritsma was pre-war and of a quite different sociology. Iêda got quite a kick out of all this. She had once thought her tall, thin, blond, big-footed, stubborn, hard-headed husband was unique in the world. But then she met Jorritsma and the Wiarda clan and discovered there was a whole province full of people like that. What a hoot!

We stayed over in Friesland at the Hotel Europa in Leeuwarden to give us more time to see the countryside and meet people. After a couple of days we drove back to Amsterdam proceeding this time along the eastern and more rural side of the Zuider Zee. Through Sneek, Lemmer, Emmeloord, and Lelystad. We had never done that before. It is an area of huge land reclamations (the Northeast Polder and Flevoland), some already settled and for sale as the water is drained from the Zuider Zee.

Some areas were so newly drained that for thirty to forty miles no towns or villages had sprung up yet. Almost all of it is below sea level. Seeing this side of Holland makes you appreciate the country and its accomplishments more. It is one big, gigantic hydraulic project. Water and land are never far from each other. There are still vast areas under water. Life is precarious: one pull of the plug or breach of the dikes and half the country would be submerged. Most houses are precariously built below the level of the drainage canals. But there are also many backups and safeguards; the system is purposely small-scale and compartmentalized so, if one dike or dam breaks, others will hold. The whole country is an engineering wonder.

On the way back to Amsterdam, I was pondering the question of why my grandparents, all four of them, would have left Friesland back in the 1880s. The answer is obvious: Friesland was poor; America offered better opportunities. In the mid-1880s, the future looked better in the New World than in the Old, and for a long time it was. But now things have equalized; by some measures The Netherlands is better off than the United States. Given the prosperity, it's hard to feel sorry for the Old Country now. This also helps explain why emigration from The Netherlands is presently way down as compared with then.

In Friesland people were poor; land was scarce; there were social rigidities; and opportunities for poor people like my relatives were limited. There was no future; people thought with their feet by getting out. By emigrating to Michigan, Grandpas Wiarda and Drooger did well, moved up to the middle class; their children and grandchildren (me) did even better and became university-educated professionals. Would that have happened if they'd stayed behind in The Netherlands? Doubtful. But now Holland—and Friesland—have matched U.S. living standards; whether the opportunities in the Old County are as good as in the United States I could not say without living there for a longer period.

Back in Amsterdam we received a visit from the urban, big-city Wiardas who had been alerted by Jorritsma of our presence. The man was tall and handsome, a former KLM pilot; his stately wife, a former KLM hostess. They brought candy for our children and Dutch chocolate liqueurs (in a tulip-shaped bottle!) for us. They both spoke Portuguese and had lived in Portugal. He informed us that he had known my Aunt Julia in Indonesia back when he was still flying for KLM. I wondered silently if he was the one she had been in love with then, a well-known family story. He also informed us that there was then a prominent Wiarda (Girardus) on the Dutch Supreme Court who later became president of the European Court of Justice; we would eventually discover the judge's daughter, Elise, as our "long-lost cousin" living in Washington, D.C.

It was a very pleasant get-together. He went on to tell us more family stories. We talked of religion, and he told me the Dutch churches had been full during the war but now attendance was limited mainly to the elderly, the very young, and (his words) "common people." He told us there were other Wiardas in Australia and South America. He informed us that in the fifteenth century there was a Wiarda family fund for those who wished to pursue the ministry, but recently there had been no takers and the fund had dwindled to such a low level it was no longer worth administering.

What wonderful family lore. Our visitors were very nice; they had even brought their son Elly, well-brought-up and polite, to play with our kids. At one point, the wife interjected good humoredly to tell us that she—like ourselves— was skeptical of all this family history, didn't believe there was a family castle and that most of the Wiardas were not nobles or aldermen but humble peasants. Probably true—that's why they emigrated. Nevertheless, it was great fun to meet our Dutch cousins, to hear all this lore, and to find our Dutch roots, however fanciful some of the stories (did we really eat Saint Boniface?) might be.

Family Reunion, 2005

Our third extended trip to The Netherlands, where we operated as more than just tourists, came in 2005. The occasion was a Wiarda family reunion in Dokkum, Friesland. This proved to be the most friendly, enjoyable, and tension- and harassment-free of our eight trips to the "Old Country."

Iêda and I had been in Germany anyway on a State Department-sponsored lecture tour. The Wiarda family reunion fit neatly into our schedule. We had been in Hamburg where she had lectured at the University of Hamburg and I, at Helmut Schmidt University and Keel University. Just before heading to the airport for the flight to Amsterdam, I had also met with prominent German journalist, Josef Joffe, one of the most arrogant and unpleasant men I have ever met. But Joffe had two saving graces: he told me he was the last German to still be supportive of American foreign policy; and, it turned out, as a young exchange student he had attended high school (and learned his excellent English) in Grand Rapids, Michigan! He knew my hometown thoroughly, even the neighborhood where I had grown up.

For reasons unknown, my travel agency had booked me into an unwanted and more expensive business class seat, while putting Iêda back in economy. When I questioned why, the clerk, without responding, put Iêda also in business class. Not a bad deal for her, but it didn't answer my question. So I again queried the clerk: why not put both of us in economy, which is what we had originally requested, and give us a refund of the price difference. At that point, the clerk got huffy, rude, and downright insulting; to give me a refund, she would have to reissue the ticket and actually have to do some work. Perish the thought! It wasn't worth arguing about, but I thought, "Oh, oh, is this going to be another one of those trips where we encounter Dutch rudeness and arrogance all rolled into one?" Fortunately, this proved to be the only unpleasant encounter on the visit.

Flying KLM, I noticed that the airline logo bore an uncanny resemblance to the bird, a Dutch swan, that was on the Wiarda family coat of arms. So *our* emblem is now becoming the *national* logo. Flying into Amsterdam from the east, we cross over the southern tip of the Zuider Zee, over the myriad canals that are so typically Dutch, and over that flat countryside, all below sea level, carved out of the reclaimed polders. In The Netherlands, of necessity, almost all houses are on waterfront property! On this trip we avoided going into central Amsterdam; maybe that's why we had a better impression of the country this time.

At the car rental agency, the clerk who helps us is Elizabeth Terpstra. It's obviously a Fresian name. We kid a little about that. Then when I tell her I want the car to drive to Friesland, her only response is "Why?" Because from her point of view, as compared with Amsterdam, Friesland is a boring, rural, and small-town area. By moving to Amsterdam, she has escaped what she viewed as her boring past. She could not conceive that anyone would *want* to go to Friesland.

We got on the Beltway, or Ring, Route A10, around Amsterdam. Then A8 north and A7 to Leeuwarden, the provincial capital. Another twenty miles northeast and we arrived in Dokkum. En route we cross over the Zuider Zee—the fifth time I've taken that route. It's obvious within a few miles that the Dutch highway system, the national infrastructure, and the country's prosperity have advanced greatly since we were there last.

Friesland is famous for its productive, exceedingly healthy black-and-white cows (and wonderful milk and cheeses), and we see plenty of these, as well as advertising billboards full of them, on our drive. Cows are almost worshiped up here (replacing Calvinism?) and referred to as "our mother" because they are the source of much of the province's wealth. We have our picture taken in front of one of these that shows all the products derived from a single cow. There are also abundant sheep and goats but no pigs—too smelly for Dutch nostrils.

At first, we had thought of staying in Leeuwarden because it's bigger and livelier, but Dokkum proved to be a wonderful little town. It's absolutely spotless, as a Dutch town should be, surrounded by water and canals (one of the Wiarda cousins drove his boat to the family reunion), and with its downtown area beautifully restored. I see *none* of the poverty, malnutrition, and absences of opportunities that drove my four grandparents to abandon the area and emigrate to America a hundred and twenty years earlier. I learn at the reunion, incidentally, that while my ancestors emigrated to America at that time, others went to South Africa, Brazil, Australia, while still others went only from Friesland to Amsterdam where they also moved up. One (Willem) became the attorney for the city of Amsterdam and another (Gerardus) became chief judge of the Dutch Supreme Court and eventually head of the European Court of Justice in Strasbourg.

Absent available hotel space, we stayed in a small B-and-B on the outskirts of Dokkum. The owner might be the only person in all of The Netherlands who doesn't speak English—not good if you're running a B-and-B. She was very hospitable and tried her best, but the facilities were not the greatest: we had to share the bath with her teen-age children; her ducks, chickens, pigeons, and the frogs (of course, on the edge of still-another canal) woke us up at 4:00 A.M.; and across the street was a refugee camp for Kosovar, Bosnian, Somali, Albanian, Iraqi, and Afghan political dissidents—good from a human rights point-of-view but not exactly whom you'd want as near-neighbors if you're trying to run a B-and-B. Can anyone imagine all these unhappy people living together harmoniously, let along with close-by Dutch neighbors?

At the B-and-B a note and map awaited us from Sybring Wiarda, head of the family association, inviting us to join the group for cocktails at the Isherburg Restaurant. So after checking in, that's where we went, careening through Dokkum's darkened, narrow, canal-front streets. And there they all were in the bar of the Isherburg: about seventy to eighty persons, all with the name of Wiarda. I doubt if ever in the history of the world that many Wiardas had ever been gathered together in one place at one time. There were German (von) Wiardas, Dutch Wiardas, Australian Wiardas, South African Wiardas, English Wiardas, and American (my cousin Tom, myself, and Iêda) Wiardas.

Everyone was extraordinarily nice to us and flattered that we would journey all the way from the United States to join the reunion. We saw none of that Dutch arrogance and rudeness we had observed on earlier visits. Sybring and his wife Ulrique Wiarda (she had gone on a high school exchange in Gaylord, Michigan); Edzard and Utta Wiarda (she, the daughter of the Dutch naval attaché in Washington); the family genealogist Remmo Wiarda; the von Wiardas from Germany (who had surprised me the year earlier by attending a lecture I gave in Hanover). The Australian and English Wiardas were the granddaughters of a Wiarda who had fled The Netherlands about the same time my grandparents did, but as a pacifist and to avoid serving in the Dutch army, not so much for religious or economic reasons. He ended up in South Africa just in time to be drafted into the Boer War so he fled again, this time to Australia.

It must have driven Iêda crazy to have so many Wiardas all gathered in one room. It was a little disconcerting to me, too, because *everyone* was named Wiarda, so we only used first names. To give a sense of the flavor, there were, in addition to the already named, Mignon, Ariette, Sietze, Tjalling, Tjitske, Eslke, Wiardina, Jan, Adrianus, Aaltje, Hanna, Willem, Klaas, Robartus, Taco, Estker, Kunna, Siurt, Wendy, Felicity, Georg, Bucho,

Enno, Uwe, Hermann, Diddo, Christoph, Gottfried, Franke, Kerburg, Minthia, Margaret, Lisalotte—Wiardas all. Plus their families! Quite a clan gathering.

The next morning was the family association meeting, also held at the Isherburg. It was very well organized with coffee, sweet rolls, name tags, and genealogy tables. Sybring, a physician by training and a good politician by instinct, presided as president of the association. He skillfully made introductions in Old Fresian, Dutch, German, and English. Then, much to our relief and so as not to offend either the Dutch or the German branches of the family, he decreed that English would be the lingua franca of the meeting. For it turned out the Wiardas who had migrated to Germany (to Emden on the border, the East, Fresian Islands, and eventually Hamburg) four generations back were more prolific than their Dutch cousins; there were now more German than Dutch Wiardas, and considerable tension (going back to World War II and the Nazi occupation of The Netherlands) between the two groups. But Sybring, himself a sailor as well as a physician, navigated these shoals skillfully and presided over a harmonious meeting. The Wiarda family association had been organized in 1965 so this was its fortieth anniversary; it met every third year.

The business meeting was followed by a splendid lunch at the Isherburg. We then formed a caravan of cars to visit the *terpin* in the area, terpin being manmade mounds (the highest in the area is twenty-eight feet) on which the early Fresians, before there were dikes and canals, built houses and churches to stay above the flood waters. The terpin are archeological treasures because the mounds contain, in layers, all sorts of buried items including animals and people. The names in the Hegebeintunm terpin church graveyard—De Vries, Boersma, Jansma—were the same Fresian names I was familiar with from Grand Rapids. That evening we went in another car caravan to the town of Anjumon nearby Lake Lanwersmeer for a dinner-boat tour that took us around the lake, past a flock of those famous Dutch swans again that are on the family logo, and up to the dam and sluice gates that hold back the often-rampaging North Sea.

In between, we took a walking tour of Dokkum. In addition to being a charming little town, Dokkum is famous as the place where Saint Boniface was killed when he came to Christianize the Fresians. The town is festooned with banners, markers, and postcards of this event, and a statue of Saint Boniface. As a Protestant and a Calvinist, I'm not much in favor of all this celebration of a Catholic saint. And it turned out, Saint Boniface was killed, not for grand political or religious reasons, but in a single, but botched (he resisted) robbery. Nor, in contrast to earlier Fresian lore, was he eaten!

The next day the whole family boarded a large ferry at Anjum on the north coast to go up to the North Sea Islands (Schiermonnikoog) forty-five minutes away. The islands are nature preserves; no cars allowed; and wonderful for day-long picnics and tours. We rented bikes, toured all around the island, and took in the sights. There are (more) happy, contented Fresian cows here, beautiful flowers, a lighthouse, an old German pillbox that goes back to World War II (part of the German defense line stretching the length of western Europe's coast), as well as an allied cemetery containing American, Canadian, British, French, and Australian remains. I spotted an oil-drilling platform offshore in the North Sea; I hadn't known The Netherlands had oil or gas and, when I inquired, was told that Holland had ambitions to use the petroleum to surpass Norway as the world's richest nation!

It was Sunday morning and, as we strolled through the main square on the island, Iêda and I discovered a Reformed Church that actually was having a service. So we walked in, settling in the balcony so as not to disturb the service, already half over. Much to our surprise, the Church was full—the first time we'd seen that in all of Europe. And there were children and young people—again a unique occurrence. But Ulrique, Sybring's nice wife, informed us that, after much debate and in the name of multiculturalism, diversity, and the separation of church and state, the Reformed Church (and its schools, hospitals, charities, etc.) was no longer being subsidized by the state or, if it was, at much lower levels, and was no longer to be privileged as the official state church. These were further nails in the coffin of an already-dying Reformed church and tradition.

Our Wiarda clan settled into the patio and living rooms of the elegant Graaf Bernstorff, a combination hotel-apartments-restaurant. There we had lunch and the most delicious apple pie/strudel (with ice cream) I'd ever had—as good as Vienna! Because I hadn't known what it would be like on this excursion and thought it might be dull, I'd brought my briefcase full of work along. I'd like to say that only a Wiarda would do this—bring work along on a family vacation outing—but, in this case, surrounded by Wiardas, I'd have to say only a *Howard* Wiarda would do that. Iêda and I discovered the Graaf Bernstorff had a separate library room so after lunch that's where we happily settled in for a couple of hours: she, to read for a time (discovering a Sigfried Wiarda in a *History of Friesland* volume) while I scribbled off a few pages on the manuscript (this one) I was then working on.

In the evening, as the formal part of the family reunion wound down, we got together informally for drinks and dinner with some of our favorite family members: Sybring, Ulrique, Ezard, Utta, Wendy, Felicity, Remmo, and Jan. Several of these had brought their camping trailers along and, European style, after the reunion were heading on holiday to Spain, Italy, and the South of France. Ulrique and Utta regaled us with stories of culture clash from their days in the 1960s (my era!) of dating American men. It was a fun evening with nice people. I suspect we got to know this group better than others because their English was better, while the others were timid about speaking it. The atmosphere among this group was so nice it was like having a barbecue in your own back yard.

The next morning cousin Tom, Iêda, and I drove into Leeuwarden, actually the suburb of Goutom, that small village where the Wiardas had originally come from. Once an isolated rural area, it was now all but swallowed up by the expanding provincial capital. It was much more built up, with nice, middle-class suburbs, than it had been when we visited previously in 1973 and 1979. Tom had not been here before; it took us only a short time to spot the church spire that marked the spot.

And there it is: the "Wiarda School" with the family swan on top and a new addition on the building; it's a weekday and parents are dropping off their children, staring at us as we snap pictures of the school. We also locate a "Wiarda Street" not far away in Leeuwarden and (this is new) a "Wiarda Bike Path" in Goutom. A curious omission for which we had no explanation is the absence of any Wiarda gravestones in the adjacent church cemetery; the Wiarda ancestors must be buried elsewhere.

A new addition, however, and in some ways the highlight of the whole trip, was our finding the new Wiarda Monument, nestled in a flowered area between the school and the church. That had not been here on previous visits. It's a four-sided granite monument with lettering on all sides in the four languages of the family: Fresian, Dutch, German, and English. The founding year of the family, or as far back as our records go, 1369, is chiseled in on all four sides. The carved inscription reads, "On this spot, in about the year 1400, the Wiarda estate (in the European sense of that term, implying a castle, lands, probably peasants) was founded. It lasted until 1882." Readers will recall from chapter 2 that is the year one of our ancestors, rather than pay taxes on it, burned down the castle—or at least that is the family lore. No wonder my grandfather was left a poor orphan and had to emigrate! But now thanks to the political influence of cousin Willem, the city attorney of Amsterdam, the monument and grounds around it are well cared for by the municipal government.

A bit later we recrossed the Zuider Zee, drove down toward Amsterdam, and dropped Tom off at the airport. His wife Dot is from Northern Ireland, another Calvinist enclave where I've never been; she was visiting her family there and Tom was flying back to Belfast to join them. Meanwhile, Iêda and

I continued our Dutch holiday by driving down to Utrecht, the former academic and religious center of The Netherlands, then east to Arnhem, eventually over the border to Düsseldorf, Cologne, and Bonn where I resumed my German lecture tour.

While driving along Iêda and I were discussing why this trip to The Netherlands was so much more pleasant and free of rude encounters than on any previous excursion. We came up with four reasons, all interrelated:

1. We stayed completely out of Amsterdam and the big cities, with their often aggressive, money-grubbing atmosphere.
2. We spent all our time in small towns and rural areas which are very pleasant and where people are more traditional and friendlier.
3. We had no business to transact and, therefore, encountered no rough edges or bustling entrepreneurs seeking to take advantage of us.
4. We were enveloped in a family gathering and allowed the family to take care of us, make arrangements, and run interference for us.

On Balance

The Dutch economy is one of the wonders of the world. Here you have a small country, without significant resources, that for decades, even centuries, has been one of the world's high flyers. The Netherlands is one of the globe's most prosperous economies with a per capita income and a standard of living and social services that are among the world's highest and best. There is almost no poverty in The Netherlands and, at the same time, it is one of the world's most egalitarian and socially just societies. There are many good reasons for living in The Netherlands.

There is something efficient and even magical about the Dutch economy that makes it the envy of Europe. It even has its own name: the "Dutch" or "Polder" model. The Dutch model is neither as socialistic as that of the Scandinavian countries nor as free-market-oriented as the American. Rather, it occupies a "golden mean" somewhere in between that combines an extremely dynamic and productive economy with the benefits of the modern welfare state. Dutch taxes are high in order to support the country's progressive welfare system, yet the Dutch have built incentives into their system that allow private entrepreneurship and investment to flourish. In many respects, Holland has the best of all possible worlds: a dynamic private economy like that of the United States combined with the best features of the European social welfare system.

For a long time there was a close association between Dutch Calvinism and the country's phenomenal economic success. That association was best captured in the justly famous book by world-renowned sociologist, Max Weber, *The Protestant Ethic and the Spirit of Capitalism.* Weber, to set the record straight, did not argue that Calvinism *caused* the Dutch success; rather, that Calvinism, through its emphasis on logic, the rationalization of society, the rule of law, and the notion that the "elect" of God should also demonstrate their Godliness through this-worldly success, provided a set of beliefs in which capitalism could flourish. As the old Dutch proverb puts it, "God gave us only sand, sea, and wind, but he also gave us John Calvin and that was enough." While other countries in seventeenth-century Europe remained locked in feudalism and mercantilism, the Dutch had already broken the chains of this old society and were wholeheartedly dedicated to the modern world that emphasized tolerance, freedom, and open markets.[5]

By today, with the exception of some rural and "Bible-Belt" areas, the Dutch have largely abandoned their Calvinism. The Netherlands is presently one of the most secular nations on earth, with less than 4 percent of the population as regular church attendants. I have to confess that this bothers me greatly about The Netherlands. The country has increasingly abandoned one of the most important and distinct features of its culture, religion, and society, with terribly negative consequences. It is the abandonment of this religious heritage that accounts nowadays for some of the country's least attractive features: the widespread drug use, the open and flagrant prostitution, the legalization of euthanasia, the open acceptance of sexually deviant behavior, and so on.

But the issue is more complicated than that. For we have argued here that, while The Netherlands has largely abandoned its Calvinism at the formal religious level, it continues to practice a form of Calvinism underneath. I am convinced that the frequent rudeness my family has experienced in The Netherlands, the verbal efforts to correct our mistake even if it involves such minor violations as playing in the park or stepping into the bicycle lanes, the superior-than-thou attitudes frequently encountered—all emerge out of the legacy of Dutch Calvinism, now no longer expressed in religious form but still present in secularized versions of moral purity.

It is a paradox that even Dutch tolerance, expressed in such extremely liberal and seemingly open-minded policies toward drugs, sex, gays, mercy killings, and political asylum, is a form of secular religion that has long been at the heart of the Dutch tradition grounded in Calvinist notions of ethical calling, moral purity, and absolute certitude. Nowadays, the Dutch are ashamed of their Calvinism and are fast backtracking from it,[6] but they cannot escape that easily and, when scratched a little, Dutch society and culture are still permeated with Calvinist operating principles. Even their intolerance toward intolerance is infused with a kind of Calvinistic messianic certainty that I find troubling.

Recently these issues have come to a head in the ritual killing of Dutch anti-Muslim filmmaker Theo Van Gogh, a series of retaliatory (Calvinist) church burnings by Muslims (now one-tenth of the Dutch population), and increased Dutch questioning of their commitment to diversity, tolerance, and multiculturalism. For when ritualized murder is committed against someone whose sole infraction was to exercise freedom of expression, and when other anti-Muslim public figures are threatened with violence and require police protection, then it is plain that something is wrong with the Dutch model. Neither assimilation nor pluralism seem to have been successful in dealing with the presence of so many Muslims in the once strongly Christian and Calvinist Netherlands.

This is a complicated issue for which there are no easy answers. But if it forces the Dutch to go back to their roots, stimulates a renewed discussion among the Dutch as to who they are as a culture and people, and forces a reconsideration both of national values (including traditional Calvinist values in both religious and modern secularized form) and of where other, non-Western, non-Calvinist peoples fit into that culture, then it will have served a useful purpose. No one expects the modern, free-thinking Dutch to return to traditional Calvinism, but it might be useful for them to acknowledge the religious origins, in part, of the free and wealthy society which they presently enjoy.

Notes

1. Royal Ahold, which owns numerous grocery store chains including Giants, Winn-Dixie, and Stop & Shop, was caught cooking its books to make its profits seem greater than they were. It is now attempting to recoup its financial position and its moral stature. What made the Ahold practices especially scandalous is that in the cozy, Calvinistic world of doing business in The Netherlands, such manipulation of the books is not supposed to happen.

2. A wonderful essay that captures all this nicely is by Dutch political columnist Leon de Winter, "Tolerating a Time Bomb," *New York Times* (July 16, 2005), A21, published originally in Dutch in *Elsevier* magazine.

3. Details are provided in my book, *Adventures in Research* (forthcoming).

4. Ibid., chapters 11 and 12.

5. The issue has long been controversial. Recent scholarship has suggested it was the humanist Erasmus of Rotterdam, more than Calvin, who championed private property rights, freedom of conscience, and free markets. Either way, it was a Dutch phenomenon.

6. In my travels I have had numerous encounters illustrative of this point, but one brief story will suffice. One time when traveling in Hong Kong I came across a group of young Dutchmen roaming around the world and drinking themselves silly until

their money ran out. So I bought them all ice cream cones, told them about my Dutch Calvinist enclave in Grand Rapids, and urged them to visit Michigan sometime to see firsthand another Dutch, but New World, settlement. Whereupon one of the young men piped up, "Oh, if it's Calvinist, then I wouldn't want to visit there at all," a sentiment that was echoed by the others. I understood this sentiment but also find it sad that young people like this want to abandon and even repudiate their own tradition and heritage.

CHAPTER SEVEN

The Americas: The Dutch in Brazil, Suriname, and the Caribbean

With Dutch independence from Spain finally achieved and consolidated by 1609, the establishment of national unity under the Estates General, and the founding of the Dutch West Indies Company in 1621, The Netherlands was in a strong position to begin exploring the transatlantic region as it had earlier explored the Indian Ocean and the South Pacific. Independence, the consolidation of national identity, and innovations in finance, banking, sailing, and navigation unleashed in Holland a tremendous flurry of energy and exploration in the 1620s and 1630s that carried over for several succeeding decades and elevated the Dutch to the very front ranks of nations. In rapid order the small Dutch republic defeated Spain, displaced Portugal, surpassed France, and challenged Great Britain for global dominance.

It was a remarkable accomplishment for such a small, resource-poor, and heretofore insignificant nation. By the mid-seventeenth century The Netherlands had acquired a truly global empire, was the world's leading commercial and trading nation, had taken its place as among the top two or three global powers, and was certainly the world's leading maritime nation. Its vast empire came to include the Moluccan or Spice Islands, Java, and Sumatra in the Indonesian archipelago; Ceylon (now Sri Lanka); Formosa (Taiwan); important ports and trading depots in Malaysia, India, China, Indochina, and Japan; areas of West, East, and South Africa; ports and refueling stations around the Indian Ocean and the Persian Gulf; Brazil; six Caribbean islands; and New York/New Amsterdam and much of the Central East Coast in North America. Australia, New Zealand, The Philippines, Borneo, and other islands were initially explored by the Dutch but not colonized. Except for a slipup in strategic planning that enabled a British fleet to defeat its forces, the United States, or at least a good part of its eastern seaboard might have remained a Dutch colonial possession.

That The Netherlands should conquer and control such a vast world empire is quite remarkable; at least as remarkable is that all these conquests occurred within a very short time period. That is, from the turn of the century and the early 1600s (the Moluccas, Australia, Indonesia, etc.), reaching its high point in the 1620s and 1630s (Brazil, New Amsterdam, the Caribbean), and continuing through mid-century (South Africa). It was a vast global empire, as big as the Spanish and Portuguese empires that preceded it (powers whom the Dutch often defeated or displaced) or the British that followed.

But by the 1670s some of the steam and energy had run out of this fantastic enterprise. The Dutch had become rich (the wealthiest nation on earth at that time), complacent, and less driven. They lost some of their colonies. Just as they had displaced the Spanish and especially the Portuguese in their colonial possessions, now the Dutch were displaced by the British in New Amsterdam, Ceylon, India, and elsewhere in this vast empire.

In this chapter we focus on the Dutch in Brazil, Suriname, and the Caribbean; subsequent chapters explore the Dutch presence in East Asia, Indonesia, and South Africa. I have personally visited the Dutch enclaves or "fragments" in all these areas, so some of this account is in the first person. But because the Dutch empire was so big, it is next to impossible for one person to explore all these areas and all the legacies the Dutch left behind. The present account, therefore, is what I have discovered so far; I look forward to further adventures in "Dutch territory."

Brazil

In the early decades of the seventeenth century, the Dutch were exploring all up and down the east coast of South America, from the Orinoco River (Venezuela) in the north where they ran up against Spanish power to the Rio de la Plata in the south, another important Spanish colony (and soon, in part because of the Dutch threat, to be elevated to the rank of a viceroyalty). The Northern part of this coast, what my generation as a kid learned of as the three Guianas—British, Dutch, and French—and is now independent Guyana, independent Suriname, and French Guiana, was still largely unexplored and all but deserted, making it quite easy for the Dutch to stake out its claims and trading outposts there!

But the southern part, what we now know of as Brazil, was Portuguese territory, discovered as far back as 1497 and colonized by Portugal some three decades later. Portugal was a small country, however, with limited resources; it had not strongly settled or fortified its colonies and they were vulnerable. From 1580 to 1640, reflecting Portuguese weakness, the Spanish and Portuguese crowns had been unified under Spanish Hapsburg rule. Looking at the world in 1600, The Netherlands had already decided that the vast but thin Portuguese empire was the weak sister in this partnership, and that is where they decided to strike. The first Dutch conquests of areas previously colonized by Portugal came in the first two decades of the seventeenth century in the Moluccas and other parts of Indonesia and Asia; by the 1620s they had decided to strike in Brazil.[1]

The Dutch were not exactly newcomers to Brazil. In the previous century, even while Brazil was already under Portuguese rule, the Dutch had been exploring its coasts and were important in the Brazil trade. During several periods, in fact, the Dutch had emerged as the dominant trading partner of the Brazilian planters, often to the chagrin of the Portuguese crown that strove (not very successfully) to maintain its own trading monopoly and to keep the "heretical" (Calvinist) Dutch out of this staunchly Roman Catholic enclave.

Nor were the Dutch necessarily unwelcome in Brazil. After all, many of the Portuguese settlers in Brazil were *marranos*, Jews who had been forced to convert to Catholicism or face the dreaded Inquisition. For them, the prospect of a greater Dutch role in the colony was welcome news because (1) the Dutch were far more tolerant than the Portuguese, and (2) they might even allow the marranos to freely practice their Jewish religion again, which is precisely what happened when the Dutch conquered Brazil.

The first Dutch attempts at military conquests came in the form of sieges and bombardments, and then a brief occupation of Bahia in 1624–1625, and then again in 1627. However, it was not until 1630 that the Dutch secured the northeast Brazil city of Recife militarily and then cemented their control over the former Portuguese colony. The capture of Recife gave the Dutch effective control over what was, then, the most important part of Brazil, the northeast, which was the center of the plantation system and the all-important sugar industry.

Dutch rule in Brazil was enlightened and progressive, especially after the arrival of Johan Maurits (his family home is now the Mauritshuis Museum in The Hague) of Nassau-Siegen.[2] He introduced honest, effective government, allowed Jews and Catholics to practice their religion freely, and treated both slaves and Amerindians with a degree of fairness not practiced previously. He championed free trade, increased productivity, and expanded Dutch control over other, larger areas of the colony. He brought real development, infra-structure building, trade, production, and modernization to the "sleepy," al-most moribund Brazilian colony for the first time.

Johan Maurits, however, who was the cousin of the ruling stadholder back in The Netherlands, is perhaps best well known for the artistic renderings and scientific advances that he brought to Brazil. Between 1637 and 1644 he brought to Brazil some of the most accomplished painters and scientists of his time. Some studied tropical diseases for the first time; others studied the still largely unknown tropical flora and fauna of Brazil; still others mapped the ge-ography of the country; another group did astronomical and meteorological observations. It was for Brazil a period of science, empericism, rationalism, and nascent capitalism. Perhaps the best known of the forty-six scholars, sci-entists, and artists Maurits brought to Brazil were the painters Frans Hals, Frans Post, and Albert Eckhout.

In the centuries before cameras and other modern means of pictorial rep-resentations, the sketches and paintings of these men constituted the first de-tailed images of the New World that Europeans had ever seen. These artists and painters filled their portfolios with sketches of every aspect of local life and culture. They painted pictures of tropical birds, flowers, fruit, and animals that no one in Europe had ever seen before. The paintings were remarkably realistic, in color, with such vivid detail that they could be used (and often were!) in botany and biology textbooks. For a long time these paintings by young Dutch masters were the only pictorial representations available in Eu-rope of what the flora and fauna of the New World looked like. The paintings were important in shaping the European image of America.

Among the most famous of the paintings was a set that Eckhout painted of the native Tupi Indians of Brazil. Iêda and I had the opportunity to view the originals of these paintings in the National Museum of Denmark in Copenhagen. The portraits are remarkable for their detail, honesty, and the remarkable colors, facial expressions, and skin tones that Eckhout managed to capture. The most famous of the paintings shows a Tupi woman strolling along nonchalantly wearing a knapsack and little else. In her hand she car-ries a human hand; out of her knapsack, a human foot protrudes—her snack for the day! Obviously, she is a cannibal—and, by her stance and nonchalant air, an unapologetic one besides.

Now, there *was* cannibalism in Brazil at this time by some indigenous ele-ments, but Eckhout has clearly exaggerated its importance. Moreover, because this painting is so famous, it has profoundly influenced, in the absence of much firsthand knowledge, European views of Latin America. I am convinced that most Europeans, who know even less about the area than do most Americans and almost never travel there, believe that is what Latin America actually looks like: very primitive, populated by "noble savages," living à la Rousseau in a state of nature, corrupted by European (and now American) colonialism and imperialism, and awaiting a heroic leader like Fidel Castro or Hugo Chávez who can deliver them from their oppression. Of course, this view is entirely inaccurate and completely ignores the immense progress, dynamism, development, and middle classness of Latin American society. But it does help explain why Europeans still think of Latin America in such primitive terms, and it all goes back to those early paintings by Albert Eckhout.

As compared to the Dutch colonies in Asia (especially the Spice Islands), the Dutch enterprise in Brazil was never very profitable. Moreover, thinking they had little to fear from weak Portugal, the Dutch had not adequately fortified their Dutch colony. In addition, with the departure of the enlightened Johan Maurits in 1644, the colony lost its most ardent enthusiast. Soon the colony started to run downhill. Portuguese elements who still lived in the colony and in other parts of Brazil grew increasingly discontented with Dutch (Protestant) rule. The Portuguese besieged Recife; beset by troubles elsewhere in its then vast empire, the Dutch were unable to come to its defense. In 1654 the city fell and Dutch rule in Brazil came to an end. To their surprise, the Dutch residents of the colony were treated courteously by their Portuguese (Catholic) captors.

The fall of Recife, which many had thought to be virtually impregnable, was a shock to the Dutch and to the Dutch West India Company, and may have marked the beginning of the decline of their vast, worldwide empire. At the time, some observers commented that they thought it would be easier to conquer Amsterdam than to take Recife. Whatever ambitions The Netherlands might have had to global superpower status were now dashed. Other parts of their empire, including Manhattan's New Amsterdam colony, would soon fall as well.

Few traces remain today of the Dutch presence in Brazil. The street design of waterfront Olinda, where the Dutch actually settled and which is now a suburb of greater Recife, shows the Dutch influence; the water and sewer system of the town and the irrigation system also go back to the original Dutch design. There is a row of Dutch-design houses, but they are of a much more recent vintage. If they want to convey some measure of elite status on their children, people in northeast Brazil may baptize them using such Dutch names as Wanderlei or Maurits. There are still remnants of the fortress the Dutch had built in Recife and other ruins that archaeologists are presently digging up.

The reconquest of Recife by Portugal from the Dutch is portrayed in Brazilian textbooks as a great nationalistic victory. But Iêda tells me that in her Brazilian school in Belo Horizonte the message was just the opposite. That the Dutch, in contrast to the Portuguese, brought modernization to Brazil. That they were progressive, rationalists, products of the Enlightenment. That the reforms ushered in by Johan Maurits and the Dutch helped lift Brazil out of its torpor and into the modern or post-feudal world. That this was a glorious, uplifting, modernizing period in Brazilian history. That the energetic, hard working, and Calvinist Dutch were infinitely better than the lethargic, Catholic, past-their-prime Portuguese. Even that—heresy of all heresies—Brazil would have been better off in the long run if it had stayed under Dutch rule rather than reverting to the Portuguese! But that was not to be and, for better or worse, Brazil remained a Portuguese colony until it became independent in 1822.

The Dutch government has tried, a bit half-heartedly, to revive and invigorate its historical as well as current presence in Brazil. In addition to its embassy in Brasilia, it maintains a consular presence in Recife seeking to remind people of its earlier role and burnish its reputation for enlightenment and progress. But the nationalistic Brazilians would often prefer *not* to be reminded of the earlier Dutch conquest, often seen as a blot on their Luso-Brazilian nationality. Hence, when Queen Beatriz of The Netherlands came to Recife for an anniversary celebration, the Brazilian government chose to downgrade her visit by not having the president accompany her during the ceremony. It is plain that the Brazilian government, its foreign ministry, and the president's office do not share the same enlightened, progressive, modernizing image of the short-lived Dutch conquest of Brazil as did Iêda's school.

Suriname

On the isolated northeast coast of South America, north of Brazil, are three enclaves, the legacies of earlier colonialism, that are almost completely unknown, that almost no one ever visits, and that fit in only uncomfortably with the rest of "Latin" America. These are, from north to south, the former British Guiana (now the independent country of Guyana), the former Dutch Guiana (now the independent country of Suriname), and French Guiana (now organized as a part of metropolitan France).

The main colonial powers in Latin America, Spain and Portugal, considered this coast and its interior territories so worthless and forbidding that they never settled them or established colonies there. There was no readily available gold or silver on this coast, few Indians to enslave (and those that were there were primitive and cannibalistic), and nothing to recommend it.

Spanish and Portuguese colonial neglect, therefore, left the door open along this coast to Dutch, French, and British incursions and, eventually, settlements. That is why these parts of South America speak, respectively, English, Dutch, and French and not Spanish or Portuguese. They remain as isolated outposts, still cut off from the main currents of not just Latin American life but also of larger global developments—although Guyana and Suriname have recently joined the Caribbean free trade community CARICOM and are planning an association with the South American free trade organization MERCOSUR. Even now these territories are so isolated that from the United States it takes *two* days to get there, one of the few areas in the world that still require two days flying time.[3]

The Dutch, British, and French did not want to confront the centers of Spanish power in Venezuela and the Rio de la Plata directly, although, as we have seen, they were less reticent about attacking the weaker Portuguese colonies in Brazil. But once driven out of Brazil, the Dutch, along with the British and French, were content to explore and eventually settle that uninhabited, unclaimed coast that lies between the Esequibo and Amazon Rivers. Much of that coast is swampy, unattractive, malaria-infected, hot and steamy, and generally uninviting, so the colonial settlements there remained small and not well defended. Among the three main powers, the Dutch, British, and French, control over the colonies passed back and forth several times. At some times the Dutch were the main power in the region; at other times, the British; at still others, the French—depending on which country happened to have the largest fleet in the area at any one time. It is safe to say that, of the three, the Dutch were the predominant power for the longest time and over the largest territory, at one time controlling much of Guyana (one of whose principal cities is New Amsterdam—just like the New York version) and all the way down to Cayenne, the capital of French Guiana. It was only at the beginning of the nineteenth century that the three-part division into British, Dutch, and French Guiana was more or less settled; and even today, in the southern or Amazon jungle parts of these territories where the lines and borders are obscure, there are still unresolved territorial disputes.

Our focus here is on the main, formerly Dutch colony of Suriname. Right at the beginning it is essential to make an important distinction among the main Dutch colonies, and to fit Suriname into this paradigm. Malacca, Cape Town, Curaçao, and New Amsterdam (the one in Manhattan!) were all essentially coastal depots or *trading centers*. They were commercial enterprises, hubs, shipping centers. In contrast, Suriname (and Indonesia and Ceylon and essentially the interior of South Africa) were mainly *plantation* centers. They were founded to farm, settle, and exploit the land and resources.

Although the Dutch had explored the coasts of the Guianas in the six-teenth century, it was not until the seventeenth century that they settled and colonized the area. They settled on an embankment up the Suriname River a few miles from the Atlantic coast and built a fort (still standing, now re-stored) which they called Fort Zeelandia after a province in The Nether-lands. The original colony was small, just the stockade and a few huts, but af-ter the Dutch were expelled from Brazil in 1654, the settlement received an influx of new colonists from there as well as from The Netherlands, and it be-gan to prosper. As usual, the Dutch proved to be especially good at draining swampy land and starting new farms.

Especially important in the life of the colony in these early decades were the Jews. A little background is necessary. When the Inquisition was estab-lished in Spain (1478) and slightly later (1496) in Portugal, the Sephardic Jews of these countries were forced to convert to Catholicism or else to flee. Some of these "New Christians" or marranos went to the Portuguese colony in Brazil; a larger number fled to the more tolerant Netherlands where they could practice their religion and their trades freely. When the Dutch then took control of Brazil from Portugal, many of the Jews in the colony wel-comed them as liberators, practiced their religion openly once again, and threw in their lot with the Dutch against the Portuguese.

But when Portugal regained control in 1654, most of the Jews had to flee. The largest percentage went back to The Netherlands. But some of them, we know, found their way to Curaçao, to Jamaica and Barbados, to New York (New Amsterdam), and to Newport, Rhode Island, home of the longest lived, continuous congregation in the Americas. And some of them moved only slightly north to the French and Dutch Guianas where they organized rural settlements and began to farm. Within a few years the small Jewish community in Dutch Guiana was reinforced by the arrival of more Jewish families from Amsterdam, some of whom had earlier been part of the Por-tuguese colony in Brazil, then had gone back to The Netherlands, and now were crossing the ocean yet again to resettle in Suriname. Dutch tolerance toward the Jews set an example for all of Europe as well as Latin America.

I have been in the place (Jodensevanne—Jewish Savannah) where these Jews, eventually numbering over five hundred, settled. It is located some sixty to seventy miles up the Suriname River from the coast in the midst of what can only be described as a dense, Amazonian, tropical jungle and rain forest. You drive for thirty miles on rough, unpaved roads, passing huge, of-ten tipsy (no weight restrictions on these roads) trucks carrying raw bauxite ore to the Alcoa plant. Eventually the road gives out entirely (the bridge has collapsed) and you cross the Suriname River on a small, two-car, put-put ferry. On the other side the "road" narrows to become a rutted trail with trees and vines on all sides; in the Amazonian rain forest the vegetation grows so fast that it can obliterate a road in a matter of days. You have visions of boa constrictors, anacondas, and all manner of poisonous snakes, to say nothing of the piranhas and crocodiles (cayman) in the waterways (all of which are present here), swooping down and carrying you away, just like in some C-grade horror movie.

And then, there it is: Jodensavanne The signs and historical markers are in English and Dutch. The first sight is the Jewish cemetery: you know it was a patriarchal society because the women's grave markers show their husbands' names; the husbands' tombstones do not mention their wives. An extraordinary number of persons seem to have died in their thirties, but from what: disease, dysentery, or the sheer exhaustion and loneliness of living in this inhospitable, God-forsaken place? Next comes the temple, completed in 1685 with parts of the walls still standing: I have a piece of one of the stray bricks to go with my collection of fragments from the Acropolis, the Pantheon, and Old Jerusalem. Steps lead down to the waterfront, along with a sign warning that, if you go in the water, you should put your toe in first and not your whole body in case there's a school of piranhas nearby!

Here is where they came, these mid-seventeenth-century refugees from the Inquisition, from anti-Semitism, and from a hostile Europe. The Dutch were more tolerant than anyone else, but even here in Suriname the Jews found it prudent to establish their colony in isolation far from the coast and from the urban centers where they might still be persecuted. To this steamy jungle only a few degrees from the equator came an initial contingent of twelve families, mainly from Brazil and French Guiana originally; they were joined a few years later by a couple hundred more from Amsterdam. By 1685 the colony had swollen to over five hundred Jews plus over nine thousand slaves. Here they cleared the land (sandy), planted sugar cane and pineapples, and fought off disease, wild animals, and Amerindian attacks. Men outnumbered women by a ratio of about 4:1 so there must have been considerable miscegenation involving both Negro slaves and Amerindians; one of the signs says that the women present were not of the highest moral repute because no one else besides thieves, jailbirds, and prostitutes would have been willing to come to this lonely, isolated place.

The colony flourished for about half a century. Then decline set in. The living conditions were too harsh (no air conditioners, gigantic mosquitoes, diseases like malaria); there was a financial crisis; and late-eighteenth-century tolerance decrees made it easier to live in the capital city or even return to Europe. By the early nineteenth century, only a handful of the original families was left; they were supplemented by German and Polish (Ashkenazi) Jews which introduced a split in the Surinamese Jewish population (Sephardic vs. Ashkenazi) that continues to this day. Today, no one lives in Jodensavanne but it is maintained as an historical site by a neighboring Amarindian (Arawak) village. However, in the capital of Paramaribo come of the wealthiest of the original Sephardic families (Fernandes, Da Silva, Cohen, Pereira) are present and still influential.

Meanwhile, along the Atlantic coastal escarpment and near the mouth of the Suriname River, the Dutch had established their own slave-plantation system devoted mainly to sugarcane, then, along with the spices from the Moluccas, serving to enrich what had heretofore been a quite boring and tasteless (literally) European cuisine. Along with the gold and silver that Dutch pirates like Piet Heyn captured from the hapless and unprepared Spanish and Portuguese fleets, these were among the most valuable commodities in seventeenth- and eighteenth-century global international trade. The Dutch went energetically into the slave trade (which current Surinamese politicians, playing on Dutch guilt, never let them forget), with most of the slaves being brought into the commercial center of Curaçao and then sold to plantation owners in Suriname, other islands, and the U.S. South.

The Dutch plantations were largely confined to the Surinamese coast and along the major rivers. But many of their slaves escaped, went deep into the jungle, and hid out there, sometimes for centuries. Then, as now, there were no roads penetrating into the interior and, hence, no way to chase down, capture, and bring back the escaped slaves. Many of these escaped slaves, called "Bush Negroes," reverted to traditional African ways, language, religion, culture, and dress. Deep in the rain forest they continued to exist, an African "sub-fragment," in this case, cast off in the seventeenth century both from its original African moorings *and* from the Dutch slave plantation society that had shipped them across the Atlantic. Modern anthropologists have rediscovered these isolated and often "lost" communities and have found them still using utensils, speaking a language, and practicing religious precepts used in the West Africa of the seventeenth century from which they came. More recently, some of these Bush Negroes have migrated out of their forest areas to the capital city of Paramaribo where they have set up new urban communities or slums, often on public land. How to assimilate these isolated groups (when they move into the city they are referred to as Maroons) into modern Surinamese society is a real problem.

Another important group in colonial Surinamese society was the Huguenots, members of the persecuted French Protestant and Calvinist community, either from France itself or from the French community in Cayenne.

The Huguenots assimilated quickly into Surinamese society, as they did in South Africa, both because they were white and because they were Reformed or Calvinist. Like the Dutch, they established plantations, became slave-owners, and were part of the white elite. Perhaps the most famous of the Huguenot families was that of Salomon du Plessis, a leader of the French-speaking community who was always disagreeing with the Dutch governor, and whose much-married daughter, Susanna, is infamous in Suriname as the cruelest slaveholder in the entire colony.

The Dutch colony went into general decline in the eighteenth century. There were financial crises and downturns back in Amsterdam; the French colony of Haiti emerged as a stiff competitor as a supplier of sugar; and it was difficult to get colonists to settle in Suriname. The situation was one of colonial neglect and lethargy. At various times The Netherlands all put lost interest in their South American colony.

But with the end of Napoleonic rule in The Netherlands and the reconstitution of the Dutch state in 1813, there was renewed interest in the colony and new efforts to exploit its wealth. To that end, over the course of the nineteenth and early twentieth centuries, the Dutch brought in successive waves of laborers and indentured servants from its own and also then-British colonies to perform manual labor. Slavery had been abolished in 1863 so these foreign laborers now replaced the slaves. These included Indians from India (called Hindustanis), Indonesians (also a Dutch colony), and Chinese. In most cases these several waves of imported laborers were brought in without their wives and families; miscegenation in these circumstances was inevitable. They, in turn, mixed not only with each other but also with the Bush Negroes, Amerindians, and even the Dutch settlers. The result is one of the most complex, ethnically mixed, and diverse societies anywhere in the world.

There are tensions, of course, and all politics in Suriname is basically ethnically based. The Hindustanis, according to official records, are the largest group and therfore are dominant,[4] but the Indonesian, Maroon, Bush Negro, Chinese, Jews, and Amerindian communities—all except the white ex-pat Dutch groups—have their own political parties and interest associations. Politics involves balancing off and rewarding each ethnicity in an ever-changing and very delicate kaleidoscope. The incredible racial diversity, if you are an American and used to American racial categories, is enough to blow your mind: I have met people with Chinese names who, to me, looked very black; persons with Dutch names who were Amerindian or Hindustani; Indonesians who looked Japanese; and a great variety of other combinations. All your ethnic stereotypes, of whatever kind, are blown away by a visit to Suriname.

One more ingredient was added to this fantastic racial and ethnic mix in the late-nineteenth, early-twentieth centuries. These were—are you ready for this?—a group of farmers from Friesland (my ancestral territory) and the neighboring province of Groningen who came to the colony looking for economic opportunities they did not have at home. Understand that these were not plantation owners and slave holders (the early Dutch colonists) but humble peasants and family farmers wanting only to settle and farm. They formed their own communities (one is called Groningen) out in rural Suriname, intermarried with each other and seldom within the other ethnic communities, and continued to speak Fresian. Over time they did quite well for themselves as farmers, producing for both local and international markets. It occurred to me that my Fresian grandparents, rather than migrating to Michigan, could have easily ended up in Suriname. And then what would I have become? Life's contingencies!

This simmering cauldron of races and ethnicities, described above, changed over time: slavery ended; the plantations became less important; literacy rose; urbanization accelerated; and a middle class developed. Then, with the rise of Third World nationalism, anti-colonialism, and Third World liberation movements following World War II, a variety of new tensions was added to the brew. The Dutch sought to extract themselves from a no-longer-acceptable colonial and imperial situation, while local groups jockeyed for independence and to inherit power after the Dutch left.

Independence for Suriname came in 1975. But the Surinamese leaders had learned how to play on Dutch (Calvinist?) guilt over racism, colonialism, and imperialism. Independence was thus accompanied by a "golden handshake" from the Dutch government amounting to one-and-a-half billion dollars, to be used by Suriname to ease its way to freedom and to develop the country. But many Surinamese were frightened of the consequences (chaos, ethnic strife) that might follow independence and preferred to retain their ties to The Netherlands—and their Dutch passports. Then, when dictator Desi Bouterse seized power (1980–1991), violated human rights, and killed prominent opposition leaders, a mass exodus from the country followed. Today, over 300,000 Surinamese (almost half the population) live in The Netherlands where conditions and opportunities are much better than in their home country.

Suriname is a funny place, almost surreal. Driving into Paramaribo from the airport, I noticed a "De Vries Nightclub" and a "Van den Bosch Casino" as well as a "De Vries Bank." There is an entrepreneurial spirit here that is unmistakably Dutch, leavened by other ethnic and cultural influences. In the center of town is a statue of Queen Wilhelmina but also one of the rebellious slave, Cujo Presente, who burned the entire city to the ground in the eighteenth century and then was himself martyred (burned to death) by the Dutch colonial government. Interspersed with evangelical meeting houses are hundreds, if not thousands, of Buddhist temples, Islamic mosques, and Hindu shrines. If you believe in multiculturalism, diversity, and ethnic and cultural pluralism, Suriname is the place for you. It may be the most ethnically diverse country in the world.[5]

But Suriname is also a poor and deeply divided country. Its per capita income is only about $1,000 per year, among the poorest in the Western hemisphere. Though it has abundant bauxite ore, timber, and, apparently, vast oil and natural gas reserves, its main export commodity may well be drugs. Suriname is on its way to becoming a drug economy, a narco state. Unlike other Dutch enclaves where I've been, it is not a very clean country—perhaps a sign of how little Dutch it now is. Nor are public spaces maintained, kept up, or cleaned in the Dutch fashion; Paramaribo seems more tropical, run-down, and Third World than Dutch.

Nowhere is this more apparent than in the downtown area of the capital. Recently this district has been declared a World Heritage area by the UN. That is because almost all the inner city buildings, all made of wood and reconstructed after the eighteenth-century burning, have a quaint, historic, colonial appearance. But like the rest of the city, many of these buildings are run down, decrepit, and suffering from wood rot in the tropical steam heat. Even the famed Peter and Paul Cathedral, designed to look like a medieval church but constructed completely of wood, is rotting away in its beams, pillars, and foundations. When such old buildings are afflicted by deep wood rot, they are tremendously expensive to repair, and it may not be worth the effort. As the son of a carpenter, I learned early on that such old buildings may be "quaint" but they are cheaper and much easier to tear down and rebuild from the bottom up than to repair. Meanwhile, built completely of wood, the whole of downtown Paramaribo looks to me like one giant fire trap waiting to be set off in a giant conflagration, just as it was in the eighteenth century.

The Dutch presence in Suriname today is declining but still important. Suriname is an independent country, but many Surinamese have relatives in The Netherlands (from the earlier exodus), went or go to school there, and travel there frequently. Suriname Airlines has one Boeing 747 which flies back and forth to Amsterdam every day, always full. The Dutch embassy is still the largest one in Paramaribo. The Dutch language is still the official language and is widely used, especially by the elites and in business transactions, although the local street language is a form of papiamiento (a mix of Dutch, Portuguese,

Spanish, English, Indian, and African languages), and English is increasingly used as an international language. For me as an American, it was a pleasant relief to go to a place where someone else (the Dutch) are the "colonialists," "racists," and "imperialists" instead of, as usual, the United States.

For the American embassy, too, the Dutch presence here is useful. It takes some of the pressure off the United States to solve all of Suriname's problems. It serves to deflect blame away from the United States and toward The Netherlands. On many issues (drugs, human rights, democracy, corruption) the U.S. and Dutch embassies work closely together.

But the Dutch presence in Suriname is in decline, and The Netherlands government has given notice that it does not intend to prop up indefinitely the Surinamese economy. That is, in fact, why I was initially invited there: to give a series of lectures on regional and globalization issues and to suggest to Suriname alternatives besides the Dutch connection. The Dutch have issued a five-year plan under which they will dole out the remaining $250 million of the original 1.5 billion golden handshake in five installments of $50 million each. The Dutch are trying to "basket" their aid in alliance with other donors so they are no longer held responsible for everything that happens in Suriname; they are also trying to reorient their aid away from projects that imply a long-term commitment on their part. After this five-year period, Suriname is on its own; the Dutch will officially separate from and wash their hands of their now four-centuries-old colony. Whether they will actually be able to do that given ongoing Dutch guilt over colonialism, racism, and imperialism is another matter.[6]

The Dutch ambassador told me that there are only two or three hundred Dutchmen left in the country, not exactly a large neocolonial presence—although there may be ten thousand Surinamese who hold Dutch nationality and Dutch passports. There is still some limited Dutch investment here (although in this domain, too, the Americans—Alcoa, others—are moving in); many of the engineers, mining technicians, and aid administrators are Dutch; and, around the pools of the hotels where I stayed on my two trips there in 2004 and 2005 (Krasnapolski, Torarica), I would estimate 80 percent of the tourists are Dutch. Some of this Dutch presence will remain, of course, and The Netherlands will continue to be the destination of choice for many Surinamese. There are, in addition, ongoing efforts to integrate Suriname more closely into CARICOM and MERCOSUR. But in the long run, I am convinced Suriname will be sucked into the American orbit of trade and political relations (to say nothing of use of the English language) and away from the Dutch—as are, nowadays, most countries in the world.

Naturally, given my background, while in Suriname I went in search of the Dutch Reformed Church. I did not find much. Suriname was always a commercial plantation enterprise; the Dutch did not try to proselytize among the Amerindian, African, or Asian ethnic groups that they brought in. In addition, the Reformed Church was so closely associated with hated colonialism, slavery, and imperialism that, when those ended and independence arrived, the Dutch Church was discredited as well. The situation in Suriname was similar to the situation of the Dutch Reformed Church in Indonesia (also discredited by its association with colonialism) and in South Africa where it was associated with the hated and racist apartheid system.

There is now a full-time Dutch Reformed minister in Paramaribo, who is attempting to revive the Church, and several Dutch churches in the countryside where there are still communities of Dutch (and Fresian!) settlers. There are also Pentecostal, Evangelical, and Moravian churches (the latter going back to the seventeenth century in Suriname), but they are not Dutch. I found only three Dutch Reformed Churches in all of Paramaribo. And even the "Dutch Cathedral," a historic and beautiful church in Church Square, the central square of the ancient capital, is now used more for secular ceremonial occasions than it is for religious services.

In my interviews in Suriname the Dutch Reformed were referred to derisively as "black socks guys," whose church included only white colonials, and whose music came only from the dull and slow *Psalter Hymnal*. To maintain its existence, the Dutch Reformed Church has entered into a cooperative agreement with the Lutherans. But by now the Dutch religion and the Dutch church are almost gone.

The Dutch "fragment" in Suriname is fading from view. Set down in the seventeenth century as a slave-plantation society, and then reinforced in the nineteenth century by the successive importation of waves of indentured laborers, it was later discredited as one of the world's worst examples of colonialism, racism, and imperialism. As a fragment, it failed to modernize and progress, remained locked in place for centuries, was fixated on an earlier time and society, and began to change only when rising independence sentiment *forced* change. Now, some thirty years after granting Suriname independence, the Dutch are still struggling to disassociate themselves both from this earlier and ugly legacy and from their obligations to Suriname. It is not a glorious history or a pretty picture. Meanwhile, for good or ill, Suriname is bound over time to become America's responsibility and no longer that of the Dutch.

The country as a whole, meanwhile, is facing a severe identity crisis. Who are we as a people and nation? Are we Dutch, Asian, Caribbean,

African, South American, what? For good reasons, the country has a love-hate relationship with the Dutch. Though despised for its colonialism, racism, and participation in the slave trade, The Netherlands is still viewed by many Surinamese as a land of opportunity; they were educated there; and they have family in Holland. Though independent, Suriname is still closely tied to the Kingdom of The Netherlands and receives preferential treatment in the Euro zone that it would be foolish to give up. But now it is being encouraged and pressured to join up with CARICOM and MER-COSUR. In addition, English is gradually becoming the country's second language and, as reflected in my work there with the university, the research institutes, and the U.S. embassy, the United States, over time, is replacing The Netherlands as the main outside actor and presence in Suriname affairs.

As the Dutch ambassador to Suriname told me, "We have a high visibility here [as the former colonial master] but few real concrete interests."[7] And, in fact, there are by now few Dutch companies in Suriname and few commercial links. "Our presence here is winding down," he said, "whether the Surinamese are prepared for that or not." That is a true statement but, at the same time, it is also true that Suriname, isolated for so long by geography, culture, and distance, is more Dutch than Curaçao or the other Dutch islands of the Caribbean. That is Suriname's fate, whether it or the mother country want it that way: it is still tied inextricably to The Netherlands. But, at the same time, other winds of change—nationalism, the lure of the U.S., Caribbean and South American ties—are also in the air.

Curaçao

While the Dutch were exploring and settling both the North and the South American coasts, they were also exploring the area in between, the Caribbean islands, the Spanish Main, and the isthmus of Central America. The Dutch did not wish to provoke a direct confrontation with larger, more powerful Spain as they had with smaller, weaker Portugal; but they did probe for weak spots in the Spanish empire, preyed upon Spanish treasure ships, and, when they found vulnerabilities, moved in to seize colonies of their own.

It is not well known that The Netherlands still controls six islands in the Caribbean. These include the Leeward or "A, B, C" islands of Aruba, Bonafire, and Curaçao along with the smaller, so-called Windward Islands of Saba, St. Maarten (which is half French), and St. Eustatius. St. Eustatius should be known to Americans as the first country to extend its congratula-

tions to America upon its achievement of independence, for which imperti-
nence it was then burned to the ground by its then British colonial masters.

Of these six, Curaçao is the largest (thirt-eight by seven miles) of the islands and the most Dutch. So it is here that we concentrate our analysis. I
have been to Curaçao on three separate occasions. It is what the World Bank
calls a "middle-income country." Its per capita income is in the range of
$10–12,000 per year, far higher than Recife or Suriname. There is poverty
here but not the grinding, society-wide poverty that one sees elsewhere in
the Third World. There is a substantial middle class. It is clean like a Dutch
enclave should be; the streets are washed but no longer by hand and certainly
not with wooden shoes on! There is a spirit of business and enterprise here
that is quite Dutch, but it is often laid-back and relaxed, Caribbean style. An
interesting fact is that most of the Dutch who came here originally came
from the Southern Netherlands and were, therefore, Catholic (80 percent)
rather than Protestant or Calvinist.

The Dutch government still subsidizes Curaçao to the tune of about $200
million yearly, a whopping amount for so small an island. That is more on a
per capita basis than the United States gives to Israel, the largest recipient of
U.S. aid. While the Dutch are generous with their stipends, they are very
stingy with passports, visas, and citizenship. If they were not, half the Curaçao population of 150,000 would likely move to The Netherlands. Already
facing a crisis over immigration and the assimilation of Arab, Moluccan,
Surinamese, and Indonesians into Dutch society, The Netherlands is not eager to see (they say this privately) large numbers of Caribbean blacks, Rastafarians, and druggies coming into their country.

Curaçao was originally a Spanish colony, discovered by one of Columbus's
lieutenants, Alonzo de Ojeda, in 1499 while exploring the Spanish Main
(the Caribbean coasts of Venezuela and Colombia). The first Spaniards to
settle on the island came in 1527. A century later, in 1634, the Dutch and
their West India Company conquered the island, expelling the Spanish and
the few remaining Indians to neighboring Venezuela, which is thirty-five
miles to the south and whose mountains are still clearly visible from Curaçao
on non-polluted days.

It is important to remember that Curaçao was mainly a Dutch commercial
center, not a plantation colony like Suriname or Indonesia. There are, or
were, plantations on Curaçao (now converted mainly into tourist restaurants) but the island is too small for large-scale plantation agriculture and
most of the island, consisting of rock, coral, and desert scrub, is inhospitable
to growing things. A glance at the map will show that in colonial times Curaçao was on the main east-west and north-south trade routes and, therefore,

became the center of a flourishing North and South America and circum-Caribbean commerce. Almost all Caribbean trade in the seventeenth century passed through Curaçao. It was also the center of the slave trade, with slaves being brought in from West Africa to Curaçao, sold or auctioned off there, and then shipped to Brazil, Suriname, Barbados, Jamaica, and the U.S. South. It is not among the most glorious accomplishments in Dutch history: the slave trade, the breakup of families, the forced displacements, the cruelty, the treatment of humans as commodities to be bought and sold—these are among the reasons the Dutch are not especially well-liked throughout the Caribbean. In the slave trade as well as other commercial enterprises, the Dutch were very aggressive businessmen.

As the main trading center in the Caribbean, Curaçao's small, picturesque capital of Willemstad was also a center for the slave trade. Blacks were brought here from Africa, often in inhuman conditions and auctioned off to slave-owners throughout the Hemisphere. In 1795 there was a slave revolt on the island parallel to that which occurred the same year in French Haiti, but the Dutch brutally suppressed the rebellion, cut off the heads of its leaders, and threw their bodies to the sharks. As in Suriname, Indonesia, or South Africa, the Dutch Reformed Church in Curaçao defended slavery with the use of scripture. Even today there exists a residue of hatred among some of Curaçao's blacks toward whites and toward the Dutch, in particular.

As early as 1651 the first Dutch, Sephardic Jews arrived on the island. They came directly from Amsterdam, but in the next few years (note the date, three years before the Dutch and the Jews were driven out of Brazil) their ranks were supplemented by Jewish families migrating north from Recife, French Guiana, and Suriname. Over time, quite a number of these Jewish families prospered in commerce, banking, real estate, and, let us face it, the slave trade, and are among the wealthiest persons in Curaçao. Their beautiful synagogue, which has a floor of sand to symbolize the Israelites wandering for forty years in the desert, is the oldest synagogue still in use in the western hemisphere—even though the ones in Recife, Suriname, and Newport, Rhode Island, were founded earlier.

Iêda and I have twice visited the synagogue and interviewed the congregation's president, Rene Maduro, who is the scion of the Maduro bank family and numerous other commercial enterprises in Curaçao. Part of the ritual in the synagogue still is to give thanks to The Netherlands and the ruling family of the House of Orange for rescuing the Jews from their persecutors and the Inquisition, giving them refuge and religious freedom, and allowing them to settle both in Amsterdam and in its American colonies. There are pictures of both Queen Juliana and Queen Beatriz in the synagogue.

Peter Stuyvesant, before moving on to New Amsterdam/New York, was governor on Curaçao from 1642–1645, arriving eight years after the Dutch first took hold of the colony. Because it was on the main trade routes and strategically important, all the major powers of the time sought to wrest Curaçao from the Dutch. There were French and British invasions, and Spain sought to re-conquer it. To defend against the repeated invasions, the Dutch built fortresses that they steadily reinforced. What had begun as a simple stockade grew into the more substantial Fort Amsterdam which still stands today at the entrance to the city.

Fort Amsterdam was built at the point where the Caribbean Sea opens into Saint Ann's Bay, one of the best natural harbors in the entire Caribbean. Saint Ann's Bay is a protected (from storms as well as marauders) inland bay connected to the open sea by a narrow channel. Both the fort and the surrounding city of Willemstad occupy the eastern side (the "Punda") of the harbor entrance; across the channel is the fast-growing newer part of the city called the Otrobanda (the Other Side). Willemstad is named after the Dutch stadholder William III.

Someone from The Netherlands would feel right at home in Curaçao. In addition to Fort Amsterdam, there is the Juliana Bridge (named after the former Dutch queen), Wilhelmina Park (named after another queen), and the Scharloo neighborhood where the early Jewish merchants first built stately homes. Almost all the place names and street names are Dutch; Breedestraat (Broadway) is the main thoroughfare of Willemstad as it is of Manhattan. The red tile roofs of the houses are also a familiar sight, with many of the original tiles brought from Holland and used as ballast in the sailing ships.

As you walk through the archway of Fort Amsterdam, which is really the entrance to the old city, you discover another world. It is calmer, quieter, and more traditional than the hubbub of busy, touristy, capitalistic downtown Willemstad. The fort, which was once the center of the city and the island's most important barracks, is now the seat of the governor's office, the Fort Church, the Council of Ministers, and government offices. It has been beautifully restored, painted (yellow stucco—for the Dutch), and kept up. One night, as a guest of the U.S. consulate in Curaçao, I attended an elegant reception up on the parapet of the fort.

If you're interested in Dutch or island history as I am, there is plenty to do in Curaçao. Both the Fort Church (Dutch Reformed) and the Jewish synagogue have small but wonderful museums attached to their sanctuaries. The Curaçao Museum is a poor and struggling public museum; it has a statue of the Dutch stadholder William of Orange as well as handmade Dutch furniture, a rich collection of maps that go back to colonial years, and Dutch tools and kitchen implements that look like things my grandmothers used to use. The new Maritime Museum, a nice walk across the (Queen) Wilhelmina Bridge, is a superb (and air-conditioned!) museum that tells the story of discovery, pirates, and colonial rivalries.

But because I'm Dutch and have this Christian Reformed background, I also made plans to attend the services of the Fort (Dutch Reformed) Church within the fortress walls. A first indication that this was not a thriving congregation came when I asked around at the hotel, on the streets, and even among employees in Fort Amsterdam, and no one knew when or even if the services began. When I got there, only a handful of people were in the pews; as the service began, forty people were in attendance, three-quarters of them Dutch or German tourists. The congregation has a lively, gracious female minister, imported (of course) from Friesland (Sneek) in The Netherlands, and the service is all in Dutch. The names of the members (totaling about two hundred—most inactive) are familiar to me from growing up in Dutch Grand Rapids: De Vries, Van Eps, Visser, Muller, and so on. The Fort Church, as well as its minister's salary, as with many other activities on Curaçao, is subsidized by the Dutch government.

Unlike many of the American Dutch Reformed Churches which have modernized their services to attract and keep young people, the Fort Amsterdam church has no special music, no choir, sings exclusively from the *Psalter Hymnal* (again, all those boring half notes), and has no special programs for young people. It *does* have, fortunately, a nice coffee hour after the service, as well as the museum room that has wonderful materials from Curaçao's and the Fort Church's history. At the coffee hour I learned that on the entire island there are only two other churches with a strong Reformed orientation, and two of these are more in the evangelical or spiritualist mode than in the logical, rationalist, Calvinist mode of the Dutch Reformed. In Curaçao, as in Suriname, and as in The Netherlands itself, it appears that Dutch Calvinism and the Dutch Reformed Church are a dead or certainly dying influence. Almost no one goes to church anymore.

The Dutch influence is fading in other ways as well. While Dutch is still the language of the elites and of official government discourse, the vast majority of the population speaks a form of papiamento, which is a combination of Spanish (from before the Dutch conquered the island), Portuguese, English, Dutch, and African languages. It is different (more Spanish, less Dutch) than the papiamento spoken in Suriname. Similarly with the population: there are only a few hundred Dutchmen in Curaçao, while the overwhelming majority of the population is black, African, colored, or from other islands in the Caribbean. Nevertheless, because of the colonial background, many residents of Curaçao hold valued Dutch (now European Union) passports.

In 1954 Curaçao became an autonomous part of the Kingdom of The Netherlands. Unlike Suriname, it is not an independent country. Rather, it has a governor appointed by the Dutch queen, an elected parliament, and an island council. Public administration, the courts, the legal system are all, here as in the other Dutch Caribbean islands, a reflection of the system in The Netherlands. It is transitioning to greater autonomy.

Though the governor is appointed by the queen, in fact the governor is chosen by the Curaçaoese and ratified by the crown. Similarly with the parliament and island council: technically the Dutch government has control over these bodies but in reality they are elected by the Curaçao people. However, there are still close ties with Holland, and Dutch advisers are still present at various levels of the Curaçao government. I have witnessed tall, blond, red-faced (from the tropical sun, not good healthwise for those of us with Nordic complexions) Dutch military officers smartly saluting as Curaçao officials arrive and depart. At the same time, the Curaçao government in recent years has not been especially known for its honesty, efficiency, and probity. But that has not prevented the government from moving toward greater autonomy, though still within the Kingdom of The Netherlands.

There are many issues in Dutch-Curaçao relations that are sensitive and complex. One is the issue of Curaçao independence: so far its leaders have seen the advantages of remaining a part of the Kingdom of The Netherlands (and, therefore, a part of the European Union), but there is widespread sentiment for independence and the current arrangements may not be permanent. A second issue is race: Curaçao is predominantly black and "Caribbean," and its relations with its white, Dutch, former slave-holding colonial masters is often fraught with racial friction. A third issue is language: should the official languages be Dutch and papiamento, and what about English which, as elsewhere, is becoming de facto, the second language of the island.

Drugs are also a complicated issue: many islanders are Rastafarians; drugs are a part of religious and cultural traditions; and islanders tend to have a tolerant attitude toward their use. But enforcement of anti-drug laws is carried out mainly by white U.S. and Dutch coastguard officials: again, the race issue. Finally, there is the matter of passports: initially all islanders, as Dutch citizens, were to receive them and, therefore, be able to travel back and forth freely to Europe; but recently, and now even more so with anti-immigrant sentiment rising in The Netherlands, the mother country has put increasing restrictions on Curaçaoese access to Dutch passports and on open immigration. The Dutch-Curaçao relationship is loaded with possibilities for greater tension and conflict.

Outside of Fort Amsterdam, the Dutch influence in Curaçao is a mixed one. For me, it's refreshing to see all those Dutch place and street names. That good, Dutch Amstel and Heineken beer is available in every bar and corner grocery store. Although in many of the outlying luxury hotels the guest list is mostly Americans looking for sun, beach, and a vacation, in downtown Willemstad, I would say that 60–70 percent of the strolling tourists are Dutch. I've noticed that in other former Dutch colonies as well: now that The Netherlands is a rich, affluent country, more and more of its people on their vacations are exploring these colonial enclaves in various parts of the world.

Because of its sunny, warm weather, yet cooled by ocean breezes, Curaçao is a very pleasant place to live. A new phenomenon is the wave of Dutch ex-patriots who are flocking to the island, not as temporary tourists but as permanent residents. Some are seeking cheap and easy drugs; others like the beaches and underwater sea life; still others, the warm, bright days compared to often-dreary and wet Holland. My own conversations with these ex-pats leads me to think they mainly want to escape the rat race, find a nice, laid-back place like Curaçao, and drop out for a time. They may stay there permanently or they may go back to Holland some day. There are both rich and upper-class ex-pats on Curaçao and poor, stoned-out ones.

Playing upon this Dutch wanderlust, as well as on the Dutch sense of guilt about its former colonial empire, is a curious institution in Curaçao: the Kurá Hulanda Hotel. The creation of Dutch multimillionaire Jacob Dekker, the Kurá Hulanda is more than a hotel; it is a museum, a business center, a restored eighteenth-century village, a center of art and anthropology, and a boutique hotel all rolled into one. The rooms are large, with high ceilings, and decorated with island-made furniture; there is also a pool, bar, and restaurants.

But the really unique feature is the Kurá Hulanda museum which focuses on the slave trade, portraying the Dutch as consistently cruel and oppressive and the native Africans as purely innocent victims of Dutch colonialism, racism, and imperialism—meanwhile, completely ignoring the role of African chiefs, both as slave holders and slave traders. The museum appears to be a product of the 1970s–1980s "dependency theory" which succeeded in blaming the West (in this case, the Dutch) for all of the world's problems. The museum *does* provide valuable insight into often neglected Dutch, African, and American history and has some wonderful display items and information that is not well known. While I find its heavy-handed biases and one-sidedness off-putting, the Dutch tourists that I talked to at the Kulá Hulanda found it to be "inspiring" and "wonderful." Apparently the Dutch enjoy wallowing in all that (Calvinist?) guilt; meanwhile, in both Suriname and Curaçao, local politicians have cleverly learned how to manipulate Dutch guilt over racism and colonialism to their own financial and political advantage.

The Kulá Hulanda is located on the west side of the Emma Bridge, a curious floating pontoon bridge that opens to the side for passing boats and is driven by an outboard motor, in the Otrobanda section of Willemstad. As you look across the channel leading into Saint Ann's Bay, you see on both sides a skyline of Dutch architecture that looks like it could be a city block in Amsterdam. But then you notice the buildings are painted in pastel colors, a reflection of island as compared to more conservative Dutch preferences. And, furthermore, that many of these are of recent vintage and not a reflection of Dutch colonial history. They were created strictly to draw tourists, to appear quaint and historical—a kind of Potemkin Village facade to impress visitors to the island and especially to appeal to the passengers on the gigantic Caribbean cruise ships that now ply the Saint Ann's channel. Perhaps that could be a symbol of the island: the Dutch influence and Dutch culture are fading, or exist mainly at facade levels, as Curaçao becomes more and more a reflection of Caribbean island culture, politics, and society.

Conclusion

Recife, Suriname, and Curaçao were once flourishing Dutch colonies in America. Recife and Suriname were plantation societies, while Curaçao was a commercial hub. In all three of them the Dutch presence, culture, and even religion were strong—at least for a time. All three were products of an integrated, systemic enterprise called the Dutch West India Company.

But in all three, the Dutch presence is either gone or fading fast. The Netherlands, a small country, never had the resources, especially the population surplus, to settle these territories effectively, to have its culture, including the Reformed religion, sink deep roots in the soil, the way Spain, Portugal, and Great Britain did with their American colonies. Instead, the Dutch provided mainly a facade, a set of overseers, plantation owners, and commercial elites. They did not penetrate the colonies they settled deeply, nor were they much interested in proselytizing among the natives or the slave laborers and indentured servants whom they brought in. The result is that the Dutch influence has all but completely disappeared in Recife and is fading rapidly in both Suriname and Curaçao. Many of my interviewees wagered that, in these latter two, the Dutch influence would be largely gone in only a matter of five to ten years.

What is striking is how little the Dutch are doing, either to preserve their heritage and culture in these former colonial outposts or to retain their influence there. In fact, just the opposite is the case: the Dutch seem to want "out" of these areas as quickly as possible. They are doing very little either to modernize the structures and institutions of these territories to adapt them to the modern world, or to put the resources in to ensure that these former colonies retain at least some vestiges of Dutch civilization.[8]

In a curious twist on the "fragments" theme, the Dutch in my area of Western Michigan seem to be much more with it in these respects than are the Dutch in The Netherlands or the three areas covered in this chapter. For the Dutch in Western Michigan are very interested in their own history, have done some wonderful historical renovations, and have opened new research and study centers to explore their own past. Not so in Recife, Suriname, or Curaçao, however, or even in The Netherlands where the Dutch are ashamed of this colonial legacy and wish to liquidate it as soon as possible. Moreover, in their music, their religion, their culture and religious services, the Western Michigan Dutch seem to be much more progressive and forward-looking than their forbears in The Netherlands who have continued to lag behind and are locked into old-fashioned religious practices and ways of doing things. It is another instance in which the New World has surpassed the Old, the former colony has done better than the mother country in adapting its beliefs and institutions to a new and changing world.

Notes

1. The best source still is Charles Boxer, *The Dutch in Brazil* (Oxford: Clarendon Press, 1973).

2. A wonderful, full-color, beautifully printed, coffee-table book is Paulo Herkenhoff, ed.), *O Brasil e os Holandeses* (Rio de Janeiro: Sextante Artes, 1999).

3. It was along this isolated coast that Robert Louis Stevenson set his famous novel *Treasure Island*. Then, as now, it was a remote, secretive, and hidden area that attracted few visitors.

4. The last Surinamese census was done in 1972 and it showed the Hindustanis as the largest group with 37 percent of the population. No census has been done since then: the Hindustani-dominated government says that is because a new census would upset the "delicate balance" in Suriname, but the real reason is Hindustani fears that the black or Maroon birth rate is greater than their own and would show a black plurality that would deprive the Hindustanis of political power.

5. Edward Dew, *The Difficult Flowering of Suriname: Ethnicity and Politics in a Plural Society* (The Hague: Martinus Nijhoff, 1978).

6. My interviews at the Dutch embassy in Suriname with Ambassador Henk Soeters, political counselor Hans de Voogd, and aid administrator Natalie Den Bruggen de Hooss (Hans's wife) indicated that the Dutch public and its representatives in parliament no longer felt the same guilt concerning their former colonies as did an earlier generation. We shall see how this works out.

7. The Dutch Ambassador Soeters told me that, for a gathering of ambassadors from The Netherlands to all the Latin American countries, they were all asked to read my book on *The Soul of Latin America.* (New Haven: Yale Uniersity Press, 2001) Of course, they all recognized mine as a Dutch name. But of the group, only the ambassador to Suriname had met me personally.

8. The parallel here with another small but much poorer country, Portugal, is striking; see Howard J. Wiarda, *The Legacy of Portuguese Rule in Asia: Reasserting Influence in the Post-Colonial Era* (Lisbon: Portuguese Center for the Study of Southeast Asia, 2002).

CHAPTER EIGHT

Dying Memories:
The Dutch Empire in Asia

In 2001 I had received a major research grant from a Portuguese foundation, the Oriente Foundation, to conduct research in Asia. The Oriente Foundation, headquartered in Lisbon, sponsors studies, publishes books, and celebrates the explorations, culture, civilization, and conquests of the Portuguese in Asia. Though it mainly focuses on historical research of the sixteenth, seventeenth, and eighteenth centuries, as a political scientist I wanted to do research on the lasting and contemporary impact of Portuguese political ideas and institutions in Asia. I knew that Portuguese explorers had been all over Asia—India, Malaysia, Indochina, Indonesia, The Philippines, Formosa, China, Korea, Japan—in Portugal's glorious sixteenth century, but I wanted to see if Portuguese ideas and institutions of local government, public administration, state-society relations, corporatism and organicism had had a lasting impact on Asia. So I wrote up a proposal to test this idea, sent it off to the Oriente Foundation, and, much to my surprise since they are a quite conservative (history is less controversial than political science), stuffy organization, received a handsome grant to support my studies.[1]

So off to Asia I went in the fall of 2001. That year was a sabbatical leave year from my university, the University of Massachusetts, so I could take my leisurely time in exploring Asia and the Portuguese presence. I had previously traveled and done research in Japan, China, South Korea, Taiwan, Hong Kong, Singapore, and The Philippines, so on this trip I decided to concentrate on Japan (but only the area in southern Japan where the Portuguese settled), Macau, Goa (in India), Indonesia, and East Timor.

113

My first shock came in Nagasaki, Japan. Nagasaki is best known as the site of one of the only two (the other being Hiroshima) targets of nuclear weapons used in war but, with its natural harbor facing the East China Sea, it was also the place where Portuguese missionaries, merchants, and conquistadors first landed in Japan. The Portuguese were in Japan from 1541 to 1639—what Charles Boxer has called "the Christian Century" in Japan.[2] But when the Portuguese were expelled definitively in 1639, the Dutch moved in. Indeed, for the next two hundred years and more, 1641–1852, until American Admiral Perry arrived on that latter date, the Dutch were the *only* foreign presence in Japan.

As I roamed around Nagasaki gathering materials and doing interviews for my monograph on the Portuguese legacy in Asia, I discovered the Dutch had actually been more influential in Japan and for a longer period than had the Portuguese. In fact, as I subsequently pursued my research design around Asia—Hong Kong, Macau, India, Indonesia—I found that was generally the case. *Wherever I went in Asia looking for the Portuguese, I found that the Dutch had also been there*, usually stronger, for a longer time, and with greater wealth and influence. Hence, the idea for a future project, parallel to the Portugal one, on the Dutch in Asia. This chapter, largely focused on Japan, and the next on Indonesia, are the first fruits of that endeavor.[3]

The Dutch in Asia

The extent of the Dutch explorations and empire in Asia and the rest of the world in the seventeenth century is simply incredible. The Americas, Africa, Asia, the Middle East, the South Pacific—name the area and the Dutch were there, usually as traders and merchants, often as conquerors.

In this brief chapter, we can only begin to describe the vast extent, complexity, and geographic spread of the Dutch empire. Provided here is only a shorthand guide to the areas conquered. More extensive treatment of the Dutch role in Japan is offered later in the chapter; the important Dutch possessions of South Africa and Indonesia are treated in separate chapters.

Getting There

The Dutch generally followed in the seventeenth century the route the Portuguese had taken to Asia in the sixteenth century. It is striking when reviewing the list of Dutch colonies and trading depots that they, with their superior ships, navy, and sailing instruments, settled in almost the exact same colonial centers and strategic posts as had the Portuguese a century earlier. It could be said that the Dutch built upon and extended what the equally pioneering Portuguese had done earlier, meanwhile giving their empire its own special Dutch character.

The Dutch recognized early on that to secure their Brazil and Caribbean colonies, described in chapter 7, it would be essential to control the West African coast. Not only because that was the center of the slave trade but also, given the prevailing westerly wind flows, because West Africa would be the jumping-off point for European sailing ships headed toward South America and the circum-Caribbean. To take advantage of the prevailing wester-lies, it was best to drop down from Europe in a southerly direction, skirt the Canaries and West Africa, and then cross the Atlantic from there. To guard these routes and trading posts, the Dutch sought in the 1630s and 1640s to explore and conquer areas of the West African coast including present-day Mauritania (named after Dutch Prince Maurits), Guinea, Ghana and the en-tire Gold Coast, Angola, Namibia, and South Africa. In several of these ar-eas, the Dutch were active for a period of time and held the territory, but found it either unprofitable or indefensible strategically and eventually with-drew, giving way to other powers. Other than South Africa, the Dutch were never involved in the "race for colonies" in Africa as were the other colonial nations.

At the tip of the African continent, at the Cape of Good Hope, lies the large, former Dutch colony of South Africa. The Dutch settled the area and established Cape Town as a trading and refurbishing depot in 1651, mainly for ships bound for India. At first, the Dutch presence was limited to the Cape; only later would they effectively settle the interior. South Africa is so important in our account of Dutch "fragments" that it merits a separate chapter.

Rounding the Cape, the Dutch explored the large island of Madagascar and took control of the Mauritius Islands (similarly named after the Dutch stadholder) and held them until they were occupied by France after the Dutch left in the early eighteenth century. One of the Dutch commanders on Mauritius was a former pirate, Hubert Hugo; another interesting feature about Mauritius worth following up on was the French Huguenot (Calvinist) community sent there in the late seventeenth century after the persecution of Protestants and the Saint Bartholomew's massacre in France in 1672.

Moving up the Indian Ocean, we come to Ethiopia, then called Abyssinia. The Dutch East India Company's efforts to establish contact with an Ethiopian government were both unsuccessful and read like a farce. Rather like the sometimes comic-opera efforts of British colonials branching out from India to find a mythical kingdom in isolated and primitive Afghanistan, as portrayed in the movie *The Man Who Would Be King*.

The Dutch then moved farther around the perimeter of the Indian Ocean exploring the Gulf of Aden and the entry to the Red Sea, the foot of the Arabian Peninsula where Yemen is now located, and the entry to the Gulf of Oman and the Persian Gulf. Already in 1611 the Dutch were exploring the coast of Persia (now Iran); in 1651–1652 an ambassador from the Dutch East India Company had taken a fantastic journey throughout Persia with the aim of establishing a major trading depot there.

Since India was so long a British colony, we tend to forget that the Dutch were in India before the British—and the Portuguese even before that. Neither The Netherlands nor Portugal was a large enough country to be able to colonize, settle, and conquer large, populous India, so they mainly limited themselves to trading enclaves on the coast. These included such areas as Gujerat, the coast of Coromandel, the coast of Malabar, Bengal, Suratte, as well as Goa where the Dutch and Portuguese fought mightily for control. The Dutch did not try to Christianize India but in Bengal they did seek to favor the "Syrian" or "Thomas-Christians" (so-named because St. Thomas is supposed to have traveled to this part of India in the first century, and because "everyone" in that state is named Thomas) and sought to turn them into their special agents in India.

At the southern tip of the Indian subcontinent lies Ceylon (now Sri Lanka) which the Dutch also controlled from 1638–1796. We think of Ceylon, like India, as a former British colony which it was, but for over one hundred and fifty years the Dutch influence was enormous. There is still in Sri Lanka over two hundred years later a "white tribe" whose names and antecedents go back to Dutch colonial days. And in the city of Gaull on Sri Lanka's southwest coast—one of those cities all but destroyed in the Christmas, 2004, tsunami—there is still a row of Dutch architecture-style houses that looks remarkably like Curaçao or Amsterdam.

The key gateway to the rest of Asia was through the Straits of Malacca, which has the Indonesia island of Sumatra on one side and the Malay Peninsula on the other. The Dutch were already (since 1615) penetrating the interior of Sumatra in pursuit of the pepper trade; they also controlled parts of the Malay Peninsula and captured the strategic city of Malacca, which controlled all passageways in the straits, from the Portuguese in 1641. Control of this essential "choke-point" (as it's known in the strategic literature) enabled the Dutch to dominate all the main sea lanes to Asia.

Arriving in Asia
Even before seizing control of the Straits of Malacca, Dutch ships were exploring the farthest reaches of Asia and the South Pacific, engaging in trade,

and establishing their hegemony. Once again, anyone who looks at a map will be astounded by the extent of the Dutch explorations and colonial empire in Asia.

The most valuable of the Dutch colonies in these days (hard to believe now) were the so-called Spice Islands, today part of the archipelago that is the nation of Indonesia. The Spice Islands, in turn, consist of three sets of islands: the northern Moluccas (further divided into four sultanates), the southern Moluccas consisting of the regional capital of Amboyna, and the eastern Moluccas or Banda. The Dutch defeated and drove out the Portuguese from here, settled and helped Christianize the islands, and monopolized the spice (nutmeg, cloves, peppers) trade. The sociology of and the relations between the islands and the Dutch (and now the Indonesian nation) and the several tribes, religions, and chieftaincies within them are incredibly complex. Suffice it here to say that many Moluccans after Indonesian independence opted to settle in The Netherlands where they are still not fully assimilated into Dutch society. Also interesting is the fact that the Moluccas have been the scene of probably the fiercest fighting between Christians (a legacy of both Portuguese and Dutch rule) and Muslims in all of strife-torn Indonesia.

The Celebes Islands, en route between Batavia (present-day Jakarta, Indonesia) and the Moluccas or Spice Islands, were explored by the Dutch as early as 1600. A few years later they established a trading post in the Celebes and began to Christianize the natives; there and in the Moluccas were among the few places the trade-oriented Dutch actually sought to convert the native population. Meanwhile, the Dutch were already involved in the pepper trade on the large island of Sumatra, and on the island of Java (from which the Dutch word for coffee—because it came from there—derives). Dutch traders in 1619 established their capital (Batavia) and made it the principal port for trade throughout the entire archipelago.

Exploring farther afield, the Dutch discovered the larger islands of Borneo and New Guinea. The Dutch mainly explored the southern coasts of Borneo (pepper again) and the western half of New Guinea (ditto). It is these Dutch explorations and the dividing lines subsequently drawn that explain to this day why both of these islands have borders that indicate divided sovereignty: southern Borneo is Indonesian, while northern Borneo is divided between Malaysia and Brunei. Similarly, western New Guinea is claimed by Indonesia while the eastern half (known as Papua New Guinea) is independent.

Contrary to much popular opinion, it was the Dutch who discovered Australia and New Zealand (note the name, after a Dutch province) and not the British. The Dutch sailor William Jansz in 1606 was the first European to sight Australia, the world's largest island, and explore and map its coasts.

However, the Dutch never settled or colonized this territory (no spices, therefore "worthless") and left both of these large islands to be settled by the British a couple of hundred years later.

Since the Dutch rarely challenged stronger powers, it is especially interesting to learn that Dutch fleets also explored and then attacked The Philippines, which had been under Spanish control since the early 1500s. But the Dutch were smart: they did not attack The Philippines when Spanish power was still at its height but waited until later, when Spain was already in decline, to launch their attacks. But the Dutch were already over-extended and were never much of a presence in The Philippines. Nevertheless, the idea of a potentially Dutch-controlled and Protestant Philippines is intriguing, another of those "what ifs" of which history is so full.

From 1624 to 1662 the Dutch were also in control of the island of Formosa, today's Taiwan. Like other powers before and after, the Dutch saw Formosa as a strategic jumping-off point for trade with both mainland China and Japan. Here, too, in a settled colony, the Dutch were involved not only in trade but also in missionary activity that was quite successful for a time. Even today a good part of Formosa is Protestant, stemming from the early Dutch and later British and American missionary activity. The Dutch citadel in Formosa was called (of course) Zeelandia; in 1662 it was captured by Kok Sing, one of the last defenders of the Ming dynasty.

The first Dutch incursions into China came both by way of Formosa and through the Pescadores Islands in the South China Sea. Note how many of these place names—Formosa, Pescadores—have Portuguese-origin names, all places the Dutch took over from the weaker Portuguese. The Dutch were in the Pescadores and on mainland China as early as the first decade of the seventeenth century, but they never established a permanent colony there. They sent several trade and ambassadorial missions to the mainland in the seventeenth century, but China was already then so big and so populous that the Dutch rightly calculated they had no chance of conquest. There were plenty of profits in trade to be made elsewhere.

If one studies a map of these regions carefully, one realizes how extensive the Dutch colonies, settlements, and trading posts in Africa, the Middle East, and Asia were. It was a huge and vast colonial empire. The last and farthest link in this "imperialist chain" (as Vladimir Lenin put it) was Japan.

Japan

My purpose in going to Nagasaki, a more traditional Japanese city on the southern island of Kyushu (the people are smaller; less English is spoken) had been to explore what remained of the Portuguese legacy (if any) here. Nagasaki, with its wonderful, protected, deep-water natural harbor facing out onto the East China Sea, had long been the route by which first the Chinese and then the Portuguese had penetrated the Japanese islands. I had known intellectually and from my history readings that the Dutch had been here, too, but I had not realized the full extent and longevity of the Dutch presence. For over two hundred years, long before U.S. Admiral Perry's "opening" of Japan to American trade, the Dutch were virtually Japan's only connection to the outside world, and certainly to the Western one.

I had arrived extremely tired in Nagasaki on a Saturday night after a sixteen-hour flight and an extremely long, thirty-six-hour day. Early the next day, on a Sunday morning in the rain, I went off to do a preliminary reconnoiter of my research terrain concerning the Portuguese legacy. Within three blocks of my hotel, I stumbled onto a short, one-block street, really only a narrow walkway, called "Hollander's Slope." It's a shaded, flagstone street that leads up to what was once the foreigners' settlement on the top of the hill. A brochure advertises the neighborhood as "historic" and it is, but the houses here only go back to the nineteenth century.

The houses look like the old wooden structures I've seen at La Romana or Panama or other places where colonials settled a hundred or more years ago. It's known as Hollanders' Slope because at one time, since the Dutch were the only Westerners allowed into the country, all foreigners were referred to as "Hollanders," no matter their actual country of origin. And, therefore, even if they were not all Dutch, the street leading to the foreigners' housing enclave was also called Hollanders' Slope.

As the Portuguese and their Catholic missions were martyred or forced out of Japan because of Japanese fears they also had imperial designs on the islands, the Dutch came in. The Dutch in Japan were mainly traders and merchants, however, not proselytizers. They, and specifically the Dutch East India Company, had no interest in either converting or conquering the islands. Rather, as in New Amsterdam (Manhattan) and other Dutch commercial centers, they were in it purely in capitalistic, profit-making terms—that is, for the money. To prove their bona fides in this respect, the Dutch merchants were obliged to trample on and stomp images of the pope and the Catholic saints. This the Dutch were happy to do since, as one of the leaders of the Protestant Reformation and of a strong, nationalistic movement that was anti-pope, anti-Catholic, and anti-Spain and Portugal, they had no love for the pope, the Roman church, or the Catholic saints. By these shows of anti-papal and anti-Catholic sentiment, the Dutch earned their Japanese trading monopoly that they maintained for the next two centuries.

Not fully trusting the Dutch much more than the Portuguese, however, the Japanese confined them to a small island in Nagasaki harbor that they kept carefully policed and isolated. Dejima Island is the former Dutch East India Company "factory" or trading post in Japan. A small island of only 25,000 square meters (about four acres), it was built up in 1636 from a sandbar at the mouth of the river that flows into Nagasaki harbor. It had been created in that year as a way of confining the Portuguese who up to then had been allowed to live anywhere in Nagasaki. But in the next few years, all Portuguese were expelled from Japan and the Christian (Catholic) religion banned. Hence, when the Dutch arrived in 1641, they, too, were confined to this one small island. From then until 1852, when Admiral Perry forced his way into Japan, Dejima was Japan's only window and port of entry and exit to the outside world.

Dejima Island long, narrow, and curved—is shaped like (depending on your point of view) a banana, a quarter moon, or perhaps a boomerang— There are warehouses and houses along the two long sides of the island and a third row in the middle. Often the houses of the Dutch doubled as warehouses for silk, tea, spices, and other exports; ships would pull up and dock literally at your back door. Two parallel "streets" (really, just dirt paths) separated the rows of houses and storage barns. The East India Company also maintained an administrative headquarters on the island.

The island was connected to the mainland by a causeway and a small bridge. The bridge was guarded night and day by Japanese samurai (warriors) who kept strict control over people coming and going. There were always three to five guards; visits across the bridge were limited to officers of the Company and persons used as language translators. Others were allowed to pass only by a permit from the district government.

For the Dutch residents of Dejima, it was a tight, restricted, confined existence. They were not allowed to travel to other parts of Japan or to have Japanese visitors on their island. The big event of the year (or maybe several years apart) was the arrival of a Dutch merchant ship from Batavia (Indonesia), Ceylon, India, or Amsterdam. The Dutch brought in sausages and salted meats to trade with Japan, along with animal heads and skins that the Japanese had never seen before. They also traded in sugar, spices (from the Moluccas), dyes, and rare woods. Occasionally, employees of the Company joined with their Japanese kitchen help in festive occasions.

A new museum on Dejima shows the Dutch warehouses, docks, houses, scales, and administrative centers. It pictures the Dutch dressed as patroons, with broad-brimmed hats, black breeches, and white shirts and kneesocks— straight out of a Rembrandt painting. It shows monkeys and other exotic animals brought to Japan by the Dutch. It pictures servants, includes a pool table (on this confined island, life could be pretty boring), and shows that the Dutch brought knives and forks to Japan for the first time as well as new foods, flowers, and agricultural products.

The Dutch are pictured, as in Brazil, as having brought modernization to Japan. They were great naturalists and scientists. They brought map-making as well as the systematic study of plants and animals to Japan—quite a number of which they had imported from Indonesia and other Dutch colonies. They brought in new foods and commercial products. Much more than the earlier Portuguese, the Dutch introduced Japan to the modern or modernizing world.

Of course, Dutch power waxed and waned—and waxed again, as it did elsewhere in the Dutch colonial world. Some of these changes were due to the greater, or lesser, vigor of the Dutch domestic situation and, hence, its colonial enterprise; and some to the rise of other competing powers, such as England and France. Thus, the high point of Dutch power was the seventeenth century, the "golden century" in Dutch history, while in the eighteenth century, with both decline at home and the challenge of other, larger powers, the empire went into decline. It was revived again in the nineteenth century when Dutch colonialism was revived and, along with the colonialism of other European powers, reached its apogee.

In 1810 The Netherlands, along with much of the rest of Europe, was conquered by Napoleon. England planned to take advantage of this opportunity to plunder and seize the Dutch colonies in Asia, especially Indonesia, as well as South Africa. To that end, England sent the famous Thomas Raffles (of Singapore fame) to Asia to take control of the Dutch areas of India and the Indonesian archipelago. However, in a story that every Dutch school child is taught, Blomhoff of the Dutch East Indies Company refused to hand over control of Dejima Island to England. Hence, from 1810 until the liberation from Napoleonic occupation and the founding of the Dutch Republic in 1815, this tiny, little, four-acre island was the only place in the world flying the Dutch flag and the pride of the Dutch people.

There is a little-known American twist to this story as well. In school we are taught that Admiral Perry was the first American to visit Japan. Not so. Between 1810 and 1815, when The Netherlands had lost its independence and was under the heavy hand of Napoleon and the French, it asked an American ship then visiting Jakarta, Indonesia, to stop by the Dutch "factory" on Dejima to inspect and show the flag. So as not to rile up the Japanese, the Americans were asked to pretend they were Dutch and to fly the Dutch flag during their visit, and were given instructions on how to speak a few words of the difficult, very guttural Dutch language. This they did—and reported back to The Netherlands on their visit. I was told in Nagasaki by one of my interviewees that there is a house in Salem, Massachusetts, that once belonged to one of the sailors on the American ship that commemorates and contains mementoes and artifacts acquired on that voyage to Nagasaki, but I have not had a chance to visit this museum or see what it contains. It's a fascinating story: forty years before Perry (1852), an American ship with American sailors had already landed in Japan.

With the restoration of Dutch sovereignty in 1815, the Dutch took a renewed interest in their Asian colonies, including their small Dejima Island outpost in Japan. Trade was resumed and the Dutch sent a new wave of scientists, merchants, and scholars to Japan. The most prominent of these was a von Siebold, of German extraction but a Dutch citizen and employed by the East India Company. Siebold was a doctor who served as the Company's physician, but he also conducted scientific research on Japan. He married a Japanese woman, built a beautiful house in the hills above Nagasaki (the house is now a museum; by the nineteenth century, foreign residents were no longer confined just to Dejima), and their daughter became the first Western-trained Japanese physician. Men like Siebold made major contributions to the development of Japan, as well as re-introducing Japanese culture, largely lost for a time, to Europe.

But once the Americans came into Japan in the 1850s, and then as other major European countries subsequently also entered into diplomatic and trading relationships with Japan, the always-small Dutch enclave in Dejima/Nagasaki lost its privileged position. For over two hundred years the Dutch had been Japan's only eye on (and trading partner with) the world. But after Perry's voyage, Japan opened up to other foreigners, and the Dutch, a relatively small and not especially significant country by then, rapidly lost not only its monopoly in Japan but its place of special importance as well.

Today the Dutch influence in Japan has waned; it is just one country among many with which Japan maintains good relations. There are Dutch words, especially those having to do with trade, foods, commerce, and cooking, in the Japanese vocabulary; but most Japanese speakers are not even aware that these have Dutch roots. Nor has the Dutch government done very much to print brochures, set up road signs, establish a museum, or incorporate the Dutch period into Japanese history textbooks. I have found in my travels in Japan, and particularly in Nagasaki, that almost no Japanese are aware of either the Portuguese or the Dutch role in the history of Japan. No one believes that Dutch influence could or should be revived in Japan; on the other hand, for historical reasons alone, one would think the Dutch government would be interested in making better known its early—and important—history in Japan.

Today, there is no Dutch "fragment" in Japan. The number of Dutchmen in Japan on Dejima Island was never more than a hundred and it never constituted a full-fledged colony. Nor did the Dutch ever settle, let along conquer, the Japanese islands or become assimilated in Japan. Instead, the Dutch formed a very small enclave; they were dedicated almost exclusively to trade as distinct from missionary and "colonizing" work, and they were confined to this tiny, little island, Dejima, where their overall cultural influence on the rest of Japan was extremely limited. In terms of the overall thesis of this book, the Dutch experience in Japan does not count for very much; their influence is purely historical rather than ongoing. At the same time, it would be nice if the Dutch government showed more interest in this fascinating history and did a little more to publicize it, both in Japan and to the outside world.

Notes

1. The research on Portugal in Asia is reported in Howard J. Wiarda, *The Legacy of Portuguese Rule in Asia: Reasserting Influence in the Post-Colonial Era* (Lisbon: Portuguese Center for the Study of Southeast Asia, 2002).

2. Charles Boxer, *The Christian Century in Japan, 1549–1650* (Berkeley: University of California Press, 1967).

3. I have also published a travel account of these research explorations; see Howard J. Wiarda, *Adventures in Research* (Lincoln, NE: Universe, 2006), especially the chapters on Japan and Indonesia.

CHAPTER NINE

Indonesia: The Epitome of Colonialism and Imperialism

Indonesia is the world's fourth largest nation in terms of population (behind only China, India, and the United States) with over 220 million people. The Indonesian archipelago of islands stretches over 3,300 miles (wider than the United States) reaching all the way from mainland Asia to Australia. It contains in this chain over 13,000 islands, speaks over five hundred different languages, and encompasses a great diversity of cultures, ethnicities, and religions, including Hindu, Buddhist, Confucian, Muslim, animist, and Christian. How to hold all this diverse territory and peoples together and integrate them as a single nation-state is the great theme of Indonesian history.

Background and History

The colonization of Indonesia by the West was part of that great outward expansion of Europe that began in the fifteenth century with Columbus's discovery of America in 1492 and continued in succeeding centuries. Portugal and Spain were the world's first great global empire-builders, staking out vast domains and acquiring colonies in far-flung regions of the world.

The Portuguese were the first of the European powers to explore the Indonesian archipelago and establish bases there. Portuguese caravels began appearing in the islands in the early sixteenth century and soon the Portuguese had a virtual monopoly over the profitable spice trade. Especially valuable were the Moluccan Islands, also known as the Spice Islands, because of their abundance of peppers, nutmeg, cloves, mace, ginger, and cinnamon. The importation of all these spices to Europe greatly improved what previously had been a very bland European diet all through the Middle Ages and was an extremely lucrative trade for the power that controlled it.

The Dutch arrived in Indonesia a century after the Portuguese. In 1596 the first Dutch fleet of four ships arrived in the islands, returning home with a profitable cargo of spices. This initial foray whetted the Dutch appetites for more, both spices and profits, and in 1600 the Dutch East India Company was founded. The VOC (its Dutch initials), like its later counterpart in the Americas, the Dutch West Indies Company, was motivated almost exclusively by profit. But it was not just a trading company; rather, it operated almost as a right arm of the Dutch state and had the authority to build forts, wage war, conclude treaties with indigenous peoples, and administer justice to subject populations. Its appetites were voracious.

Already by 1603 the Dutch had invaded and occupied the Banda Islands, part of the Moluccas. Within two years the VOC had chased the Portuguese out of their trading posts and military bases on Amboy and Tidore, also part of the Moluccas. Over the course of the next few years the Dutch rid Indonesia of just about all of the former Portuguese outposts—except East Timor. By the end of the first decade of the seventeenth century, the VOC had taken complete control of the Spice Islands, was working to establish a trade monopoly, and had begun to consolidate its empire in Indonesia.

The Dutch were not particularly nice or even Christian about how they established their empire—or maybe they were just like other colonialists. When local chiefs in the Banda continued to sell some of their spices to England in defiance of Dutch monopoly practices, the VOC killed or deported virtually the entire population, replacing it with indentured servants and slaves whose absolute loyalty they could count on. Within twenty years the Dutch had not only consolidated their monopoly that they vigorously enforced, but also extended their rule to other islands.

Leading the Dutch efforts during this period was the legendary Jan Pieterzoon Coen who was the VOC's chief representative in the islands and, simultaneously, functioned as governor-general of Dutch state interests. Coen was ruthless in pursuit of monopoly, territory, and greater profits for the Company. To keep prices high, he was not against destroying large native nutmeg and clove plantations; he also vastly expanded Dutch holdings on the large island of Java. It was Coen who established the capital of the Dutch Indonesian empire at Jakarta, razing the old city to the ground when the locals objected and rebuilding and re-christening it as Batavia after the legendary kingdom in The Netherlands itself that had resisted Roman domination.

Dutch incursions into Java and the other large island of Sumatra involved the VOC in the internal politics, rivalries, and civil wars of the various Indonesian kingdoms there. It was difficult, maybe next to impossible, for The Netherlands, a small country, to completely conquer, settle, colonize, and subdue the entire Indonesian archipelago. So the VOC contented itself with pitting the local kingdoms off against each other, playing divide and conquer, making tactical alliances with local groups, and working through the native power structure, meanwhile gradually expanding the VOC's suzerainty and monopolies. This long struggle to expand its control lasted until the mid-eighteenth century, a full century-and-a-half after the initial Dutch conquests in the islands.

But by then The Netherlands was itself a weakened country, had lost the vim and energy of the early seventeenth century—the "Golden Era" in Dutch history—and was facing renewed competition from England and France who sensed the Dutch weakness. In addition, the VOC had become by this time less efficient and dynamic and increasingly corrupt and short-sighted, determined, as a phrase at the time put it, to "shake the pagoda tree"—greedily to eke every ounce of profit out of its Indonesian possessions. As a way of stemming the tide, it introduced new cash crops on Java, including coffee—hence, the Dutch word for coffee, java—but by then the Company's fate was sealed.

The Company had also been corrupted by its own office-holders and was deeply in debt. When, at the end of the eighteenth century, French troops occupied The Netherlands, they allowed the Company's charter to lapse. Thus ended the Company's sometimes glorious, sometimes inglorious, always tumultuous two-hundred-year history. It also marked the end for a time of Dutch colonial control in Indonesia.

French troops had occupied The Netherlands in 1795; in 1808 Napoleon had put his brother Louis on the Dutch throne. In addition, when the VOC's charter had been allowed to expire, possession of the Company's vast colonial possessions had reverted to the Dutch government, now under French control. Louis Napoleon appointed a Dutch official imbued with the ideals of the French Revolution (liberty, equality, fraternity), Herman Willem Daendels, as governor-general of Indonesia. But he had no sense of the local customs and ways of doing things, nor of the delicate balance the Dutch had long maintained between colonial overlordship and the indigenous power structure. Daendels quickly earned the hostility of the Javanese elites and tribal/feudal leaders that quickly weakened the colony and paved the way for a British takeover from the French in 1811.

Thomas Raffles, best known as the founder of Singapore a few years later (and for whom Singapore's famed Raffles Hotel is named), was appointed lieutenant governor of Java by the British East India Company. Raffles, like Daendels, had good intentions and introduced a number of enlightened reforms in Indonesia (abolition of forced labor, free choice of crops for Indonesian peasant farmers, abolition of the slave trade) but was in power too briefly to carry them out. For at the outset of the British campaign against Napoleon, the British government had promised the Dutch government in exile that, in return for its support in fighting Napoleon, England would at the end of the war return all the occupied colonial territories to The Netherlands. This the British did over the objections of Raffles, so that in 1816 Dutch authority in Indonesia was reestablished.

Dutch rule during the nineteenth and early twentieth centuries was very different from what it had been in the seventeenth and eighteenth centuries. While the earlier system had often been cruel and sometimes bloody, it also involved the VOC's efforts to get along with and accommodate local power structures and practices. The new program, called the Cultivation System, was not nearly so benign or enlightened. Indeed, it brought new forms of debt peonage and virtual slavery to Indonesia. It also helps explain why even now Dutch colonialism and virtually all things Dutch are strongly despised.

Under the Cultivation System, Indonesian farmers and peasants were obliged to devote a large share of their lands to growing cash crops—indigo, silk, sugar, coffee—that the Dutch colonialists could sell for huge profits in Europe. Much of Java, and soon Sumatra, too, became a gigantic plantation system producing for the world market. Local elites in Indonesia also profited from these arrangements since they served as middlemen between the farmers and the Dutch exporters and were used by the colonial government to help maintain order and authority on a local and regional basis, thus retaining their historic status and power. The Cultivation System was tremendously profitable, accounting for between a quarter and a third of all Dutch government revenues until the 1860s and financing the construction of the Dutch state railroads. The system was so successful financially that the British government used it as a model for its own colonial exploitation in Africa and India.

But the Cultivation System also bred exploitation, greed, and oppression by both Dutch and Indonesian overlords. In some areas of the country, the system amounted to a form of slavery; it also slighted production for local, home-grown markets with the result that consumption of "poor people's food" (e.g., rice) went down, and many peasant farmers faced decreased living standards and even starvation. An exposé of the abuses of the system published in 1860 had a powerful effect (like Harriet Beecher Stowe's *Uncle Tom's Cabin* published just before the Civil War in the United States) on liberal public opinion in The Netherlands and led to significant reforms.

But once the worst abuses of the system had been corrected, Dutch colonial rule continued much as before. It was exploitive and, at the same time, hugely profitable. New crops, such as rubber, were introduced; tin mines were opened up; and Royal Dutch Shell began exporting Indonesian oil. The economy continued as basically a rapacious, export-oriented, exploitive, colonial system. The system's worst features were reformed after the 1860s, especially the Cultivation System which reduced Indonesian farmers to peons; but it was still top-down, repressive, and oriented toward the greater enrichment of the mother country and not the colony. Even now Indonesians fault the Dutch not just for their colonialism and imperialism but also, in contrast with the British in India, for failing to educate them, failing to create an Indonesian system of public administration, and, in general, for failing to prepare them for independence.

While the period 1870–1940 was generally quite stable in Indonesia, a number of major developments important for the main themes of this book occurred during this period that demand our attention. The first of these was continued Dutch expansion and conquests into new islands and areas of the archipelago: Sumatra during much of the nineteenth century, Bali (today's tourist center) in 1906, Aceh province (where the 2004 tsunami hit) in 1908, and West Papua in 1920.

The second was expanded missionary activity among the native populations. Under the VOC the Dutch had been more profit-oriented than proselytizers, but in the nineteenth century, with a religious revival taking place in Europe and Holland, Dutch missionaries fanned out over the islands to convert the natives. They had some success but also misfortunes. During my own stay in Indonesia, I vividly remember my guide telling me, with great pride in his voice, that, when the first Christian missionaries came to his village in central Sumatra, "we ate them!" How's that for a conversation-ender?[1]

A third development had to do with expanding the Indonesian population. As the economy grew in the nineteenth and early twentieth centuries, so rather rapidly did the Indonesian population. But the Dutch colonial masters took some of this excess population and shipped it off to Suriname, another Dutch colonial territory (see chapter 7) in South America, where there was a labor shortage. The Indonesian laborers shipped off this way often had no idea of their destination, were not given a choice in the matter, could not bring their families along, were carted off in conditions of debt peonage, and had no records of their place of origin. I have already written of my encounters in Suriname with persons of Indonesian descent who had spent immense amounts of time and money searching for their origins, villages, and family roots back in Indonesia, but to no avail.

A fourth consequence of rising Indonesian prosperity was the arrival in the islands of many ethnic Chinese, coming either from China directly as a result of nineteenth- and twentieth-century civil wars or from other Southeast Asian outposts, such as Malaysia, Singapore, or Hong Kong. Hardworking and frugal, many of these Chinese immigrants, now numbering over 2 percent of the population, prospered in Indonesia as merchants and traders.

Many of them were also Christian, having been converted either earlier in China or after their arrival in Indonesia. When I was doing research there in 2001 on the role of religion and the Muslim-Christian conflict, I discovered that in Jakarta and elsewhere many of the Christian churches, including Reformed churches, consisted mainly of ethnic Chinese congregations. They were despised (and sometimes firebombed) by the Muslims, not just because they were Christian but also because, as ethnic Chinese, their wealth and elevated social position (many Chinese families employ Indonesian maids and gardeners) were resented by the poorer Indonesians.

One final aspect of Dutch rule in the nineteenth and early twentieth centuries commands our attention, and that involves the changing nature of Dutch colonial society itself. Early (pre-nineteenth-century) Dutch settlers had been known as *blijvers* (best translated as sojourners): persons who represented a tiny Dutch minority on the islands, came without their families as traders, soldiers, and merchants, and adopted an "Indies" style of life that combined and often integrated European and Indonesian elements. But in the nineteenth century, new generations of Dutch immigrants (called *trekkers*) brought their families along, settled in Dutch or whites-only enclaves, and lived a European life style separate from—and usually disdainful of—the Indonesians around them. These Dutch/white communities were, as the Dutch usually are, immaculately clean, Dutch-speaking, with Dutch architecture, and quite comfortable and affluent. They were also completely cut off from the "dustier" and far poorer Indonesian life that swirled about them. The parallel here with the Dutch-based, Afrikaans community in South Africa is remarkable; even the term used—trekkers—is the same. We shall have more to say on the parallels, and differences, between Dutch South Africa, Indonesia, and also Suriname later in the discussion.

Indonesian national self-consciousness, and eventually the desire for independence, began to rise in the early twentieth century. The Indonesian National Party (PNI) was organized in 1927; in the 1930s there was considerable ferment in favor of independence, and in the 1940s a series of events precipitated independence. First, when Hitler invaded and occupied The Netherlands in 1940, it put the issue of independence on hold, while also demonstrating to Indonesian nationalists that the Dutch were not invincible. Second came the Japanese invasion of the archipelago in 1942 and a Japanese occupation until 1945, which drove many of the Dutch out and reinforced the belief the Dutch could be defeated.[2] Third, when Dutch rule was restored after the war, The Netherlands was by now ambivalent about continued colonial rule.

Indonesian nationalist forces were stronger; and Holland was so devastated by the war and its aftermath that it could no longer afford the costs of its old empire. In 1949, after three years of ongoing struggle with Indonesia, the government of The Netherlands granted independence to Indonesia.

There is a Wiarda family involvement in these events. For in the late 1940s, my globetrotting Aunt Julia Wiarda was stationed in Indonesia with the U.S. State Department. As a U.S. government employee, Aunt Julia supported the official American position that was in favor of Indonesian independence. But her fiancé at the time, a pilot for KLM airlines, favored continued Dutch control. Family lore has it, though we cannot be certain, that the romance foundered over this issue. And Aunt Julia, though extremely attractive, never married.

Not all groups or islands in the archipelago favored independence. One of the groups that did not was from the Moluccan Islands, part of the Spice Islands chain that had been strongly Dutch (and Christian) since the early seventeenth century. In April 1950, only a few months after Indonesian independence, they proclaimed the Republic of South Molucca, with its capital at Amboyna. South Molucca, especially, was mainly Protestant Christian; it had a long history of collaboration with Dutch rule; its soldiers had formed an indispensable part of the colonial military; and it was one of the few parts of Indonesia where pro-Dutch sentiment was strong. In addition, the Christian Moluccans feared being swallowed up in the larger Muslim population of Indonesia. But by November of that year, the South Moluccan Republic had been suppressed. In the following year, some 12,000 Ambonese soldiers and their families were allowed to emigrate to The Netherlands where they formed a government in exile. They were assigned to settle in the isolated, far-eastern parts of The Netherlands near the German border where they were promptly forgotten by the Dutch government and people. Only years later, when they spectacularly hijacked a Dutch train, did the plight of the Moluccans surface again.

Indonesia's more recent history is familiar to us. The new republic was organized by independence leader Sukarno, a charismatic, populist, and nationalist leader who called his system of rule "Guided Democracy." Indonesia was an exceedingly poor country; it had received no training in self-government from the Dutch; the military continued to dabble in politics;

and various parts of the archipelago preferred to go their own separate ways. Sukarno presided over a chaotic regime and was challenged by both Muslim and left-wing extremists; in 1966 he was replaced by the military and a right-wing authoritarian regime under General Suharto. Suharto ran a repressive regime that clamped down on the extremists as well as on democracy, but under his rule considerable economic growth took place.

Suharto also clamped down on Indonesia's regional and centrifugal forces, centralized control, and sent his army into formerly Portuguese-controlled East Timor to prevent it from achieving independence. Among Suharto's strategies for centralizing power and preventing parts of the archipelago from spiraling out of control was that he, like Stalin in Russia, moved vast populations around with considerable loss of life, so as to prevent local or regional ethnic consciousness from growing that might challenge national unity and authority. To that end, he moved large numbers of Muslims from other islands into the Moluccas and other Christian territories, thus diminishing the Christian presence and preventing them from going in independent directions. This policy is also at the root of the conflicts in Indonesia between Christians and Muslims that persist to this day.

After thirty-two years in power, Suharto was ousted in 1998. At that point, Indonesia began a more democratic course. This is around the time I came to the country.

The Dutch Legacy

Dutch rule in Indonesia at the time of independence was bitterly hated and resented. The Dutch had ruled Indonesia for three-and-a-half centuries; they had practiced slavery and debt peonage; they had treated the Indonesians with disdain. Nor had they educated the Indonesians or, unlike the British in India and the Caribbean, prepared them for independence. True, the Dutch brought economic development and "civilization" to Indonesia, but their attitude, like that of all colonial powers, was extremely patronizing and condescending. It is hard to discern anything particularly Christian or especially Calvinistic about Dutch colonialism in Indonesia; even Dutch missionary activity among the islanders was extremely limited. Christianizing the population was always secondary to profit-making. Small wonder, then, that not only were the Dutch despised at the time of independence but that those hatreds and resentments persist to the present.

The result of this hatred is that today, beyond a few hundred persons (in a population of 220 million), there is no "white tribe" of Dutchmen, nor a Dutch "fragment" in the sense of a cultural-religious enclave as the term is being used in this book, in Indonesia. They have all been driven out or have gone home to The Netherlands—or perhaps to South Africa, Australia, Canada, or the United States. Immediately after independence, there were several thousand Dutch who stayed on hoping they could reach an accommodation with the new rulers of Indonesia and make a go of it, but now that number has dwindled to a few hundred—maybe fewer.

Indonesia is very much unlike South Africa in this regard. In South Africa the numbers of Dutch, rebaptized and reconstituted as Afrikaners, was in the millions, fully 10 percent of the population. Moreover, the Afrikaners considered themselves fully African; they had broken their ties with the European mother country. South Africa was their home; they were there to stay.

Indonesia was a very different situation. First, the numbers were so much smaller: mere thousands even at the height of colonial rule compared with the millions of Hollanders in South Africa. Second, the Dutch in Indonesia never broke with the homeland as their South African cousins had. On the contrary, they continued to look back to Europe as their home; they sent their children there for education; their culture and civilization remained entirely European; Indonesia for them (except for a handful of planter families) was never a permanent abode. Instead, it was a colonial outpost to which one went only temporarily; even if one settled in for a number of generations, "home" was always back in The Netherlands.

Indonesia is, therefore, much more like Suriname than it is like South Africa. Both were plantation societies set down in the tropics within a few degrees of the equator. Both countenanced slave labor. In both the Dutch presence was always superficial and its contacts with the local society were largely limited to the upper levels. In neither place did Dutch culture, religion, and ways of doing things penetrate deeply throughout the entire society. Nor did they establish universities for their own people (like Pretoria or Stellenbosch in South Africa) or other institutions of civil society that would signify they were there in substantial numbers and that they intended to stay permanently. Instead, the Dutch exercised colonial overlordship and domination, but they seldom mixed with the native peoples. Plus, the number of Europeans in both these colonies was always infinitesimally small, too small to have more than a surface impact on local cultures. The plantation "model" in Suriname and Indonesia was very different from either the commercial model of New York and Curaçao, or the permanent settlement model of South Africa.

The result is that evidence of the legacy of the Dutch presence in Indonesia, fifty-five years after independence, is slim—and it is fading fast. Almost no one in Indonesia speaks Dutch anymore, and those who do speak it are of an older and aristocratic generation whose numbers and importance are dying out. KLM Airlines still flies into Jakarta but that is because it brings hordes of paying European tourists to South and Southeast Asia, not because of close ties between colony and former mother country. There are many Dutch words now in the Indonesian language but, as in Japan, almost no Indonesians know what they are or that they are Dutch.

Nor is there a special relationship between The Netherlands and Indonesia as there is still between the former mother country and Suriname. The Dutch feel a certain sense of guilt over their former practices of slavery, colonialism, racism, and imperialism; and they have an active embassy and a foreign aid program in Indonesia, but neither of these is large-scale. And, except for the Moluccans, there are not large numbers of Indonesians in The Netherlands (although some of the best Dutch restaurants are Indonesian) nor a large-scale flow of people, commerce, tourists, and diplomatic relations between the two. The Dutch are curious about all their former colonies and may go there briefly on vacation, but Indonesia is not a place high in their consciousness; and they certainly do not want significant numbers of Indonesians migrating to Holland.

Nor are there many physical reminders of the former Dutch presence in Indonesia. Touring around the countryside one still sees examples of Dutch colonial plantation houses, but these are few and far between. In Jakarta in the old part of the city (called Batavia after the original Dutch republic) there are still examples of Dutch architecture, but many of these buildings are badly in need of repair and restoration; some appear to have succumbed to mildew and wood rot in the steamy tropical climate. One has the sense that, in terms of the Dutch language, architecture, culture, and influence, after one more generation in Indonesia it will be completely gone.

When I first landed in Indonesia in the fall of 2001 (shortly after the 9/11 terrorist attack on the Pentagon and the World Trade Center) and as the United States was retaliating by attacking the Islamic Taliban in Afghanistan, it was a very dangerous time to be there. Anti-American demonstrations were taking place daily before the U.S. embassy; Christian churches were being systematically bombed or burned and their members harassed; Westerners were being accosted and beaten up on the streets; and in the big, international hotels roving gangs of thugs were demanding to see the guest registration cards and then going to the rooms of Americans to harass and beat them. It was a very scary environment; I didn't know whether it was more dangerous to try to pass as an American or a Dutchman.[3]

I immediately went off to explore the city. My first stop, down the main thoroughfare Jl. M. H.Thamrin, was Independence Park and the U.S. embassy located there. Quite a number of the buildings here, even in this down-town area of office buildings and tall skyscrapers, go back to the colonial era. They were one-story, with tiled roofs, and "tropical-colonial" in appearance, like the colonial outposts we had visited in India and Latin America.

The U.S. embassy was an armed camp: barbed wire, Jersey barriers, and at least four levels of armed security. Political counselor Brian Nichols had arranged some of my interviews; he also briefed me on the current political and religious situation. He told me that the great majority of people in the Moluccas (the Spice Islands) were Protestant Christians, going back to the early Dutch colonial period. To counterbalance this majority and ensure that the Moluccas stay within the Indonesian state, long-time dictator Suharto had transplanted thousands of Muslims to the Moluccas. It was the Muslims who had triggered the earlier and ongoing attacks on the Christian commu-nities, leading the Christians, since neither the government nor the army was protecting them, eventually to form their own protective militias. Churches were burned and firebombed; Christian pastors were kidnapped and killed; the Muslims laid siege to the Christian communities. Eventually the Christians retaliated, leading to a situation of near-civil war. What was once *the* center of Dutch Protestant influence in Indonesia had become a "very dangerous" place from the Embassy's point of view; it was seen as "un-stable, uncertain, and susceptible to a sudden eruption of violence."

Additional insights into the fading Dutch presence and influence in In-donesia were provided by my next-day host at the Center for Strategic and In-ternational Studies (CSIS—named after the Washington version), Clara Jae-wono. Clara, who was my age and had been educated at the University of California/Berkeley, told me that, as a little girl growing up in the 1940s (just before independence), she had received a thoroughly Dutch upbringing. She spoke fluent Dutch but told me her generation was the last to speak it. She had been educated in a Dutch school but told me her teachers were Dutch Catholic nuns, not Protestants or Calvinists. Even in the 1950s, after inde-pendence, she said that the ability to speak Dutch conveyed social status and that education in Dutch names, etiquette, and ways of doing things was pres-tigious and a sign of upper classness. But "no more," she said, "all that is gone."

The next day I went off to visit the National Museum, or what in In-donesia is called the Elephant Museum, on Independence Park. It is housed in what was once a grand, sprawling, Dutch "terrace house." It has wonder-ful displays of ancient Indonesian history (Hindu, Buddhist, etc.) but senti-ment against the Dutch is still so strongly negative that its sections on the Dutch colonial period are weak, incomplete, and portrayed in entirely nega-tive terms. My guide and interpreter told me as we chatted that Protestants

in the Moluccas and elsewhere in the archipelago were being forced to con-
sent to Islam (including circumcision) or else face death.

In the afternoon I took a grand tour of the district known as Kota or Old
Batavia. This was, for centuries, *the* center of the Dutch community in Indonesia; indeed, it was once the administrative center of that great Dutch empire that stretched all the way across the Indian Ocean and beyond, from
South Africa to Dejima Island in Japan. Much of the district is run down, but
there are some wonderful old Dutch colonial houses here, including that of the
last of the Dutch governors-general. There is a Dutch Museum with a great display of Dutch-made furniture and ceramics (including Delft tiles), and some
wonderful panels devoted to the once all-important spice trade. Nearby is the
Dutch-built Kota train station, the port area of Sunda Kelapa that grew to become the most important harbor in the entire Dutch empire, and the historic
cobblestone square of Fatahillah, surrounded by museums, historical monu-
ments, and Dutch-style architecture. Looking at these many run-down buildings, it is hard to believe that Batavia was once a walled city, virtually impregnable, and maybe the most important in the entire Dutch empire.

The high point was a visit, drink, and snack at the famed Batavia Café.
This was once a famous place, languorous and dark, a hangout for the Dutch
governmental elite as well as for foreign dignitaries. It is one of those places,
like Raffles in Singapore or the Manilla Hotel, where shady businessmen,
slinky women in dresses cut to the hip, and spies from all over the world
gathered in earlier, colonial times to drink, eat, and socialize—to see and to
be seen. To me, the Batavia Café seemed to be straight out of a Graham
Greene novel, a throwback to an earlier time when everything was hot
(slowly turning ceiling fans and no air conditioning), tropical, and not a bit
seedy. Here is where the likes of Ernest Hemingway, Marlene Dietrich, Mar-
lon Brando, Humphrey Bogart, Fred Astaire, and Agatha Christie hung out;
even Queen Juliana of The Netherlands ate here once. When I was there,
they were playing Glenn Miller music on the stereo; the place looks like the
bar in *Casablanca*. Somehow I felt right at home here; maybe I should have
been born in an earlier time. Already at 10:30 in the morning the few ex-pats
there were into heavy drinking.

As I exit the Batavia Café there is a roaring sound as upwards of 150 to
200 motor scooters (scooters, not Harleys) pull into the plaza in front of the
restaurant. It turns out this is the gathering place every morning for the
young Muslim attack forces where they decide who or what targets to zero in
on that day. They all have helmets and sun visors on to hide their appearance, and bandanas they can pull up to screen out a potential teargas attack.
And there I am right in the middle of the gathering, in fact surrounded and

trapped by the circle of motor scooters. It's a scary moment, especially if you know the viciousness of some of their earlier attacks on foreigners and Christians. But I've been in this kind of hostile environment before, mostly in Latin America but occasionally in the United States as well, during the 1980s when I was called on to go out to university campuses and abroad to explain President Reagan's Central America policy.

So we begin, these young toughs and I, a conversation. I quickly find out that, as expected, most of them are university students; quite a few speak English. I ask them about their programs and ideology and get an earful in return, meanwhile letting on that I'm a professor of political science and international relations in Indonesia to carry out a research project on civil society—actually true; but I don't mention the Dutch connection.

Well, that certainly gets their attention, and we have a long and fascinating discussion; it is out of this conversation that some of my own conclusions about civil society in Indonesia emerge. For I realize that the people I'm talking to, mostly Muslim radicals, make up, or at least are a good part of, civil society in Indonesia; further, that when the international civil society and human rights groups advocate aid to civil society in Indonesia, they are often aiding the very groups, such as in Aceh and other provinces, whose separatist agendas would tear Indonesia apart and destroy it as a nation. This the government cannot permit which is why it often takes repressive action against these groups. As long as we're talking political science and international affairs, my guerrilla/terrorist interlocutors seem to forget that I'm American (and Dutch!); we have a spirited discussion (including about how to come as an exchange student to the United States!), and at the end I pass between the motor scooters and go on my way.

I spend the next few days in Jakarta contacting and meeting with Dutch Reformed (Reformed Evangelical) pastors and church members. What a fascinating set of encounters that turns out to be. Among the things I learn in these meetings:

- There are twenty-seven churches with about three thousand members in this denomination; there are several other Reformed or Dutch-descended churches and congregations, but they are struggling for members and their very existence.
- The Evangelical Christian Church and the allied Church of Christ have several of their young people studying in seminary at Calvin College in Grand Rapids, Michigan—my home town.
- While many Protestant and Christian churches had been attacked or bombed in the past, the situation in 2001 was "quite safe." As one pastor

told me, we are "lying low." The Protestant churches in Java (the Moluccas was another story) were staying out of the headlines, seeking not to provoke the Muslims, and emphasizing they were not the enemies of anyone.

- Christianity in Indonesia is not well accepted, either by the Muslim majority or by Indonesian nationalists. It is identified with all the wrong countries and issues: with the Dutch, with colonialism and imperialism, with America and anti-Muslimism, with separatism (in the Moluccas), and with the deeply resented Chinese minority.

- The Dutch had actually made few efforts to Christianize Indonesia. The Moluccas is the main exception, and in some areas of Java and Sumatra. But for the most part, the Dutch did not seek to convert the local populations.

- The situation in the Moluccas remained, according to my interviews, "very dangerous." This was *the* center of Dutch—and Protestant—influence. As one of my interviewees put it, conditions were "quite volatile and could explode again at any time."

- Quite a number—perhaps by now the majority—of the Reformed churches in Indonesia were those of the overseas Chinese. Many of the Chinese Christians had been converted to Christianity in China, before they emigrated to Indonesia. They are resented in Indonesia not just on religious grounds but also on ethnic and economic (the Chinese tend to be wealthier) grounds.

- It was especially striking that, in my search for a continuing Dutch Calvinist tradition in Indonesia, I found none. *All* my interviewees denied that they were a part of a "Dutch" or "colonial" church. To a person, they denied having any connection with either the Dutch government or the Dutch Reformed (state) Church. I am not sure if there is *any* Dutch Reformed Church still functioning in Indonesia. The situation is, again, like that of Suriname, where the Dutch Reformed Church has, in the aftermath of colonialism and the discrediting of all institutions associated with the colonist power, similarly all but been completely snuffed out.

- In contrast, and especially interesting given both my background and our "fragments" thesis, the Reformed churches of Indonesia identified far more and had considerable institutional connections with, the Christian Reformed Church of the Dutch community in Western Michigan than with the "mother church" in The Netherlands. So this is another new twist on the fragments thesis: that over time the relations between the several colonial or former colonial "fragments"

(Michigan, Indonesia) may be closer than those between the fragments and the original mother country (The Netherlands).

Conclusion

Dutch influence and the Dutch legacy in Indonesia are fading fast. With the passing of the present generation of people in their sixties and seventies (a small minority in youthful Indonesia), that legacy and history of language, religion, culture, and etiquette will be completely gone. It will be only a historical memory and a few displays in the historical museum. It will become like Dejima Island, a history and series of episodes, irrelevant and long forgotten by most of the population, and of interest only to a scattering of the historically minded.

In many ways this is a shame, at least from my point of view; but then I have a special—and very narrow and perhaps idiosyncratic—interest in the subject. However, given the history of Dutch colonialism, racism, and imperialism in Indonesia, to say nothing of the facts the Dutch failed to educate the Indonesians or prepare them for independence, this anti-Dutch feeling was probably inevitable. But now a new generation is rising in Indonesia that is less hostile toward Holland, or perhaps has just forgotten, was never educated, or doesn't care. At the least, therefore, the Dutch government, in addition to the development projects it is already financing, ought to be putting some money into historical markers, museums, directional street signs, postcards, or good coffee table books tracing the history, cultural and economic contributions, and the lasting impact of The Netherlands in Indonesia.

The theory of fragments breaks down in Indonesia, as it did in Suriname. There is no Dutch "fragment" left in Indonesia to speak of, or only a very small one, and what there is of a Dutch fragment is fading fast. It took about two generations for that to happen; in Suriname we are still only one generation away from Dutch colonialism, so after one more generation Suriname's relations with The Netherlands and its Dutch background and culture will likely be at about the same place as Indonesia is now. And that is, with almost no cultural, religious, or other kind of special influence at all.

Ironically, in both countries, it is the Americans who are replacing the Dutch as the dominant outside influence, including the language, culture, and through the Christian Reformed Church in Western Michigan, the religious connection. Could it be that one of the former "fragments," the United States, has now replaced the original mother country as the dominant outside influence even in those countries that were once Dutch colonies, that once constituted other colonial "fragments" of The Netherlands? If so, we will have to take account of this new American presence and even hegemony as we further consider the fragments theory.

Notes

1. Some Indonesian tribes believed that, if you ate people, you then took on their characteristics. Hence, if you saw someone who was taller and bigger than you, whiter than you, and blonde and with blue eyes—like may Dutch people—and if you wanted those characteristics, then eating that person would make you look like him or her.

2. Irony of ironies. When I visited the atomic bomb museum in Nagasaki, a spinoff from my research on the Portuguese and Dutch in Japan, I discovered that there had been a wartime Japanese prison in Nagasaki that was also obliterated in the blast. Among those killed were Dutch—along with some British, American, and Canadian—prisoners taken in the Japanese conquest of Indonesia.

3. Upon registering, I had told the hotel clerk in the Hyatt that I was not going to show him my passport, give him my real name, or tell him my nationality. He responded that the hotel was already way ahead of me on these matters, that not only would they screen my calls and visitors but on the hotel registration I would be known as "Mr. Incognito." He was so proud of this ploy that I didn't have the heart to tell him I didn't think that designation gave me very much protection.

CHAPTER TEN

South Africa and
the Apartheid Regime

South Africa is one of the main tests of our "fragments" thesis. For not only did the Dutch colony in South Africa have a long history, but it was, in contrast to Suriname or Indonesia, also a strong history in terms of numbers of settlers, their acclimation in the South African setting, and the strength of the culture, religious beliefs, and institutions they brought with them.

In South Africa the Afrikaners, as they came to be called, numbered not in the thousands as in the other two colonies mentioned, but in the millions. Moreover, over time they had broken with the mother country, The Netherlands, whom they felt had abandoned them in their time of need, in order to remain faithful to themselves, their society, and their Reformed religious convictions. They had their own schools, universities, social clubs, football teams, political parties, labor unions, and civil society—even their own language, Afrikaans. In short, the Dutch in South Africa were not just temporary colonial sojourners in a strange land; they were here to stay. They thought of themselves as African: the "white tribe" of Africa, upholding and defending white, Christian, Western civilization in the midst of "deepest, darkest" Africa.

Getting There

On September 8, 2001, three days before the Arab terrorist attack on the Pentagon and the World Trade Center, I was preparing to leave for Brazil. This was the second leg of an ambitious, year-long sabbatical leave that had

taken me to Europe for the first six months of the year and a research project on EU/NATO enlargement, and would take me around Asia (Japan,
Hong Kong, Macao, India, Indonesia, East Timor) later that fall. My project
in Brazil and South Africa dealt with the comparative development of civil
society, but an at least equally strong reason for going there was to explore
the roots and culture of the Dutch community and what had happened to it
after the end of apartheid and Afrikaner rule in 1994, the year the saintly
Nelson Mandela was elected president.

I was actually sitting in the offices of an old friend and colleague from
Washington days, Bainbridge Cowell, in the U.S. consulate (the former U.S.
embassy) on Woodrow Wilson Avenue in downtown Rio de Janeiro, when
the planes struck the World Trade Center. I have already related this story in
detail in another book;[1] here let me simply say there was great confusion and
disorder at first in the U.S. consulate, and we soon were ordered by armed
Marine guards to clear out of the building. I took refuge at first with some of
my Brazilian in-laws until we could clarify a bit what was happening; later in
the afternoon I went back to my hotel, the Intercontinental, on São Con-
rado Beach.

I spent the next few days in consultation with embassy officials in Rio and
South Africa, the airlines, and my wife back in Washington, D.C., on
whether to continue with the South Africa part of my trip. In the meantime,
I was busily carrying out the Brazil part of my field research. And in the end,
the issue was largely decided for me. Since in the wake of the 9/11 attack all
U.S. airports had been closed and all U.S. airline flights grounded, I could
not, in any case, get back to the United States anytime soon. And because
both Brazil and South Africa were unaffected by the attack and functioning
normally, I decided to continue on with my scheduled trip, the next leg of
which called for me to fly from São Paulo to Johannesburg. Plus, I had never
flown over the South Atlantic before! So that is what I did, landing in mile-
high (like Denver on Mexico City) Johannesburg early in the morning on
Friday, September 14.

Background and History

As usual in these African and then Asian waters, it was the Portuguese who,
among European powers, got there first. The expansion of Islam throughout
the circum-Mediterranean in the Middle Ages had disrupted European trade
routes to Asia either overland or down through the Red Sea; hence, both
Spain and Portugal sought to find an alternative sea route. Bartholomew Dias
of Portugal was the first European to round the Cape of Good Hope at the

southernmost tip of Africa in 1487; a decade later another Portuguese, Vasco da Gama, not only rounded the Cape but then sailed all the way to India, thus opening up all of Asia to Portuguese, later Spanish and Dutch, conquest and trade.

But the Portuguese did not see much value in the Cape area; they were more interested in West Africa, East Africa, the Asian spice trade, and Brazil. Over the course of the next century, as the Dutch came to supplant the Portuguese in Asia, Dutch crews began stopping off at the Cape to restore their food and water supplies. In 1647 a Dutch crew was shipwrecked below Table Mountain and stayed at the Cape for a year; in 1652 the Dutch East India Company (VOC) established a permanent colony there.

The intention of the Company was not to colonize or settle southern Africa but only to secure a base for its ships traveling back and forth to Asia and to provision them with fresh fruits, vegetables, and water. But soon the colony grew and some of its members spilled out of the Cape area and turned to farming. Most of the residents were Dutch, but there was also, as in all port cities, a scattering of multiple nationalities: Germans, Frenchmen, and British. The language spoken was a kind of sailors' or port-city version of Dutch mixed with other vernaculars, which later became known as Afrikaans.[2] In religion, the Cape was Calvinist Reformed, the state religion of The Netherlands.

At the time the Dutch arrived, there were few indigenous Africans living in the Cape area. Because of that fact the colony was able to avoid during its first hundred years or so any large-scale conflict or war with the native blacks. The lack of an indigenous population also enabled the whites to claim, centuries later, that under international law, since this was unpopulated, virgin territory, they had as much claim to the land here as did the native blacks.

Over time the original Cape colony expanded northward and eastward into what are today called the Northern, Western, and Eastern Capes. The towns of Paarl, Stellenbosch, and Swellendam were among the first to be established in the lush, green, rural areas east from Cape Town. As the colony expanded, it inevitably came in conflict, similarly to the United States as it expanded westward, with larger numbers of native peoples. These were subjugated; although South Africa never developed as a plantation society, slavery and various forms of debt peonage were practiced. After the Saint Bartholomew's Day massacre in France, the original Dutch colony was supplemented in the 1680s by approximately 150 Huguenots, similarly Calvinist and fleeing persecution in France. The Huguenots constituted about 15 percent of the total white population in the Cape; their presence explains why in the present Afrikaner population one encounters names like du Toit, du Plessis, or Celliers. By this time also, the nature of the colony was changing from basically an urban replenishment post centered at Cape Town to a rural farm colony spreading farther and farther into the countryside.

This movement from city to countryside is one of the great formative factors in the history of South Africa. During the course of the eighteenth century, more and more Cape families moved out of the city and into the rural areas, steadily pushing the frontier farther north and east. There *trekboers* (wandering or "trekking" farmers) were quite independent of East India Company or government control, extremely self-sufficient, and entirely isolated in their rural settlements. They were often nomadic cattle herders rather than farmers, pursuing a pastoral lifestyle. Their only possessions might be their cattle, a wagon, guns, and the Bible. When they settled down, they were often several days' hike from their nearest European neighbor.

Like the American frontiersmen, the trekboer pioneers accomplished heroic feats of colonization and settlement. But unlike the Americans in their westerly march, the South Africans in these rural areas were outnumbered by the natives by ratios of a hundred, thousand, or ten thousand to one. The trekboers were courageous individualists, but they were completely isolated from all the main currents of the eighteenth century: the Enlightenment, the scientific revolution, rationalism, the industrial revolution, the movement toward representative government, the American and French revolutions with their ideas of liberty, fraternity, equality, and the separation of church and state or of religion and science. For the isolated trekboers, the only source of knowledge remained the Bible; whatever system of government existed out there on the frontier was theocratic, joining Biblical injunctions with governing precepts.

And this Biblically-informed, Calvinistic, theocratic society, growing up in the South African wilderness (like Israel's ten tribes wandering in the wilderness of the Sinai Desert, which is how the Afrikaners see themselves), alone and self-sufficient, strong, unintimidated, and thumbing its nose at authority and the rest of the world became the South African—specifically, Afrikaner—ideal, a romantic and often idealized vision of themselves. Although often semiliterate, speaking this strange language that not even the Dutch in The Netherlands could comprehend, but possessing guns, skin color, and a religious faith that made them feel superior, the trekboers (later shortened to boers) lived almost like rural peasants; but in comparison with the local population, they thought of themselves and were thought of as a landed gentry, a special people, God's chosen.

It is the isolation of this Afrikaner society, growing up isolated from the main currents of the modern world, yet shaped indelibly by its seventeenth-century Calvinism, and then locked into that position for centuries to come, that accounts for the fact that South Africa is the prime example of our "fragments" thesis. That is, of a fragment of Europe, established in the seventeenth century, isolated, that seemed to remain permanently on hold with its seventeenth-century characteristics.

Indeed, one can understand much of South African history in these terms. Here we have a Calvinistic society, God's chosen people, "The Elect of God," cast out into a very primitive, God-forsaken area where they are surrounded and far outnumbered by hostile tribes as well as ferocious wild animals. And if one takes the Bible literally, as the Afrikaners did, one could easily reach the conclusions in the seventeenth century that the black South Africans were closer to the animals than they were to men, lacked souls, and, therefore, could be enslaved or treated inhumanely. Or perhaps they were the "inferior" children of Ham—dark and uncivilized. The idea of a "chosen people" can thus be used to justify racial superiority, while Calvin's doctrine of predestination, which argues that the salvation or damnation of an individual is preordained of God, can similarly be employed to divide the chosen few (Afrikaners) from the primitive heathen (blacks). It is not surprising to hear that in the seventeenth century people thought in these terms; what *is* surprising in the South African case is that this ideology and belief system lasted so long and remained locked in place—right to the end of the apartheid era and even beyond.

Toward the end of the eighteenth century, the Dutch empire, as we have seen in other chapters, was in decline and susceptible to the ambitious designs of other powers. When The Netherlands was invaded and occupied by France in 1795, the British invaded and occupied the Cape colony to prevent France from seizing that strategic territory, too. The British occupation had little impact initially, and in 1803 they returned South Africa to the Batavian (Dutch) Republic. However, in 1806, in reaction to Napoleon's renewed conquests, the British reoccupied the Cape, defeated the Dutch garrison there, and forced the Dutch government to cede the colony on a permanent basis to Great Britain. This would prove to be a key turning point in South African history.

In the Cape area the British found a colony of about 20,000 whites (mostly Dutch), 25,000 slaves, and about 1,000 free blacks. Political power was limited to a small white elite in the Cape, with racial prejudice and racial differentiation deeply ingrained. It was a society that, for almost two hundred years, had been extremely isolated. In the interior, the conditions were primitive and quasi-feudal.

With the defeat of Napoleon at Waterloo, Great Britain was now the world's greatest power; it had a worldwide empire on which the sun reportedly never set; and the nineteenth century would be Britain's century just as the twentieth would be the American century. But in South Africa, it ran up against a stout, resistant, hard-headed Dutch or Afrikaner culture and society which it was never able to fully conquer or subdue.

The British takeover divided South Africa into two very different cultures and societies—three or more, if one includes the various black groups. The British settlements, including Cape Town, Port Elizabeth, Grahamstown, and much of the Eastern Cape, were English-speaking, urban, better educated, and dominant in politics, trade, finance, banking, mining, and manufacturing. The Dutch enclaves in the Western and Northern Capes spoke Afrikaans, were largely uneducated, and were farmers or pastoralists. The British colonists maintained close ties with their mother country, whereas the Afrikaners felt themselves cut off, even betrayed, and abandoned by their mother country. They lived in not-so-splendid isolation.

As the British consolidated their hold over the society, monopolized politics and government, and increasingly imposed their culture, language, law, and ways of doing things on the colony, the former Dutch, now Afrikaner, population felt increasingly alienated and even persecuted. Their response during the early and mid-nineteenth century was to flee northward into even more inhospitable territory north of the Orange River that up to now had been the far northern, outer limits of the colony. They wanted to practice their Calvinist religion as they pleased and to live according to their own laws and customs, not those of the British.

This trek, also on foot, horseback, and by wagon train, repeated, but on a larger scale and for longer distances and deeper into the wilderness of "darkest" Africa, the earlier treks of the eighteenth century; it was called The Great Trek. It reinforced in the Afrikaner the already well-established mentality of a persecuted minority, loved only by God but hated by the rest of the world, cut off even more from his roots in The Netherlands and the urban centers, and having to make it entirely on his own. To be honest, this sounds little different from many American pioneer families in the nineteenth century who went west, pushed back the frontier, conquered the Indians, and settled in areas where they could practice their religion and their individuality as they pleased without outside interference.

It has been said by some that the main reason for the Great Trek was so the Afrikaners, like the American Southerner during the same period, could continue to practice slavery, which had been abolished by the British government in 1833. I do not buy that argument. True, many Afrikaners had slaves but mainly as household servants, not as slave laborers as in the U.S. South; recall, this was not a slave-plantation society but a pastoral one in which you used African labor mainly to tend the herds—not a hard occupation—instead of as laborers in the cotton fields. Most Afrikaners, in fact, grudgingly accepted the abolition of slavery, but the British had gone farther, proclaiming the equality of the races and giving servants the right to sue their masters. This the Afrikaner did strenuously object to: he thought it obvious (remember, this is the mid-nineteenth century) the races were not equal; if accused, he would be forced to attend a hearing in a court several days' travel time away; and it would be in a language—English—he did not understand and could not function in. If the law could not distinguish between the races, he reasoned, how could it deal with reality, to say nothing of maintaining cultural, social, and racial purity?

These radically contrasting views of culture and society were bound to create conflict eventually. Initially, the Boers responded by going even farther into the wilderness, extending their treks, and establishing several independent republics, the most famous of which were the Orange Free State (after the Dutch House of Orange) and the Transvaal, which extended all the way up to the northern borders of the colony. Here, in these lonely and distant outposts, the Boers reestablished their settlements and sought to continue their hallowed, isolated, and Calvinist lifestyle. They withdrew even more into themselves and cut themselves off even farther from worldly influences.

One cannot but feel sympathy, regardless of one's sentiments about their later apartheid policies, toward these lonely and persecuted peoples. One also wonders how much different their primitive lifestyles were compared to those of my similarly isolated and impoverished forbears in Western Michigan, also at mid-nineteenth century. Two immediate answers come to mind: no comparable wild animals in Western Michigan to add to your fright, and no hostile indigenous population outnumbering you by ten thousand or a hundred thousand to one.

As they trekked north and began to establish rudimentary forms of society and governance, the Afrikaners increasingly ran into hostile opposition from the indigenous population, the Zulus. Later apologists for apartheid would claim, as they had in the Cape area, that these lands were empty and, therefore, the Afrikaners had as much right to claim the land as native blacks. But that was untrue, there *were* indigenous tribes in these areas, and even those lands that seemed empty were that way only on a temporary basis because of indigenous hunting and pastoral patterns. In fact, there were numerous bloody battles between the Afrikaners and the Zulus; many hundreds of thousands of Zulus were slain; and gradually they were confined to smaller and smaller areas. This does not sound to me much different from the killing of Indians in the U.S. west so that whites could seize their lands and confine the natives to inhospitable reservations. In South Africa these were eventually called "homelands"; in America, we termed them "reservations," but they amount to the same thing.

But the British, though sometimes ambivalent in their policies, would not allow the Boer republics to live in peace, let alone as independent entities. British law was increasingly imposed on the Afrikaners as was British civil administration and eventually British armies. The key turning points were the discovery of the richest diamond mines in the world at Kimberley in the Orange Free State in 1869, and then the discovery in the 1880s of the richest gold mines in the world near (and underneath!) the area of present-day Johannesburg. These discoveries gave the British added incentive to extend their rule northward and to quash the Afrikaner republics.

There were not one but several Boer wars in the last decades of the nineteenth century and the first decade of the twentieth. After first the Orange Free State and then the Transvaal were annexed and abolished as separate entities by the British colony, the Afrikaners rebelled in the late 1870s. Adept at guerrilla tactics, knowing the land, and fighting on their home territory, the Afrikaners under Paul Kruger (after whom Kruger National Wildlife Park was named) defeated the British and reestablished the South Africa Republic. But the Afrikaner republics had small populations, no industry, no wealth, and no infrastructure; and they could not hold out forever against the mighty British empire.

The British had to mobilize nearly half a million troops to defeat the 80,000 Boer fighters and by 1900 they had succeeded, even though desperate Boer commando raids continued for several more years. Many of the Boer fighters and their families were interned in British concentration camps where the conditions were so bad they earned international condemnation. A 1902 peace treaty abolished the Boer republics and reincorporated them into the British South African colony. Meanwhile, the fact that the Dutch government failed at any level to support their cause—and even positively disowned them—bred in the Afrikaner an even deeper resentment toward the mother country and the desire to go it alone than had existed before.

Relations between British and Afrikaners remained tense even after the war, while the interests of the 90 percent of the population that was black were ignored. The cultural and social gaps between the British and the Afrikaners remained huge; when after the war many Boer families were "resettled" in urban centers, the culture shock was immense. There they found all political institutions dominated by the British, a language (English) they did not comprehend; and they were under the thumb of the British. In addition, the proud and independent Afrikaners were forced to compete with blacks for menial service jobs. In response to the bad treatment, the Afrikaners boiled with resentment, came to see the Afrikaner language as a kind of nationalistic, "native" folk language that they could speak without fear of others understanding, and began to build up a network of (Dutch Reformed) churches, brotherhoods, and civil society that were uniquely—and separately—Afrikaner.

The Union of South Africa, which combined the former Boer republics into the British colony, was formed in 1910. English, Dutch, and, later, Afrikaans were made the official languages, but the tension between the English and the Afrikaner communities continued. The English community was mainly urban, better educated, Anglican, middle class, more cosmopolitan, business-oriented, and looked condescendingly down on the Afrikaners; while the Afrikaners remained mainly rural, less well educated, less sophisticated, Calvinistic, and, since they had become estranged even from their home country, The Netherlands, still largely cut off from ties with the outside world.

But over the course of the next several decades, that began to change. While still nursing their grudges, many Afrikaners moved to the cities, became better educated, joined the middle class, became bilingual, abandoned their strict earlier Calvinism, and eventually a few of them came to identify with the anti-apartheid struggle—although not nearly as many as now, post facto, claim that they did! At the same time, quite a number in the English community came to the realization that, if they were not eventually to be overwhelmed by the black majority, they and the Afrikaners needed to make common cause.

In the first Union of South Africa election of 1924, the Boer-dominated South African National Party (SANP) won. Its leaders included Louis Botha (the first prime minister) and the former Boer General Jan Smuts; former General Barry Hertzog, even more sympathetic to Afrikaner interests, former the National Party (NP). Soon there was new legislation restricting blacks from strikes, from skilled jobs, and from military service. In subsequent elections, the black threat was set forth as the main issue. New racial theories gained prominence; the Afrikaner Brotherhood, a secret organization that also held racist views, was organized. The Dutch Reformed Churches provided religious justification for these practices and for the later apartheid; they argued that the separation of the races had a Biblical, God-given basis, and that it was the duty of all Afrikaners to help preserve the purity of the white race in South Africa which was now viewed as the "promised land." Because they were so anti-British, many Afrikaners were pro-German in World War I; in World War II sentiment was about equally divided between the Axis and Allied causes. Meanwhile, in response to the waves of anti-black legislation, the African National Congress (ANC) was organized in 1923.

Afrikaner nationalism, fueled by a siege mentality that saw a threat from both blacks from within and global pressures from without, had been on the rise for some time. Many Afrikaners were no longer content with mere parity with the British; they aimed at dominance. A key turning point was the 1948 election won by the National Party which subsequently dominated all South African governments until 1994.

Mixed marriages were illegalized; interracial sex was prohibited; all individuals were given a racial classification; and the Group Areas Act provided for the physical separation of the races. The notorious pass laws were now strengthened that sharply restricted black movement, even separating husbands, wives, and children who had to remain in rural areas. As in the U.S. South, there were separate bathrooms, separate beaches, separate buses, separate schools, separate drinking fountains, separate toilets, and separate park benches for black and white. The racial segregation that had, in fact, existed for centuries was now given a legal and an institutionalized basis.

The Dutch Reformed Church provided legitimacy to this system, even though there was rising dissent. For its support of apartheid, the South African Dutch Reformed Church was strongly criticized by its Dutch Reformed counterparts in The Netherlands and Western Michigan, condemned as sinful and un-Biblical, and eventually drummed out of the association of Reformed churches. Nevertheless, Apartheid now became the law of the land and, as in the American South, most Afrikaners accepted the doctrine of strict separation between the races.

However, the black African population was also changing: it had been urbanized; the economy was dependent on their labor; more and more blacks had been mobilized and organized; and education levels were increasing. The ANC expanded its membership; it used terrorist techniques as well as peaceful demonstrations; and it began to mobilize international opinion to the anti-apartheid struggle. We cannot here recount the entire history of the black protest movement that in any case is largely familiar to us. Suffice it to say that black protests grew; international sanctions were increasingly imposed on South Africa; and eventually the apartheid regime was forced to cede ground. Fearing that the only alternative was civil war, a bloodbath, and the financial ruination of the country, National Party leader and Prime Minister F. W. De Klerk negotiated with the ANC and Nelson Mandela to write a new constitution and hold general elections in 1994 in which blacks could vote for the first time. The result was as predicted: Mandela and the ANC won overwhelmingly; the apartheid system was dismantled; white rule ended and black rule began.

Into South Africa

After 1994, South Africa largely disappeared from the headlines. The sanctions were lifted; Nelson Mandela was installed as president; the foreign foundations and civil society groups that had supported the black power movement pulled out; and the assumption was widespread that black rule would now solve all of South Africa's problems. As a specialist in Third World development, I was skeptical of all these claims; in addition, since no one was paying any attention to it whatsoever, I had this curiosity about what had happened to the Dutch or Afrikaner community after its fall from power. I had no sympathy for the apartheid policy but I did think, because of my ethnic and religious background, I would understand the Afrikaner better than most. I was determined to see for myself.

The clientele at the airport in Johannesburg, after landing from Brazil, was about 90 percent white, even though that's about the exact opposite of what the percentage of the white population of the country is. I made a quick judgment—correct, as it turned out—that was probably about the ratio of wealth and the power structure in the country as well: 90 percent in white hands.

On the way in from the airport, my (black) taxi driver warned me about the rising crime rate in the country. He told me especially to stay out of the center of Johannesburg where, he said, they might not only rob you but kill you as well. He said that most crime in South Africa under apartheid was black-on-black crime, but now it was increasingly, under the ANC government, black-on-white, and the overall numbers were rising. He blamed it on the high unemployment of 65 percent, including both blacks and whites.

My hotel was the luxurious Hyatt in the white Rosemont suburb of Johannesburg. Immediately after checking in, I went for a long walk through the neighborhood. I was warned by hotel security not to go out on the streets even in this wealthy area, but it was mid-morning and I was sure I'd be safe. I'm a student of architecture and am always looking for innovative home designs, but what most impressed me on this stroll was the immense amount of security, even in this nice residential area. Every house had at least one and usually two big dogs; the homes were surrounded by walls and razor wire; and in every other block there was a security patrol with two officers, armed, engine running, ready to go. I learned quickly that security was the only thriving business in all South Africa and many Afrikaners had gone into that business. Whenever I left the building, hotel security insisted that I only go in one of their cars and with an armed escort riding "shotgun" along with the driver.

I immediately signed up for a guided bus tour, the best way to see a new city quickly when you don't have much time. It turned out I was the only tourist on the double-decker so I got the grand tour: Jan Smuts Avenue, the zoo, the luxurious Valley Road, Melville, Media Park, the Post Office Tower (tallest in Jo'burg, as it's called there), Oriental Palace. On into the center of the city: Gandhi Square, City Hall, the National Library, the Rand Club.

Every single white-owned business in the city center had closed up and moved to the suburbs; I quickly noticed that mine was the single, solitary white face in the entire downtown area. As we passed through the city center, the guide told me to get down on the floorboards and hide my face; he would tell me when it was safe to get up. I thought, "This is worse than Detroit"—where I had been born.

We pass the "medicine mart": two solid blocks of herbal medicines, ground up brains, ground up testicles of several kinds, all sorts of aphrodisiacs advertised as "the African Viagra." So at one level, mainly in the Anglo-Afrikaner neighborhoods, South Africa gives off the appearance of being a nice, middle-class European country, at others it is very traditional and primitive, closer to Haiti in its poverty and backwardness than to anything else I've ever seen in Brazil or Hispanic America.

The southern side of Johannesburg (all black) is a whole world (and several centuries) away from the white suburbs in the north. The guide points out there are no trees here since this entire area is built on the castoff slag from the mine operations; "Golden Hills" as it's called ironically. Past the Turfontain Race Course: when Dutch Calvinism was in power, this was the only legalized gambling in South Africa; now there are a variety of lotteries and hundreds, if not thousands, of casinos.

Our next stop was Soweto, the huge, black township, really a slum, on the southern side of Johannesburg. This is where all foreign tourists are brought to they can express shock at the miserable living conditions of South Africa's blacks. There are parts of Soweto that are pretty bad but also parts that are up-and-coming and even middle class. I have seen far worse slums than this in Latin America, and in other parts of Sub-Saharan Africa the condition of blacks is far worse than in South Africa. My "hosts," the bus driver and the tour guide, laughed heartily when I failed to express the shock ("shocked, shocked!") at these conditions that white visitors are supposed to express. More than that, the driver, who lived in Soweto, then invited me to his nice, clean, middle-class house where we had tea and I met his nice family.

Because I'm a social scientist, I of course asked about the Dutch Reformed Church. They (driver and guide) told me it was no longer a major force here. Power has shifted, they said, to the ANC which "runs everything." Not only was the Dutch Reformed Church discredited by its support of apartheid but, like everywhere else, South Africa is becoming secularized. Few young people go to church anymore. Rugby, cricket, soccer, and the beach are more important than church on Sundays. The Dutch Reformed Church has been marginalized.

That was confirmed to me two days later when, on a bright Sunday morning, I attended a Dutch Reformed Church service. My first indication that this was a not-very-flourishing denomination was that I could not find The Netherlands Reformed Church listed in the telephone book; the concierge at the hotel could not find one; and none of the taxi drivers knew where it was. We finally located one near the zoo, off Jan Smuts Avenue, in the same Westcliff section through which I had toured two days earlier.

People at the church were very warm and welcoming. But I immediately noticed there were few young people there—always a bad sign. I was told the young people are more attracted by the Pentecostal churches when they go to church at all. The service was quite traditional as compared with services I was used to in the United States: a long (too long) sermon, no special music, singing only from the Psalter Hymnal (once more, all those boring half notes), nothing to lighten the service. I meet the minister and several of the elders; the conversation is of Armageddon, the final battle between good and evil, the last days. Wow, this is heavy stuff—too heavy for me but it reflects the siege mentality of white Christians in South Africa.

One woman told me she had just watched on TV the memorial service in the National Cathedral for the victims of 9/11 and was pleased to see President Bush and all the former Presidents there and that the United States was still a "Christian nation." Well, I had been living in Washington for the last twenty years, was very cynical about Washington policy-making, and had seen precious little Christianity at work at high-policy levels, so I replied to the woman, "Yes—more-or-less." She laughed, gave me a ride back to the hotel in her big Jaguar; we had lunch together and parted as good friends. I had the feeling, after this conversation, that maybe not all the Dutch Reformed Afrikaners were quite so rigid or uptight as they are often portrayed.

While in Johannesburg, I had signed up for a safari to go up to the Pilanesberg National Park and Game Preserve. I thought it would be hokey and touristy, but when in South Africa you've got to go on safari, right? So off we went; it was wonderful, not touristy at all; and I saw a lot of wild animals (lions, giraffes, elephants, hippos, hyenas) in their natural habitat.[3] But for the purposes of this book, what was most interesting was what I learned from the tour guide, Solly Fourie. He was from an old Huguenot family; when he learned I was Dutch and we shared a Huguenot background, he was very forthcoming:

- Many Afrikaner families have converted their farms into game preserves. They cannot make it as farmers anymore and ANC-sponsored affirmative action is keeping them out of other jobs. The only other employment is in the security industry.
- The country is still deeply divided, geographically as well as in other ways: Afrikaners in the north, English in the south.
- Many Afrikaner young people are leaving the country because they see no future for themselves here. But others are staying because they love their beautiful country and their families and friends are here.
- During the Boer War the Afrikaner forces had to live off the land so the British retaliated by burning all the farms and destroying the cattle, to say nothing of killing the wives and children of the Afrikaners. To this day, rural Afrikaners hate the British with a passion.
- This is a sharp split between rural Afrikaners (ultra-conservative, more religious, still unreconciled to black rule) and urban, better-educated, more-liberal Afrikaners.
- Afrikaans is spoken by about 50 percent of the population. English is the language of business and the big cities, Afrikaans of the north and rural areas. Blacks refuse to learn Afrikaans because of its association with apartheid.
- Tensions, anger, bitterness here are high: black versus white, Afrikaners versus English, rival black groups against each other, Afrikaners (recall, there are stubborn, hard-headed, often quarrelsome folks) among themselves.

After church on that Sunday, I checked out of the Hyatt, arranged for a taxi, and drove up to Pretoria, forty miles to the north. As we drove along, strains of the catchy Boer War song, "We Are Marching to Pretoria," were going through my head. Pretoria is a smaller, nicer, much cleaner city than is Johannesburg.

Pretoria is the capital of South Africa. It is not a commercial center like Cape Town or a banking and mining center like Johannesburg; Pretoria is mainly embassies and government buildings like Washington, D.C., but on a much smaller scale. It has lower crime and violence than other cities in South Africa, although I was warned against taking walks or going out at night. Pretoria is also the center of Afrikaner influence in the country. It owes its existence to the three main Afrikaner dreams: finding a place far enough away that the British wouldn't come, where they could dominate the blacks, and where they could practice their religion and culture freely.

After checking into my hotel, the Sheraton, I go for a long walk around the city, unheedful of the warnings I'd received. It's a beautiful city. There's a Ver Meulen Street, a Kerk (Church) Street, a Brooklyn neighborhood—I feel right at home with these Dutch names; this could be Grand Rapids or New Amsterdam. The Voortrekker monument, a memorial to the nineteenth-century trekkers who settled this area, is across the city. The University of Pretoria, mainly Afrikaner, has a beautiful campus. I locate the American embassy on Pretorius Street where I have interviews tomorrow. There's a McDonald's in the center of town—civilization! Across from the hotel is a gorgeous park area, beautiful flowers (jacaranda), a hill full of gardens. At the top are the Union, or government, Buildings. On all sides are mountains covered with flowers; the city sits like Caracas, Venezuela, in a long, East-West valley between these mountain ranges. There's no pollution.

While I'm standing on a street corner trying to read my map, an elderly gentleman comes up from behind and asks if he can help. He turns out to be not only extraordinarily nice and pleasant but also a retired minister in the Dutch Reformed Church. What a find! He spends the rest of the afternoon with me, telling me about the history and culture of the area, at the end of which he invites me to be his guest at his church's evening service.

- He is Afrikaner but of Huguenot background—Deon Joubert.
- He's an urban Afrikaner and an educated man, with advanced theology degrees.
- In his church he preached against apartheid, but his congregation opposed him.
- He also reports that the Afrikaner-dominant Transvaal (the northern province, where Pretoria is located) is very conservative and believes the world is against them—which it is. Sometimes paranoids do have real enemies!
- He reports that even today (2001) there are Afrikaner congregations, especially in rural areas, that turn blacks away or ask them to sit in the back of the church. Hard to believe. Not much diversity here.
- He insists that not all Afrikaners supported the apartheid system and that Afrikaners were often unfairly blamed for its abuses.
- He's pessimistic about the future here, telling me that, if he were a young person, he would leave.

At night I go to his church, the Arcadia N.G. (Dutch Reformed) Gemeente of Pretoria. It's a beautiful church, striking architecture, modernistic. The service is in Afrikaans, but the music is Beethoven ("Ode to Joy") and the hymns are familiar. People are very warm and welcoming; I'm asked to speak and tell them I bring "fraternal greetings" from the Dutch Christian Reformed Church of Western Michigan (where I've not actually been an active member for forty years).

The congregation is mostly elderly and mostly women. They all identify with America in its hour of need; having themselves experienced decades-long violence and terrorism, they side with the United States in its war against terrorism. Interestingly, they see this more than Americans do as a "clash of civilizations": Islam versus the *Christian* West, which includes both the United States and South Africa. But in America we are told not to view this as an anti-Islamic struggle, only a fight against terrorism and extremism. South Africans think we are naive about this; I fear their viewpoint is closer to the truth than ours. At the end of the service, practically the entire congregation comes up to shake my hand and wish me—and America—well.

During the next two days I had non-stop interviews—at Pretoria University, the U.S. embassy, the Institute for International Security, the Institute for Strategic Studies, and with local historians and military officials. The University, I learn, has 30,000 students, 6,000 of them black. The white students are mostly Afrikaner but liberal, enlightened Afrikaners. They want the present ANC, black-controlled government to succeed, not fail, because their lives and futures are also at stake. If the experiment in black rule is unsuccessful and South Africa becomes "just another" failed state, then these young, educated whites might as well leave the country, which many have already done and everyone else is seriously thinking about. For example, New Zealand's population is now about one-quarter Afrikaner; Australia, Canada, and the United States are also attractive destinations for young South Africans. There has already been a massive brain drain of doctors, dentists, engineers, and young professionals of all kinds.

In my interviews in the History and Political Science Departments at the University, I learned that, while whites are fairly satisfied with the moderate course of Nelson Mandela and his successor Thabo Mbecki, they are deeply worried about the ANC hotheads who favor a one-party regime, the immediate redistribution of wealth, and affirmative action that reserves government jobs for blacks. There is strong tension within the ANC over these issues; decisions could go either way. But in a one-party system, with redistribution of land and wealth and quotas for jobs, whites are sure to lose.

If any of these steps are taken or if they seem likely in the future, there will be massive white flight from South Africa.

At the U.S. embassy, I got a general briefing on the political and economic situation in South Africa. Most Embassy officials were still optimistic about the country's future, even while recognizing the problems and tensions. The most interesting—and surprising—things they said concerned the decline of civil society in South Africa in both the black and white communities. Black civil society was in decline because, with the end of apartheid, the foundations and funding agencies were pulling out, and better jobs could now be obtained in the public sector. Among Afrikaners, the key change was the loss of power and, hence, the loss of access to public funds. Out of power and out of money and with many people leaving the country, the whole web of Afrikaner civil society—political parties, brotherhoods, sports associations, social clubs, churches and religious groups, schools—was all coming undone.

There are two main security studies institutes in Pretoria. Michael Hough, a former mercenary and guerrilla fighter, runs the University-based Institute for International Security. It does contract work for the government and private business. Hough focuses on violence and terrorism; he told me much of the violence in South Africa stems from the poverty of the black population, but he emphasized that it also grew out of simple greed, tribal rivalries, and factional fighting within the ANC. In contrast, right-wing (white, Afrikaner) violence had almost vanished—though, he said, if blacks supported by the government started seizing private land holdings as was then going on in neighboring Zimbabwe, white farmers would likely take up arms again. Unless things got really bad, Hough predicted, most whites would stay in South Africa because all their family ties and friends are here.

Across town is the privately supported Institute for Strategic Studies where I met with researcher Richard Cornwell, researcher Antoinette Louw, and director Jackie Cilliers (another Huguenot name). As with the U.S. think tanks, much of their time (Cilliers says 80 percent) is spent in fundraising. Cilliers told me his institute no longer does traditional international security studies but is now concentrating, because that's where the grant money is, on peace-keeping, governance issues, and community policing. Cornwell was also interesting, insisting apropos of my civil society study that in South Africa the definition of civil society had to reflect the realities of the country including street gangs, terrorist groups, patronage networks, and rival tribal elements—not exactly what the advocates of civil society as a solution to the world's problems want to hear. But it certainly was relevant to my comparative study of civil society.[4]

All my interviews in Pretoria were interesting, but the most fascinating was a long lunch I had with a retired Brigadier General William Sass of the South African Defense Forces. Sass was of German (evangelical Lutheran) background but had married into a Huguenot family and considered himself Afrikaner. At seventy-five, he had seen it all.

Sass knew the history well. He explained that the Dutch Reformed Church had long been a bulwark of South African society, parallel and closely tied to the colonial state and permeating all aspects of life. During the colonial era in the seventeenth and eighteenth centuries, all the pastors and missionaries had come from The Netherlands, but when Great Britain seized the Cape in 1806 and South Africa became a British colony, that all stopped. Over time, the universities of Paarl, Stellenbasch, and Pretoria began producing their own, home-grown dominies; the universities were also leading centers for the growth of the Afrikaner language and of Afrikaner nationalism.

Sass confirmed what I had previously known: that The Netherlands had largely abandoned its South Africa colony in the nineteenth and twentieth centuries, that the South African Dutch/Afrikaner community resented the mother country because of this neglect and, more than that, that the often uninformed criticism directed at it (especially over apartheid) by the Dutch government had led South Africans over this time period to become permanently estranged from Holland. By now they no longer considered themselves "Dutch" but only "Afrikaans"; I noticed that in my interviewing because when I asked about lasting Dutch influences in South Africa, I was always immediately corrected with, "You mean Afrikan." So by now the Dutch Reformed Church in South Africa was a completely different church from the one in The Netherlands (or the one in Western Michigan, for that matter); the Afrikaner community was completely different from other Dutch communities worldwide; and there was an awful lot of resentment, anger, and hostility between these separate, but originally all Dutch, new and old world fragments.

General Sass told me that the Afrikaner community was very resentful of the way the transition to black rule was handled. He blamed it on the leadership (Prime Ministers Botha and De Klerk) who "gave everything away." He also blamed outside intervention that was too quick to condemn the apartheid regime while remaining ignorant of all the changes that had been taking place. Whites had become more urban, better educated, and less resistant to change, he said, while in the black community a new middle class was growing that offered a more moderate alternative to the ANC.

Sass believed that De Klerk should have brought other black groups into the negotiations instead of simply turning power over to the ANC, and that a more gradual and moderate transition was possible in which power would have been shared between whites and moderate blacks. Now not only have the Afrikaners been completely marginalized politically, but the prospects for future South African development and democracy are much dimmer as well. He told me the Afrikaner community is now isolated and feels itself betrayed, both by the world and by its own leadership, with all the resentments to which that gives rise.

So what is the current status of the Dutch/Afrikaner community in South Africa? Sass told me that the Dutch/Afrikaner Reformed Churches are still strong, that they do a lot of good social and charity work, that their membership is remaining solid even though they no longer receive special favoritism from the government or state aid. Second, schools especially at upper levels are still 80 percent white, that the best schools are Afrikaner schools, and that the best universities in the country—Paarl, Pretoria, Stellenbosch—are also Afrikaner, even though all of them are admitting more and more black students. Third, the Afrikaner language is still widely used; it is *the* defining idiom of the Afrikaner community; and a considerable body of literature and culture has grown up around it. And fourth, there is Afrikaner civil society. Sass acknowledged what I had heard elsewhere, that it is weaker than before; nevertheless, he said that there are networks of connections, associations, stores, families, etc. that remain important. The Afrikaners tend to patronize each other's stores and businesses; said Sass, "We take care of our own." Just like any other ethnic group I've ever heard of, except that in South Africa the setting and context for such separation are particularly volatile.

I had a wonderful time in Pretoria and would like to spend more time there. It's a beautiful city, especially when the flowers are in bloom, and I had excellent contacts and interview opportunities there. It's also, predominantly, a Dutch/Afrikaner city, but beneath the surface, here as elsewhere in South Africa, the levels of crime, violence, and fear are rising.

My armed driver the next morning to the airport is Afrikaner, as is virtually every white in the Transvaal. He tells me his family has a farm in the northwest part of the country that is 50 kilometers by 50 kilometers, or about 900 (!) square miles. But it's poor land, he says, and they can't make a go of it; hence, like most of the farmers in this area they're turning it into a game preserve and trying to attract tourists. His name is Pieters—obviously a Dutch name—but when I ask him if it's Dutch, he says he doesn't know. Instead, he calls himself "South African." It's obvious he, like most Afrikaners, doesn't self-identify as Dutch; in fact, with him as with other Afrikaners there's real hostility toward The Netherlands for having abandoned them in their time of need: when the British first occupied the colony in the early nineteenth century, during the Boer War at the end of the century, and then again during the struggle over apartheid when both the Dutch churches and the Dutch government adopted strongly critical resolutions and imposed sanctions against them. It strikes me in talking to this guy that I'm much more conscious of my Dutch roots than he is.

On to Cape Town, two hours and a thousand miles from Johannesburg. At the southernmost tip of South Africa, Cape Town was the original Dutch settlement here. The remains of the original, five-sided Dutch fortress are here and most of the streets and squares in the central area have Dutch names. I hire a taxi and go for a long tour: there's Table Mountain, Signal Hill, Devil's Peak—all the famous landmarks. But directional signs are in both English and Dutch, and it's plain that over the last two centuries, since the British conquest of 1806, Cape Town has become an English city. It's a mix, of course: there are Dutch speakers as well as English, blacks as well as whites. Crime and violence are rising, but they have not reached Johannesburg levels; on the other hand, they're higher than in Pretoria. I notice immediately that, while Pretoria is in language and culture a predominantly Afrikaner community, in Cape Town the main influences—language, business, banks, commerce, social intercourse—are British.

Cape Town is a lively, picturesque, and quite beautiful city; in other circumstances, I'd like to spend more time there. But my present interests are in Dutch influences and the Afrikaner community, and so I spend only a day in Cape Town before going on to the centers of Dutch, Afrikaner, and Calvinist power in the cities east of Cape Town, Paarl and Stellenbosch. These and other small communities are where the Dutch settled when they first moved out of the Cape colony in the late-seventeenth century and began to explore the interior and farm the land. These towns continue to be bastions of the Afrikaner culture and language and of the Dutch Reformed Church.

I stayed at the Spier winery outside of Stellenbosch, one of many Afrikaner-owned wineries in the area that has now been converted into a luxurious tourist resort complex. It's a gorgeous setting, nestled among lush green fields, endless rows of grape bushes, with steep mountains in the background. The accommodations are beautiful and the food is wonderful. The resort has cheetahs on the grounds; one half-expects a lion to jump at you out of the bushes. The manor house is luxurious but African style ("Out of Africa") with open space and large verandas. It may be the nicest resort at which I've ever stayed.

My interest here is not tourism but the local Afrikaner community. So immediately after checking in, I go for a tour of the town. Stellenbosch is a beautiful town, all whitewashed and clean—like a Dutch town ought to be. It's a small town, no bigger than our home town of Amherst, Massachusetts, and in a lot of ways is like Amherst: green, open spaces, no industry or pollution, lots of bookstores, low crime, many outdoor cafes, an historic town but away from the main centers. I walked all the streets, visited the historic churches and museums, bought postcards in the best-known place in town, Oom Samie's general store, and at the end of the day took time to attend a wine-tasting reception that one of the local wineries, eager to expand its markets to the United States, was putting on. Stellenbosch is so livable and so lovely that I'm thinking this would be a nice place to which to retire.

That is, until the next morning when I went out to Stellenbosch University. It's a beautiful campus and I was operating on the assumption that it would be like Hope or Calvin, the two main colleges of the Dutch Reformed and Christian Reformed Churches, respectively, in America. That is, Dutch Reformed, yes, but probably the liberal, educated, progressive wing of Reformed or Calvinist thinking. Was I in for a surprise!

Stellenbosch, though it receives government funds, is by no means a public, liberal, or secular university. In walking the corridors of the Arts Building looking for the offices of my interviewees, I come across both a Department of Bible Translation (mainly for translation into indigenous languages) and a Department of Dutch and Afrikaans. The University has a seminary for the training of Dutch Reformed ministers, the most important seminary in South Africa. It now admits blacks, but the instruction is all in Afrikaans. It is *the* center of Afrikaner culture in South Africa and a very conservative place.

And then I meet the faculty! I don't know if my sample is representative, but the people I meet (I'll leave the names out here but, if you're interested, see chapter 28 of *Adventures in Research*) are some of the rudest, most hardheaded, hard-nosed, and authoritarian people I've ever met in my life. They're unfriendly; it's obvious they think I'm wasting their precious time; they're abrupt and unwelcoming; and clearly they can't wait for me to leave. All my plans of retiring to Stellenbosch, enjoying the wine, the scenery, and the Dutch ambience, and perhaps teaching a course at the University go out the window in one big swoosh.

What is going on here? I can think of three analogous situations. One is the stubbornness, meanness, and sheer ugliness of the uncompromising, hard-nosed Protestant "Orangemen" (after the Dutch Duke of Orange) in Northern Ireland. Did you know that, when Great Britain acquired its vast empire in the eighteenth and nineteenth centuries, it used a disproportionate number of troops from Northern Ireland precisely because they were so tough, mean, and stubborn? That's what these folks remind me of.

The second parallel is to The Netherlands itself. Recall from our earlier trips to Holland how rudely my family was treated there, the money-grubbing nature of so many of the Dutch we encountered, and how stubborn, arrogant, and uncompromising they could be. That got me to thinking that maybe there's something in the Dutch people, the Dutch national character or the Dutch or Calvinist political culture that leads to such behavior. There are a few hard-headed persons like this, too, in Grand Rapids—lending support to the national character explanation—but they tend to be few and of the older generation, a dying breed.

The third parallel is with my experiences in the (former) communist countries of Russia, Poland, Hungary, the Czech Republic, and Slovakia. There, too, I had run into stiff, formal, hard-headed bureaucrats and government officials, ex- (and probably still) communist party members and hack politicians, still left over from the old (pre-1989) regime. And that is what I think I had seen and experienced in South Africa: the regime has changed (apartheid is gone; black rule is in) and everyone knows it's supposed to be a new era, except that the same "party" hacks (in this case, university bureaucrats and professors) are still in charge and they haven't changed their spots at all. If one thinks of the former communist countries post-1989, or South Africa post-apartheid, there are a lot of interesting parallels. Both were monopolistic, totalitarian, top-down regimes; but now a fundamental transformation has occurred and things are supposed to be different. Except there are still many continuities with the past, with the old regime.

I found South Africa to be very different from Western Michigan where I grew up. Both are "Dutch" but there is a world of difference between them. In Western Michigan the Dutch people are friendly, open, personable, and, for the most part, comfortable in their own skins. Western Michigan is conservative and approximately 80 percent Republican, but it is in the mainstreams and often liberal wings of the Republican Party. In South Africa, in contrast, people tend to be less friendly, more closed-minded, less personable, and extremely uptight.

Moreover, while the Western Michigan Dutch are conservative, the center of gravity of the South African Afrikaners is *way to the right* of Western Michigan. In part, these differences can be explained by the fact the Dutch in Western Michigan have been enormously successful, have been thoroughly assimilated by now into mainstream American culture, and are, in general, happy people. If they had just been ousted from power as the Afrikaners in South Africa have been, and if they were facing the prospect of being a permanent minority, outnumbered ten-to-one, in a black-controlled regime, maybe the Grand Rapids Dutch would be angry, bitter, and down-in-the-mouth, too.

In the end, I come back to the main theme of this book, the fragments thesis. The Dutch in Western Michigan were the product of mid-nineteenth-century Dutch Calvinism and some of the traits from that earlier time—a degree of stubbornness and hard-handedness—are still alive and well in that community. But success, assimilation, prosperity, and thoroughgoing Americanization have deeply and permanently changed the Dutch in Grand Rapids, making them nicer, more open-minded, more liberal, and less "Dutch."

In contrast, the Dutch, now Afrikaner, community in South Africa, a product of the seventeenth century and living in isolation and under siege for so long, has changed far less dramatically. It has been, on the whole, less successful, less adaptable, and less well integrated than the Dutch in Western Michigan. After World War II the Afrikaner community was changing, becoming more urban, better educated, and less parochial than it was before. But that process, in part because of the fear of black rule or revolution should they ever relax the controls, was far slower in South Africa than it was in Grand Rapids. And, while the vast majority of the Afrikaner young people I met are friendly, outgoing, and open-minded, the older generation seem to be reverting to the rigid ideology and religious and cultural beliefs of the past. Once again, the themes are "circle the wagons," "us against the world," and a paranoid life style.

But those attitudes would be a disaster for South Africa and for the Dutch/Afrikaner community there.

Notes

1. Howard J. Wiarda, *Adventures in Research* (Lincoln, NE: iUniverse, 2006), chapter 28.

2. Afrikaans speakers were (and still are) often mocked and looked down on when they went back to The Netherlands, since that language is rather crude and seen as a "street language," not refined. The fact that Afrikaans speakers in Holland were made to feel like second-class citizens in their own native country was one of the factors that led them to feel estranged from the mother country and eventually led them to separate from it.

3. *Adventures*, chapter 28.

4. Howard J. Wiarda, *Civil Society: The American Model and Third World Development* (Boulder: Westview Press, 2003).

CHAPTER ELEVEN

Back to the Origins: Geneva and the Protestant Reformation

Geneva, Switzerland, has long been one of my favorite cities. It ranks right up there with Vienna as one of our all-time special places to live and work. It combines French charm and grace with German competence and efficiency. It sits at the crossroads of Europe, both East and West *and* North and South. It is at a conjunction where French, Italian, and German cultures all come together.

Geneva is a very beautiful city, at the western tip of Lake Geneva (Lac Lemán, as the natives call it) with its magnificent views of Mont Blanc (so-called because it is snow-capped all year round), and straddling the Rhone River as it begins its journey from Lake Geneva to the Mediterranean Sea. Though small, it is also a very cosmopolitan city, home to a great number of peoples and nationalities and to a host of major international organizations: The Red Cross, the International Labor Organization, the International Health Organization, and many others. On top of all this, it was *the* center of the Protestant Reformation.

It may seem odd to include Geneva, Switzerland, in a book on the Dutch Diaspora. For Geneva is not at all a Dutch city; much like Amsterdam, Geneva is no longer the clean and immaculate city it used to be (which means, as we shall see, it has also slipped a few notches on our list of favorite cities). But as the home for several decades of John Calvin, as the birthplace and main center for Calvinism and the Calvinist faith, which then spread northward into The Netherlands and eastward into Hungary and Transylvania (see chapter 12), Geneva had an enormous impact on the religion, politics, culture, sociology, and economic life of The Netherlands and, by extension, all the colonies and fragments discussed here. In addition, many Dutch intellectuals and pastors came to Geneva to study the principles of the new Reformed faith. One additional reason for including Geneva in this book: I have lived in Geneva; I like it there; and part of my roots and origins are there.

I have traveled to Geneva on numerous occasions for short visits and lived, worked, and did research there at three times in my life. The first time my family and I visited Geneva was in 1972–1973 (we spent New Year's Eve there); it was not an auspicious beginning because we all, especially wife Iêda, got food poisoning in an Arab restaurant, the only one open at the late hour we arrived, and felt the after-effects for weeks. The second time, in 1979–1980, was also with my family; later, after the family had returned to the United States, I went back to Geneva to do more extensive work and research. The third time, interspersed with briefer visits, was in 2001 when Iêda and I returned for another period of research combined with sightseeing.

Through all these visits I have been acutely conscious of Geneva's history as the center of the Protestant (Calvinist) Reformation and have used the opportunities of my visits there not only to do my own work and research (mainly at the ILO [International Labor Organization], focused on comparative labor relations, corporatism, and the industrial relations systems of Southern and Eastern Europe) but also to explore my roots. For Geneva to me is one of those places, like Jerusalem, Athens, Rome, The Netherlands, and Western Michigan, that has had a profound and lasting impact on my life, work ethic, and cultural and social values. I am a product of Calvin's Geneva, at least as much as I am a product of these other wellsprings of the Western, Judeo-Christian tradition. During my work in Geneva, therefore, I have always taken the time to explore my own origins and formative beliefs in this Calvinist city and font of the Protestant Reformation which so strongly shaped not just my life but that of The Netherlands, too, and the entire Dutch Diaspora.

The Reformation in Geneva

The Reformation began in 1517 when Martin Luther famously nailed his theses criticizing the Roman Catholic Church to the church door in Wittenberg, Germany. Luther's critique reverberated widely because the Roman Church was, in fact, corrupt and abusive.

But it was John Calvin in Geneva who first gave scholarly rigor, intellectual substance, and organizational substance to the Reformation. Calvin's *Institutes of the Christian Religion*, first published in 1535, was a logical, well-organized, powerfully organized treatise on the Christian faith. Helped along by the invention of the printing press, Calvin's *Institutes* was an instant best-seller because it systematically laid out all that was wrong with the Catholic Church at that time and the need for reform—hence, the term *Reformation*.

The *Institutes* went through numerous editions in Calvin's lifetime; its powerful logic, argument, and systematic organization made it attractive to a broad array of European intellectuals, especially including those in The Netherlands, France, Germany, Hungary, and Transylvania. Calvin was a prolific writer and, along with the *Institutes*, his pamphlets, sermons, and in-depth interpretations of the Bible were widely disseminated throughout Europe and in many languages. In addition, in Geneva, Calvin gave structure, form, and governance to the Reformation that it had previously lacked. Calvin's great contribution was to systematize and provide coherence and organization to the work that Luther had begun.

John Calvin was born in Noyon, Picardy, in France in 1509. A brilliant student, he attended elementary school in Noyon, the College of Marche and the College of Montaigu in Paris, and then the University of Paris (today's Sorbonne), and law schools in Bourges and Orleans. He received advanced training in logic, philosophy, and theology but graduated as a lawyer; hence, in his thought the emphasis on discipline, rationalism, organization, and rigorous logic that still attracts us to Calvinism today. In Paris, Calvin was first exposed to the ideas of the early Protestant reformers including Luther; he was a member of a religious reform movement inspired by Renaissance humanism, of which the French monarchy had become increasingly suspicious. His flirtation with and eventual conversion to reformist ideas in 1534 got him in trouble with the French monarch, Francois I, and he was forced to flee the country; he converted to Protestantism while studying theology in Basel, Switzerland. It was in Basel that he wrote the first edition of his famous *Institutes*.

In the almost two decades between Luther's theses (1517) and Calvin's *Institutes* (1535), the Protestant "heresy" had gotten a strong foothold in a number of European cities: Wittenberg and Heidelberg in Germany, Strasbourg in France, and Basel, Zurich, and Geneva in Switzerland. Each of these cities and their leading theologians (Luther in Germany, Guillaume Farel in Geneva, Martin Bucer in Strasbourg, Huldrych Zwingli in Zurich, Luther's colleague Philipp Melanchthon also in Germany) preached a slightly different version of Protestantism. Calvin was actually en route to Strasbourg in 1536 when he was obliged by war-fighting in France to stop in Geneva. His planned temporary stop there turned into a two-year stay. Although he later spent three years in Strasbourg exiled also from Geneva, Calvin was most closely associated with that latter city.

Geneva in the 1520s, a city of only 10,000, was just emerging from under the dominance of the Italian Duke of Savoy. It had achieved its independence both from the secular authorities of Savoy and from the oppression of the Roman Catholic Church's representative in Geneva, a bishop appointed by the Duke. Calvin was appealed to by the small, struggling Protestant element in Geneva to help solidify the still-frail Reformation occurring there; he was likely also attracted by the fact Geneva was close to his roots in France, by its (even then) cosmopolitan and international flavor, and by its location as an international crossroads. Forbidden from returning to Catholic France, he decided to stay; Calvin's logical mind, coupled with the fiery, inspirational preaching of Farel, made them a powerful team.

But almost immediately Calvin and Farel ran afoul of the Geneva city council. The proud councilors, flush from their victory over the House of Savoy, wanted to run the city themselves and resented Calvin's and Farel's sometimes insensitive and unwelcome way of telling them how to govern. At the same time, Calvin and Farel believed that their religious beliefs and values were not limited to religion but extended into civic and political matters as well. These conflicts came to a head in 1538 when Calvin and Farel were forced out of Geneva and obliged to take refuge in Strasbourg, which was already a Protestant stronghold.

In Strasbourg, Calvin ministered and preached to the French Protestant community resident there, while also preparing a new edition of his *Institutes*. He was strongly influenced by Buber's notions of church organization and by Strasbourg's city-state system of governance. Meanwhile, Geneva had continued to fractionalize religiously, and the city council was unable to solve the problem. Hence, in 1541, after an absence of three years, Calvin was called back to Geneva by the council to help resolve the strife and bring order and discipline to the religious disputes. He stayed there until his death in 1564.

Even now, however, the Geneva city council and the Genevan elites insisted that the system of church governance drawn up by Calvin be under their control and not the churches'. Furthermore, that the city would continue to be run by them and not by Calvin or his fellow pastors. The council even insisted that *they* would appoint the ministers in the church even while they warned Calvin and his collaborators not to interfere in city affairs. Actually, there was both tension and cooperation between Calvin and the Genevan city council, but it is hard to see how anyone, aware of all these conflicts with the council, could believe the charge made by some critics that Calvin had turned pluralistic and free-thinking Geneva into a theocracy.

In addition to his theological writings, Calvin was perhaps most famous for his writings and organizational efforts on behalf of church governance.

Borrowing from what he had observed in Strasbourg, Calvin proposed four functions of church organization: pastors, doctors, elders, and deacons. Pastors were responsible for the general ministry of care of the laity—not all that different from what priests and bishops had done in the medieval Catholic Church. Doctors (Calvin, who was never ordained formally as a minister in any church, thought of himself in this category) were responsible for teaching at all levels. The elders were responsible for good order and discipline within the church—a fatherly, paternalistic function involving periodic home visitations in our time but important in the chaotic, religious situation of mid-sixteenth-century Geneva. Deacons took care of church finances.

This hierarchy of authority within the church of Geneva paralleled and existed alongside the civilian authority, but it did not overlap with it and the city fathers made sure *they* were in command, not the pastors. The system was really an extension of the "city-of-God, city-of-Caesar" metaphor of the New Testament, or of the "two swords" (secular and religious) doctrine of the Middle Ages. Calvin himself was more concerned that all these functions were carried out than that his system of governance be followed rigidly, but some later followers tended to reify his statements and elevate this particular church order into a rigid and quite absolutist system.

Calvin had a powerful, logical mind; and he wrote in the elegant French of the educated classes. He brought erudition, careful Biblical scholarship, detailed knowledge of classical antiquity, and the organized logic of his lawyer's training to all his sermons and writings. In ways that Luther—a humble parish priest—never could, Calvin was able to give the Protestant Reformation a solid, intellectual, persuasive, rationalist, structural-logical basis that it lacked before. He did for Protestantism in one generation what the Catholic Church in its organizational efforts and canon law had taken sixteen centuries to do. Year after year from his base in Geneva, Calvin churned out ever-expanded editions of his *Institutes*, detailed and nuanced interpretations and exegeses of the books of the Bible, social, political, and religious commentary and pamphlets, and volume after volume of collections of his superb and beautifully argued sermons. Almost single-handedly Calvin made Geneva into a bastion of the new Protestant faith and created an organized religion that had a worldwide impact.

In the course of his long, twenty-five-year career in Geneva, there were, inevitably, more clashes between Calvin and the city council. Both had, after all, overlapping but sometimes conflicting jurisdictions and constituencies. The city and its council were pleased by their overthrowing of the oppression of the Duke of Savoy and his appointed bishop, were proud of their independent city-state, and wanted to keep it that way. They were worried not only about the efforts of the pastors to impose their particular religious beliefs on what was a cosmopolitan and diverse community but also by the continued dabbling of Calvin and others from the French exile community in internal French politics which, in the context of those times, might result in an invasion of Geneva by the French king's armies and the loss of their hard-won independence.

For his part, Calvin did not share the current U.S. Supreme Court's view that church and state should be strictly separated and that government must be absolutely neutral and secular. His ideal was a political community in which interaction between church and state was natural and mutually sup-porting for the common good. While he accepted the historic "two swords" or "God-and-Caesar" separation of the civil and the religious, called for Christians to obey the authority over them (no right of rebellion here), and accepted the jurisdiction of civil magistrates over the clergy, he also believed rulers have an obligation to the church. They must "defend the worship of God," "remove superstition and end wicked idolatry" (no tolerance of wic-cism here), "advance God's kingdom and maintain purity of doctrine," and "purify scandals and cleanse the filth that corrupts piety and impairs the lus-ter of the divine majesty."

These are heavy responsibilities to place on the shoulders of town coun-cils. Obviously, these are broad moral injunctions; in specific cases one can easily see the potential for clashes between ministers and civil magistrates over how and when the latter should "defend the worship of God," "remove superstition," "end idolatry," "advance God's kingdom," and "cleanse the filth." It's pretty obvious, to make this contemporary, that Calvin would be in favor of requesting civil authority to keep out strip joints, curb pornogra-phy and prostitution, prohibit gay marriage, limit liquor consumption, ille-galize gambling, and enact Sunday closing laws—none of which, in my view, are such bad ideas. But in Geneva of this time there was always, as there should be, a tug-of-war between the pastors and the city government over these issues, a political process at work in which at some times one side won and at others, the other. So far as I can tell, Geneva never became a theo-cratic society like Iran under Khomeini and the mullahs.

The one great blot on Calvin's record was his acquiescence in the execu-tion of a maverick thinker from Navarre, Michael Servetus. Servetus was brilliant but clearly a heretic and, by all accounts, a miserable, antagonistic, hateful person. He had been condemned to death, not by Calvin but by the Catholic Inquisition in Lyon. Inexplicably, he escaped his fate in Lyon and showed up at Calvin's church in Geneva. But instead of granting him clemency, Calvin, who knew the case intimately and may have supplied some of the evidence involved, confirmed the Lyon court's sentence. Calvin favored a more merciful kind of execution but, convinced that Christendom was under threat from Servetus's writings, did not oppose the sentence of death by burning. Before having the sentence carried out, he consulted with Strasbourg and the other Swiss and German Protestant communities. Finding no opposition, he allowed the execution to go ahead. It is perhaps not the decision you or I would make but, in the context of those times, it was certainly understandable and hardly unique.[1]

And that is part of the final set of judgments we must make about Calvin. Calvin was a figure of his time.[2] He was a French intellectual, a highly trained lawyer, an evangelical humanist during the time of the Renaissance, a superb writer and rhetorician, and a political-religious exile. His ideas represented both a sharp break with the Middle Ages and a continuation of it. He could be both brilliant and intolerant. He was an Erasmusian intellectual, but he was not a democrat or a believer in pluralism. He was one of the key figures of the Reformation, but his religious beliefs were at the same time embedded in the spirituality of the late Middle Ages.[3]

Calvin's ideas and elegant, powerful writings ushered in a revolution in The Netherlands, England and Scotland, Switzerland, France, Germany, Hungary, Transylvania, and elsewhere in Europe. And, by extension, in America, South Africa, the Far East, Indonesia, and some parts of South America and the Caribbean. His influence marked a sharp break with the past and helped usher in the modern, rationalist, capitalistic world. For if we agree even to only a limited extent with Max Weber about the Protestant ethic and the association between Calvinism and rationality, the rise of capitalism, and the intriguing, calculating, entrepreneurial spirit, then Calvin and his influence are remarkably important in creating and developing our age. Certainly, in my own research experience comparing The Netherlands with other countries, in the comparison of development in the North and South of Europe, as well as in the chapters of this book, there is a close correlation between Calvinism and prosperity, affluence, and the well-ordered society that was instrumental in the emergence of modernity.

Travels in Geneva

1972–1973

Our first visit to Geneva in 1972–1973 was almost an unmitigated disaster. We were living in Lisbon, Portugal, at the time where I was researching a book on Portuguese corporatism.[4] On the day after Christmas, we began the first of several forays that year to explore Western Europe. Our route on this first trip took us and our used Volkswagen Beetle initially to Madrid for a couple of days to visit friends and see the Spanish capital, then to Barcelona for a quick visit, and finally onto Lyon and Geneva. We arrived in Geneva on New Year's Eve.

After a long day on the road, our two children were tired and very hungry. Plus, after living on a Spanish diet for three or four days, they wanted hamburgers. And I, as a dutiful father, tried to find them hamburgers. In those days, Geneva had no McDonald's on the Rue Mont Blanc as it does now. And, since it was New Year's Eve, almost all stores and restaurants had closed early. We drove around for a while with no success, then finally found a small restaurant up near the train station, just off the Plac du Corduvin.

It was an Arab restaurant; there was a big, flea-infected police dog inside; and it didn't look too clean or auspicious. Those should have served as warning signs, but the owner assured us he was open and could serve hamburgers. So we stayed and ate, a big mistake. Iêda took one bite and stopped eating; the kids and I, hungry if not famished, downed the whole thing.

The next morning we set off to tour Geneva. Down the Rue Mont Blanc to the lakefront, along the lake on Woodrow Wilson Avenue, back along the lake and over the bridge across the Rhone River, past the flower clock and the water fountain in the lake, into the old city, up to the Hotel de Ville (city hall) and the cathedral (Protestant, as is fitting in Geneva), past the monument to the Reformation, around Geneva's many parks and residential areas, out to the neighborhood where the ILO, WHO, Red Cross, and other international agencies and the League of Nations are located. It was a wonderful drive on, since it was a holiday—New Year's—virtually deserted streets.

By mid-morning we knew we were in trouble. Iêda's stomach was starting to give her problems and the kids and I weren't feeling too well. So we stopped the car, got out, and had a family pow-wow. The issue was: should we stay in Geneva and try to find a doctor here or should we try to head back to Lisbon and the comforts of our apartment home there by the fastest way possible. The trouble with staying in Geneva was that we didn't know anyone here; we had no contacts or telephone numbers; and on a holiday that was part of an extended weekend, we doubted if we could find a doctor who would see us anytime in the next two days. That made the Lisbon option look better. Plus we already knew a doctor we could see there; in addition, we were under pressure to get back because our kids' school started in four days.

We decided as a family not to stay in Geneva any longer but to head back to Lisbon. Back through southern France, across the Pyrenees, through northern Spain, into Portugal. In those days there were no superhighways; it took us three days plus. The kids and I were not in great shape during this frantic dash, but Iêda was sick as a dog the whole way. We had to stop every hour. She thought she was going to die. We limped back into Lisbon where she got immediate medical help and the kids started school the next day.

After she had recovered, Iêda wrote the city authorities in Geneva. Much to our surprise, we actually got an answer back. Not only did the health authorities investigate, but they found so many violations that they actually closed down the restaurant where we'd gotten sick. For us, it was a small but great victory. Does the efficiency and responsibility of the Genevan authorities have anything to do with their Calvinist past? I'm inclined to think so.

1979–1980

Our second trip to Geneva was much more successful. And enjoyable. It actually consisted of two visits separated by a couple of months. On the first visit, the family and I traveled to Geneva by train from Paris, part of a longer trip that had also taken us to England, The Netherlands, Germany, and Belgium. This was a family visit; we had a wonderful time—no more food poisoning and stomach problems. Later we traveled by train down to Rome and, after a few days of seeing the sights there, I put them on a plane back to the United States, as school was about to start.

After the family had left, I spent several more weeks in Rome doing research, then went overland and by boat to Greece for more research, back through Italy and up to Vienna, to Munich to give some lectures, and back to Geneva again for a longer period of research. All this was part of an ambitious sabbatical leave year that I had in 1979–1980 researching and writing a book on comparative Southern European (Greece, Italy, Portugal, Spain) labor relations.[5] Now when I returned to Geneva, I actually lived there for a time.

When you arrive from Paris, climb into the mountains of Switzerland, then proceed along Lake Geneva from Lausanne, it's a beautiful trip. There are sailboats on the lake, beautiful chateaus on the hills overlooking it, then a clear view of Geneva's famous fountain, the *jet d'eau*. We checked into the pension that we had reserved where the owner actually was nice to and welcomed our children (three by now). We had a fine meal in a nice restaurant—no more hamburgers in Arab places with endless health code violations.

We walked the length of the Rue Mont Blanc down to the lake. In those years the city was clean, even spotless—a Calvinist attribute. We walked across the bridge to the Rousseau statue on an island in the middle of the Rhone; most of my political science colleagues much prefer the revolutionary Rousseau, a native Genevan, to the austere Calvin. The lake water is absolutely clear and pure as it enters the Rhone. In Calvinistic cities, even the rivers are clean!

Geneva on this visit is a gorgeous city with little traffic and almost no tourists. There is no paper or even cigarette butts on the streets. (Was it Calvin or my Dutch ancestors who said, "Cleanliness is next to Godliness"?) No graffiti, no pollution, no loud noise. Unlike Brussels or Paris, there's no dog poop on the streets. It's absolutely peaceful and very pleasant here. I'm reminded of Bonn (still then the capital of Germany) that we had just visited: a small town, cosmopolitan and international, but without the hubbub and boisterousness of a big city. Sitting on the shore of Lake Geneva with my family, with the snow-covered French Alps in the distance, I was thinking, "We should have come here for a full year's sabbatical."

Early the next morning, I left my family to roam around Geneva on their own and went off to the headquarters of the ILO. I had contacted them earlier about my research project on corporatism and labor relations; they knew I was coming. The secretary met me in the reception area, took me for a coffee and croissant, got me on ID card, and showed me my office with its breathtaking view of the lake and the mountains. With her help, I also got the ILO library and research staff to begin a computer search for the research materials I needed; by mid-afternoon I already had a *mountain* of materials on hand.

The ILO clerical staff and personnel were very kind and helpful to me, but I had already noticed this was not a place where people worked very hard or put in long hours. The professional staff showed up late (around 11:30—just in time to check their mail and then head to lunch) and quit early. The dining rooms were superb and heavily subsidized: about $3.00 for a four-course meal, with wine! Moreover, salaries were high and had a variety of overseas, cost-of-living, hardship (in Geneva? What a laugh!), and special incentive escalators built into them. Plus, the facilities were superb and the views magnificent. Who would not want to keep coming back to Geneva?

That week I worked regularly at the ILO in the morning, then took the afternoons off to spend time with my family. Every day we went down to the lake. The water was perfectly clear, and the views the nicest I've ever seen: mountains on one side, mansions on the other. A variety of boats plied the lake; there were swans all around; the beach area was uncrowded. For 50 cents we could swim off the Geneva pier; one section was devoted to topless sunbathing. What would Calvin think of that? On another walk, we crossed over to the far bank, sat in the park with the clock made of flowers, took a boat tour out to the *jet d'eau* (the water comes out at 125-miles-per-hour and shoots seven tons of water four hundred feet in the air), and went shopping in the main downtown shopping district. It, too, was Calvinistically clean.

Then back to our hotel along the quay on the south side of the river. Across at the city information booth. Lots of parks, squares, and outdoor cafes. The shopping is wonderful, very elegant, and not outrageously expensive; though Geneva is ranked as one of the world's most high-priced cities (mainly because of the high rents charged all the international bureaucrats who live there), we found clothes, groceries, and living expenses to be quite reasonable.

One day we visited the old league of nations building on its beautifully landscaped lawns, overlooking the lake. On at least two occasions, I had my family join me at the ILO so they could also enjoy those wonderful subsidized meals. ILO officials explained to me how their indexed salaries and cost-of-living benefits worked; Iêda and I were thinking, how could we arrange to get appointments at one of the many UN and international agencies here? Would the austere, pleasure-avoiding Calvin have approved of such plush surroundings, such elevated salaries, such short workdays, and subsidized lunches—with wine? I'm not too sure about Calvin but know my hard-working Dutch ancestors in Grand Rapids would not.

Still another day, my older son Howard (then eleven) and I went exploring in the old city. Up the hill to the Hotel De Ville and to Saint Peter's Cathedral. In Geneva the cathedral is not Catholic but Protestant; this is where Calvin himself preached. The cathedral was then undergoing renovation (professionals had mapped and numbered every stone) but How and I were able to climb way up into the bell tower with its magnificent views of the city and the lake. Coming down on the backside of the old city, we rediscovered the Protestant Reformation Monument with its larger-than-life statues of Calvin, Luther, Farel, Knox, Zwingli, and Melanchthon—all the great Reformation leaders.

I gave a lecture at the University of Geneva (founded by Calvin) and explored the possibility of a return visit and a visiting professorship there. The University responded favorably; of course, they had no funds to pay my salary but they were happy to have me as a freebee visiting faculty member. Geneva to me was looking better and better.

When I returned to Geneva several weeks later without my family and after the research in Italy, Greece, and Austria, I settled into the same pensión where we had stayed before. By this time, I felt that I knew the city and felt at home there. On this longer stay, I came to think of myself as almost a resident of Geneva and well integrated into its cultural and social life.

My field notes, written at the time, say the following: "What a nice city this is! Very polite, finishing school manners, elegant and graceful. Very chic, cosmopolitan, and international. There seems to be a gentility in Geneva lacking elsewhere. People smile a lot, including shop owners and service people. They are invariably polite and say thank you. There's a common courtesy that is nice. A small city (250,000) atmosphere with big city culture and sophistication. Clean, neat, it takes all the tourists (like me) in stride. A Calvinistic atmosphere (scrubbed, fastidious, disciplined, orderly) without Calvinistic heavy-handedness. Let's see if we can return here."

On this return visit, I continued to go up to the ILO every day. I conducted interviews with the staff, scholars, and international labor officials. I continued to enjoy those wonderful, subsidized, multi-course, ILO meals. Meanwhile, through their computerized retrieval system, the library and research staff continued to crank out new materials for me to peruse. Research can be fun when you have an entire staff working for you.

Meanwhile, I was integrating myself more and more into the life of the community. Every day I made a point of trying to visit a new office, a new group, a new part of town, or a new part of civil society. One day I visited the Genevan Family Planning Association (an earlier research interest); another, the Women's Association of Geneva. Another day I went to a tag sale at the English-speaking Holy Trinity (Anglican) Church—it had the same kind of used stuff as tag sales back in Amherst (most often you wonder why people bought all this junk in the first place). I attended lectures at the University and visited every art gallery and museum in town. I discovered an English-language lending library operating out of one of the churches; rather like Vienna, I found that Geneva has a rich classical musical scene with Mozart, Beethoven, choral groups, string quartets, orchestras, opera, something almost every night. Without my family around, I took in lots of these, in part because I love the music, in part to combat the loneliness of being here by myself. Many of these concert venues were in Geneva's numerous churches.

On Sundays I went to church, sometimes several churches in one day. I'm not sure how religious I am but, given Geneva's as well as my own background, I felt I had to come to grips with this aspect of the city. On the one hand, Geneva's churches are suffering from the same growing secularism and popular indifference to religion as elsewhere in Europe. But at the same time, there is a religious dynamism and a pervasive religiosity in Geneva that is lacking in much of Europe. Below the surface of a modern, secular, cosmopolitan city, I discovered, is a whole other world of religious rivalries, church-based civil society activities, and competing religious factions vying to dominate the city's civil administration that can't be all that different from what it was in Calvin's day.

I went first to the 9 o'clock mass at the Catholic Notre Dame Church at the top of the Rue Mont Blanc. It was full—unusual for Europe—and seemed to have a dynamic range of activities for youth, women, and so on. The yellow pages of the telephone book indicate there are presently as many Catholic as Protestant churches in Geneva.

Then across the river to the Paroisse Protestante Church of the Saint-Pierre Fusterie, on the Rue de Marche. A beautiful church, newly restored, it was even fuller than the Notre Dame Church. It is one of the French-language Reformed (Huguenot) Churches of Geneva, even fuller today than usual because of the ongoing repairs to the main Saint Peter's Cathedral. Everyone is well dressed; this is a prosperous church of business and professional elements. Again unusual, it has a youth choir and young people participating in the service—about the first time I've seen that in all of Europe. It used the Psalter Hymnal, but in French; the young people's choir sings "You Will Know We Are Christians by Our Love," a song sung in my own home Congregational Church in South Amherst, Massachusetts. It's obvious the church is thriving; like the Catholics, it maintains a web of civil society organizations for all sectors in society.

Another Sunday I attended the Temple de la Madeleine, which is the German-language Reformed Church of Geneva. The church has been beautifully restored; here, too, the people are well dressed and prosperous, mainly bourgeois. It's interesting that here and in the other Protestant churches people attend as families, not just the old women and children as in so many Catholic countries.

From there, I proceeded to the Calvinist Cathedral of Saint Peter's in the center of the city where we had visited before. Up the Rue John Calvin, past the Theater and the Roman Museum, past the Hotel de Ville—all familiar territory. St. Peter's is again undergoing reconstruction; services today are held in the next-door Chapel of the Maccabees, attached to the main church. This has historically been *the* main Protestant/Calvinist church in Geneva, filled with history and tradition and where you would want your daughter to be married; but I'm told that, with the growth of Geneva's suburbs, people are attending church out in their home neighborhoods rather than driving into the center of the city where, as in America, you can't find a parking space. Nevertheless, this church is still *The Cathedral* and *the* center of Protestant political activities in town. Protestants are a formidable presence still, as they were in Calvin's time, in city affairs and on the city council; one of the big issues at this time was how to deal with a popular but communist mayor who was not at all sympathetic to religious issues.

Right next to the Cathedral is the Scottish or John Knox Church where I also attended services. Knox was the leader of the Scottish Reformed Calvinists in the seventeenth century who broke away from *both* the

Catholic Church and the Church of England. He took refuge in Geneva for a time and became a follower of Calvin. The Scottish Church is the English-language Reformed Church of Geneva. Though a small sanctuary, there was an overflow crowd of more than two hundred people in attendance. Calvin gave his lectures on the Bible and theology here; a plaque on the wall proclaims "that doctrine shines on the entire world." It was here also that the form of church governance described earlier was developed that became a model for all churches in the Presbyterian and Reformed traditions. A small Dutch Reformed congregation and the German Waldesian community (a religious offshoot from southeastern France that had attacked the centralizing tendencies of the Roman Catholic Church as far back as the twelfth century) also use this sanctuary for their services.

The longer I stayed in Geneva, the better I liked it. I loved to take walks along the lake, through the old city, and into the elegant shops on the Rue du Rhone or the Rue Mont Blanc. People were very pleasant and polite, with a nice kind of gentleness in inter-personal relations, not at all loud or pushy. At the ILO I had very nice colleagues and the staff was friendly and helpful; Because I was a newcomer in town, they invited me out socially on a number of occasions. Similarly with the churches: they were very welcoming; I attended quite a number of their events and get-togethers; and from them I learned a lot about the church and religion-related politics of Geneva. My social life also included attendance at Bach and Telemann concerts in the Church of Saint Germaine, a concert of the nearby Lausanne orchestra, and movies in Geneva's downtown theater. Plus a *lot* of sitting in outdoor cafes watching the Genevan world go by.

I was starting to feel like I *belonged* in Geneva. I was becoming integrated into the community. Geneva kept rising on my list of favorite cities. My notes at the time read: "Geneva has to rank right up there in my list of spectacular cities. London, Jerusalem, Paris, Vienna, and Geneva all right up there at the top—and not necessarily in that order."

But my research work there was drawing to a close, and it was time to move on. I hated to leave but my Southern Europe project called for me to do more, or renewed, field research in Spain and Portugal. So that is where I headed next, vowing that, if in the future I had a shot at another Fulbright, Geneva would be where I'd like to spend it.

2001

I went back to Geneva a couple of times in the 1980s—to lecture or to represent the U.S. government on Central America—and a couple of times in the 1990s, once to lecture and another time to attend an international conference. But these were all brief, one-day or two-day visits, not long enough to see or do very much. The next time Iêda and I spent a more extended period of time there did not come until 2001 as part of my research on EU/NATO enlargement into Eastern and Central Europe.

We immediately noticed the changes; they were starkly visible. First, the city had many more African and Middle Eastern residents than it had had before. It had always been a cosmopolitan and international city, but in earlier visits that had meant mainly white, European, and American visitors and residents. Now it was clear Geneva had become much more diverse, multicultural, and multiracial than before—both for good and ill.

The foreigners come, as elsewhere in Europe, mainly as political refugees or as immigrant laborers. Most of them here in Geneva are from Africa or the Middle East; there is a sprinkling of Latin Americans. But in Geneva there is another source of immigrants: all the myriad international agencies, bureaus, and commissions. that are located here. If you are someone assigned to one of these agencies or the 200-odd national missions located in Geneva, you can probably stay on here forever. After all, as compared with Geneva, who would want to go back to Dilli or Kinshasa? Switzerland has strict citizenship rules but liberal visa rules, especially if you are a "diplomat." And if you're here, you're *entitled* to free education, free health care, housing, food, a monthly allowance, plus, if you're not a citizen, you don't have to pay taxes. And if you can claim the threat of genital mutilation, political persecution, or either forced pregnancy or nonpregnancy (usually by genital mutilation), you can stay in Geneva forever, enjoy all the benefits, and *never* have to leave or pay. Sorry to be so cynical but that's how the system works—or fails to work.

Second and, I'm sad to say, related, the city was much dirtier and with a higher crime rate than before. It looked shoddy and unkempt. What had once been a spotless, graffiti-free, and trash-free city was now strewn with wastepaper, cigarette butts, grime, and graffiti. What had happened to the clean, spotless, Dutch-like city that we used to know?

Third, the once-elegant shops on Rue Mont Blanc and, on the other side of the river, the Rue du Rhone were now mostly gone, replaced by fast-food emporia (including Burger King and McDonald's), video stores and arcades, bargain stores, and even casinos and sex shops. It was sad to see these elegant (and high-priced) places go; the new fast-food and other stores added mightily to the trash problem. What would Calvin say to casinos and sex shops?

This led to the fourth change: the character of the city had been altered. It was becoming like Berlin, Amsterdam, or Paris with their large Arab minorities. The Genevans (and their elegant stores, I soon learned) were moving out to suburbia and the suburban shopping centers; central Geneva was being abandoned to the foreigners. When Iêda and I head into the Place de la Fusterie where we used to have coffee, pastries, and beer at the elegant sidewalk cafes during earlier visits, we discover that this area is all Arab. Headscarves are everywhere; it's mostly Arab women, smoking, drinking, and semi-liberated (including from their husbands) in the open culture of Geneva. Even the restaurants and sidewalk cafes here, we learn, are now owned by Arabs. That also helps account for the greater seediness of the city: Arabs have a different sense of the public space (it's for trash disposal) than did those Calvinistic Genevans.

The issues and situation of religion are also different as compared with our earlier times here. On our first Sunday in Geneva, I had gone out early to reconnoiter the neighborhood and search for a church we might attend. I headed down the Rue de Zurich toward the lake and only two blocks away discovered the Reformed Temple de Paquis, the Calvinist church for our neighborhood. But at 9:00 A.M. the doors are all locked; no one's around; and it's not clear if there's a service today.

Two blocks away is the American Church of Vienna. They're about to begin their service, but only five persons are in attendance. Not exactly a lively gathering, but the church does have a lending library—useful knowledge for future reference. When I ask about Calvinism in Geneva, these otherwise amicable Americans hoot and holler and tell me emphatically that they are not a Calvinist church.

They suggest I attend services at Saint Peter's (it still seems odd to me that the main Calvinist church in Geneva, with all its Roman Catholic connotations, is called Saint Peter's), which, of course, we had done before and again this time. But they also fill me in on the changing religious situation in Geneva. Whereas before the Calvinist Reformed Church had been *the* established church in Vienna and then, in the more pluralist environment of the 1970s, had had to share power and largesse somewhat with Catholics and other religious groups, now the Church was fighting for its life. Attendance was way down; membership was declining; vocations were down; fewer and fewer young people were entering the ministry. In the European context, it all sounded very familiar.

They also tell me that my original leading question—"Is there still a Calvinist tradition in Geneva?"—constitutes "fighting words" for many people here. Historically, the Reformed Church of Geneva had received financial support from both the local and the national governments, but now, as elsewhere in Europe, state support for particular religious entities was under attack and being challenged. It was similar to the U.S. (and also Dutch) debate on church-state relations and the challenges to state support to parochial schools, hospitals, and charitable bodies. The main issues were: should the government continue to subsidize religion and religious institutions, in Geneva specifically the Reformed Church; should this subsidy be curtailed or should other religious bodies get in on the largesse; should the now sizable Muslim community also receive state aid for its mosques and schools; are state funds in support of restoring the Saint Peter's Cathedral aiding a particular religious group or is this a matter of historical preservation? Again, the issues sound very familiar but often with a special Genevan twist.

So back to the hotel I go to pick up Iêda and head off for the Sunday morning service at Saint Peter's. It's *still* in restoration (for thirty years now); only about 150 people are in attendance. Even since we were here last twenty-two years before, the church seems to have declined: fewer attendees, fewer members, less activity, fewer (or dead altogether) groups for women, young people, businessmen, and so on. At the similarly Calvinist Knox Church next door, which starts a half hour later, so we can attend two services consecutively, attendance and activity are similarly way down.

After church(es), we stop for a café au lait and croissant on the Soleil Levant, the square outside the church. Then down the hill from the Cathedral, past the Hotel de Ville (all familiar ramblings for us), down the Ramp de la Treille to the Mural of the Reformation. This is also familiar, but it's good to see it again and it now, since I've studied more of the history, means more to me. For not only are Calvin, Luther, Knox, and Farel all there in their accustomed places, but so are Oliver Cromwell, Frederick the Great, and even István Bocskai from Hungary (see the next chapter) whom I had not noticed or paid attention to on previous visits. There were few people at the monument or in the park in front of it; another sign of growing secularism in Geneva.

The next day I went out to my old research terrain at the ILO. Once again, I was given an office with a view, the library and research staff put at my disposal, and treated royally in those subsidized dining rooms—except by now the price had gone up slightly. But the ILO had changed drastically in the twenty years since I'd worked there before. Earlier the theme—and the reason for the ILO's existence—had been workers' rights: the right to assemble, organize, form unions, etc. Most of us could sympathize with that. But now the main agenda was "decent work." As distinct from the earlier "workers' rights," "decent work" was seen as an entitlement, implying guaranteed employment and income opportunities, universal social protection (health, housing, education, welfare), and obligatory dialogue and power-sharing between workers and employers. A Chilean socialist, Juan Sornavilla, was now the director of the ILO and the chief architect of the new policy.

I was told by my friends at the ILO that this new focus represented the triumph of the Third World over the First, of South over North, poor countries over rich ones. And if ever implemented, the program was truly breathtaking in scope: a formula for universal socialism for which you-know-who ("rich" Americans) would pay. Yet so far as I know, this potentially ground-shaking transformation has received no attention whatsoever in the United States, in large part because the United States pulled out of the ILO over a political dispute in the 1970s and is not aware of what's going on there. If I had more space, I'd love to write more about this topic; but this is a book about the Dutch and the Dutch Diaspora and not about the ILO or labor politics.

Actually, what has occurred at the ILO is a reflection of what has also occurred at the UN in New York and at the UN's many other subsidiary organizations in Geneva. And that is the UN-bureaucratic triumph of the numerous Third World countries over the First World ones, of the poor (and darker) nations over the wealthy, white ones, and of notions of universal socialism for which the "rich" (people like you and I) will pay. Unfortunately, Geneva is the place in Europe where that triumph is most visible. That means that the once-beautiful Geneva is becoming more and more like an American city where the whites are moving to the suburbs; they come into the downtown or the UN complex only to work; and the inner city is increasingly left to the poor, darker, immigrant elements.

Yet strolling in Geneva can still be a pleasure. Every afternoon at 4:00 or 5:00, Iêda and I would walk down to the lake. Some of the blocks we passed through were not, as described above, the best, but the lake was still beautiful; the views of the mountains are magnificent; the fountain still spouts; and the sailboats still glide gracefully offshore. We'd then stroll over the bridge to the old city wall at Rue Purgatory (a Catholic, pre-Reformation name), then along the Rue Rive/Croix d'Or, or Rue du Rhone—still very pleasant. But at the now Arab-owned Mövenpick restaurant and café where we stop for strudel and ice cream, the clientele is 80 percent Arab.

Back at work at the ILO the next day, my friend and host Clair Schenker, who's lived in Geneva for over twenty years, tells me she never goes into central Geneva anymore. There's too much traffic, not enough parking, and it's not as clean as before. She tells me the ex-pat international community like herself now lives in the self-sufficient suburbs; they have their own schools, banks, post offices, and shopping malls. She says there's no reason for her to go downtown. Privately, she tells me she just doesn't feel comfortable in the city center anymore with all the dirt, grime, and (poor, dark, foreign) people on the street.

Another day Iêda and I devoted to museums. I had seen most of these before, but she hadn't. The Rousseau Museum contains details of his family tree, where he lived, and editions of all his works. Rousseau wrote broadly on music, law, religion, and politics, but he's best known for his small book, *The Social Contrast*. Rousseau was an apostle of direct, intimate, participatory democracy; in a small, educated, intimate, sophisticated city like Geneva where everyone knows everyone else, it is easy to see why Rousseau would be an advocate for this kind of democracy. You could run the Genevan canton as a small city-state; as in a small New England town meeting, everyone can participate. But even in Amherst, Massachusetts, my base of operations, a city of only 20,000, we have moved to a system of representative town meeting—I was an elected member for some ten years. Unfortunately, direct democracy isn't feasible in a polity that reaches a certain size.

The Reformation Museum is in the same building complex. It's a small museum; we were the only ones there. It traces the history of the Reformation but provides no context: why these reformers wanted to change the Catholic Church and why it needed to be changed. Actually, most of them didn't want a break; they only wanted to reform the Church from within. But when their reform effort fell on deaf ears, they concluded they had no choice but to break the tie. The Catholic response was brutal: hundreds of thousands were persecuted and tens of thousands were killed. Yet when Calvin condones the burning of only one person, Servetus, he is roundly criticized. Is that because, employing a double standard, we expect more from Protestants and especially Calvinists?

The exhibit mainly concentrates on the Reformation in Geneva. It has some of the sixteenth-century Bibles printed here, the original writings of Calvin and other Reformation leaders, and a display on how the Reformed faith spread like wildfire in The Netherlands and Hungary. It talks about the spread of Calvinism into Italy and Spain, two historically Catholic countries where the Reformation made little headway and was quickly snuffed out. Another display focuses on the Counter-Reformation and goes into detail on the persecution, torture, deaths, and human rights abuses caused by the Catholic Church. It pictures Frederick the Great of Prussia and the Dutch House of Orange as "friends of the Reformation" while portraying Mary Tudor ("Bloody Mary") of England, Charles V and Philip II of Spain, Henry IV of France, the Duke of Savoy (Geneva's former overlord), and the Austrian Hapsburgs as its "enemies." This is not a display that's very even-handed or PC; perhaps it's not been discovered yet by the thought police.

We also spent time in the Geneva Arts and History Museum. It traces the history of Geneva from prehistoric through Greek, Roman, medieval, and modern times. Julius Caesar came here and camped on the bank where Lake Geneva flows into the Rhone. The display on the Middle Ages tells how

Swiss mercenaries in this long-time neutral country came to serve in many of the world's armies, including the Swiss guards used by the Vatican. The museum has a nice collection of handmade furniture, while the painting collection upstairs has a Rembrandt painting of his mother and a masterpiece (in terms of the facial expression) of an old woman reading her Bible. The museum passes lightly over the Reformation (that's in the Reformation Museum), but it does have an entire roomful (a surprise!) of my favorite painting style—impressionism: two Renoirs, four or five Sisleys, two Pissaros, two Van Goghs, three or four Cézannes, three Monets. One of the Monets is absolutely gorgeous, full of hanging gardens and flowers, lovely red colors, maybe the nicest Monet I've ever seen.

Wrapping Up

Our trip was winding down. I finished my work at the ILO. My research work there was concentrated on updating my information and materials on corporatism and comparative labor relations, especially now in Eastern as well as Southern Europe, but I became so fascinated by the revolutionary shift in focus there—the "decent work" theme—that I determined to further explore and write about it. I collected a lot of printed materials bearing on this issue and did interviews about it with ILO staff. As expected, I found no one in the United States especially at high political levels, who was paying attention to what was going on within the ILO.

My research on Calvin and Calvinism in Geneva had also gone well. Remember, this was always a sidebar to my main research topic of comparative labor relations; it was never my intention to become a Calvin or Calvinism specialist. Rather, I'm just a layman who's interested in his roots. And without necessarily planning it that way, one who initially stumbled into this project largely by accident through my research and travel in places where Calvinism and/or the Dutch influence were strong: Western Michigan, Brazil, Hungary, Curaçao, Suriname, South Africa, East Asia, Indonesia, and The Netherlands itself. While the project began mainly as curiosity, it took on more serious, scholarly, and comparative dimensions during that incredible sabbatical leave year of 2001 when we visited so many of these Dutch-fragment places and countries in Africa, Asia, Europe, and Latin America.

We came away from Geneva with mixed feelings. In terms of the present project, Geneva was wonderful. It has this history as the cradle of the Reformation, especially its Calvinist branch. In this context, Geneva and its history are fascinating to me. While Geneva has also experienced rising secularism and growing indifference to religion, that is not all that different from the rest of Europe; through my interviews and by visiting the churches, I discovered that there are all kinds of religious undercurrents, family and clan networks, webs of religiously based civil society organizations, political and sectarian or "tribal" rivalries that are often religious in their underpinnings, that go back to the sixteenth century—or earlier, and that still influence present-day Genevan politics. If I were a specialist in Genevan history or Swiss politics, I would love to have the opportunity to explore all these themes further.

Our feelings about Geneva are more mixed. We had that horrible initial food-poisoning experience in 1972–1973. But then in 1979–1980, when we visited the city for a longer period and I lived there for a time, I began to comprehend the many layers and inner sanctums of Genevan social, religious, and political life. I came to love the city, to understand some of its complex undercurrents, and to feel at home there. It was still, in many ways, a Calvinist and a Protestant city, and a very elegant and beautiful one, but much more complex than before and forced to accommodate to a pluralism of religious and political positions. Geneva vaulted to, or near, the top of our list of favorite cities.

The present situation is more complicated. Like every place surveyed in this book, Geneva is less religious and less Calvinistic than it used to be. At the same time, it is very difficult for an outsider and a foreigner like me to penetrate and understand all its layers of complexity in a rapidly changing social environment. Geneva, while still retaining much from the past, is now less Calvinist, less Protestant, more diverse, more pluralistic, more multicultural, and more multiethnic than it once was. It is also dirtier, shabbier, less elegant than it used to be. That means it is less attractive to us, and it has fallen several notches—to seventh or eighth—in our list of favorite cities. But it remains a fascinating city, one I'd be happy to go back to, but no longer where I'd want to retire to or spend the rest of my life.

Notes

1. Perhaps the differences over these issues are generational and have to do with changing consciousnesses. My father, when asked about Servetus, said, "He got what he deserved." Our generation would probably see it differently.

2. William J. Bouwsma, *John Calvin: A Sixteenth Century Portrait* (New York: Oxford University Press, 1988).

3. In this book our emphasis has been on the social, political, and cultural impact of Calvin and The Netherlands; we have not made any judgments about the truthfulness and validity of Calvin's religious views. We are interested here in the sociology

and politics of religion, not in religion per se. And if pressed to declare whether I am myself a "Calvinist" or not, I would still have to defer. I have always admired Calvin's logic, his clear thinking, his powerful arguments, and his elegant writing style, but I also have doubts about and problems with a number of his doctrines, such as predestination. At the same time, I know that, whether I wish it or not, I am a product of a certain Calvinist culture, belief system, and upbringing that I cannot escape, and am not certain I would want to.

4. Howard J. Wiarda, *Corporatism and Development: The Portuguese Experience* (Amherst: University of Massachusetts Press, 1977).

5. Howard J. Wiarda, *From Corporatism to Neo-syndicalism: the state, organized labor, and the changing industrial relations system of southern Europe* (Cambridge: Center for European Studies Harvard University, 1981).

CHAPTER TWELVE

Struggling to Survive: The Reformed Tradition in Austro-Hungary

Almost all readers of this book will know that the Dutch in The Netherlands and the Dutch colonies in the various parts of the world explored here are heirs, and often disciples, of that particular lineage of the Reformation that began in Calvin's Geneva of the 1530s. There were in the end two main branches of the Reformation: the German/Scandinavian branch (Lutheranism) and the Swiss/Dutch/French (until 1688) branch (Calvinism). Calvinism had been born in Geneva; but by the mid-sixteenth century, it had enveloped much of The Netherlands as well and eventually became the official state religion.

While we know a great deal about the spread of Calvinism to the north, into Holland and the Low Countries, we know far less about its spread to the east, to Bavaria (today, the Czech Republic), Austria, Hungary, Slovakia, and all the way to Romania (Transylvania) and the western provinces of the Ukraine. Together, all these countries and areas were once part of the great, Central European, Austro-Hungarian Empire. I attribute this lack of knowledge about the east to the fact that in school we mainly study Western European history (Great Britain, France, Germany) and pay insufficient attention to the East. For example, when I studied European history in college, I remember studying the Reformation and the Counter-Reformation (which failed to roll back the tide of Protestantism in the North but succeeded in the East); however, in our emphasis on Western European history, I learned little of the context: how much of the East was converted to Protestantism, which countries, how the Counter-Revolution accomplished its goals, and what was the fate of the Protestant and Calvinist communities of the East after the Counter-Reformation succeeded.

It was only when I began a project on Eastern European transitions to democracy and the integration of the Eastern countries into NATO and the European Union (EU) that I began seriously to study Eastern European history and that of the great Austro-Hungarian empire. I learned that by the 1580s–1590s, the same period in which The Netherlands went over definitively to Calvinism, Bavaria, Austria, Slovakia, Hungary, Transylvania—all the countries of the Austro-Hungarian empire—had similarly been converted to Protestantism, including (and especially, depending on the region) its Calvinist form. Seventy to 80 percent, the same percentage as in The Netherlands, had, by the end of the sixteenth century, become Protestant.

But then came the Counter-Reformation of the seventeenth century. Not only did the Roman Catholic Church restore Catholicism and almost entirely snuff out Protestantism in the East, by both its restorative missionary activities and its repression and wholesale torture (it is a horrible story of massive human rights violations and even genocide); but by doing so it also eliminated the most progressive, modernizing people in the East, condemning the area to centuries of backwardness, poverty, and lack of democratization. The connection perceived by Max Weber between Protestantism and capitalism and progress never had a chance to develop in the East as it did in the West, particularly in progressive Holland. Instead, Eastern Europe sank back into feudalism, underdevelopment, isolation from the modernizing mainstreams of the West, and the Middle Ages. Much later in the twentieth century, when first fascism and then communism ruled this area, both Protestantism and progress were snuffed out even further.

Hence, when I lived in Vienna and then Budapest in 2001 and traveled widely throughout Eastern Europe over the last two decades, I became fascinated with this history and determined to explore it for myself. How could a country, really a group of countries, go from being 70 to 80 percent Protestant to, through persecution, a situation where Protestantism was all but eliminated? And what of those brave, struggling, isolated communities that managed to hang onto their Protestantism and their Calvinism?

Obviously, this is a new variation on the fragments thesis. For the countries of the old Austro-Hungarian empire were not fragments or colonies of the European colonial powers the way South Africa or Indonesia were; they were part of Europe itself. They did not struggle in some God-forsaken wilderness far from nearby shores; their "wilderness" was right at home. And while these countries are obviously not Dutch, they do present us in a related way with many of the same issues that the other fragments do: how to maintain one's religion in the face of poverty and persecution. Moreover, in carrying out my research, I discovered that at various points in the story there *are* some fascinating Dutch connections.

The History

Luther nailed his famous theses critiquing the abuses of the Roman Catholic Church to the door of the church at Wittenberg, Germany, in 1517, thus launching the Protestant Reformation. Two decades later from his base in Geneva, Calvin gave the Reformation a much more learned, organized, disciplined, and scholarly basis through the publication of the first of the many editions of his *Institutes of the Christian Religion.*

The new Reformation doctrines spread rapidly—almost like wildfire—both to the North (The Netherlands) and to the East (the Austro-Hungarian empire). Indeed, within the very decades that both Luther and Calvin taught and wrote, their ideas were being diffused widely throughout both these areas.

Since this was an era of still quite primitive communications and transportation, it is somewhat surprising that the Reformation beliefs spread so fast. In my research, I was able to confirm at least four causes for the Reformation's rapid diffusion to the east even in the face of great logistics difficulties. The first was German merchants and traders who carried Luther's ideas into the lands to the east (today's Czech Republic, Slovakia, and Austria) where, at least in the Czech lands, they found a particularly receptive audience because of John Hus's similar critique of Catholic abuses a century earlier. The second cause was the large number of East European students who went to study in Switzerland during this period and then brought the ideas of the Reformation back to their home countries. For example, at one point during the height of the Reformation, Hungary alone had over 1,000 students studying in either Calvin's Geneva, Zwingli's Zurich, or equally Calvinist Basel. The vast majority of these were studying for the ministry and became Protestant/Calvinist pastors, spreading Reformist ideas throughout their own country.

A third cause for the Reformation's rapid spread was Dutch pastoral zeal. The Netherlands, like Eastern Europe, had sent many of its best and brightest students to Geneva. Most of these returned home immediately after their studies, but a surprising number took time out to travel to the East, preach and proselytize there, and then return to Holland. Finally, there is the invention of the printing press. The system of movable type, invented close to the same time as the Reformation itself, enabled printers to mass-produce copies of the Bible or of Calvin's or Luther's voluminous writings and spread them all over the country, as distinct from the older system of solitary scribes writing out in longhand a single copy at a time of these works. Without the printing press, the Reformation would never have become so widespread as it did with such a wide mass appeal. As the popular aphorism puts it, "No printing, no Reformation."

With the base that the reformer Hus had initiated in the fifteenth century, the Reformation spread quickly in the Czech lands of Bohemia and Moravia. Slovakia was one of the main battlefields between Catholics and Protestants—to say nothing of Turks, Magyars, and other invaders—but at several points it was upward of 70 percent Protestant, including both Lutherans and Calvinists. Even Austria, the most Catholic country in Eastern Europe at this time, the home of the Catholic Hapsburg monarchy, and the center of the Austro-Hungarian empire, was at one point between 60 and 70 percent Protestant. But Austria would also become the center of the Catholic Counter-Reformation.

The Protestant doctrines were widely welcomed by the people living in the areas under Hapsburg domination. By the middle of the sixteenth century, the majority of inhabitants had been converted to Protestantism; by the 1580s the number had risen to 70 to 80 percent. Lutherans predominated in the German-speaking lands (Czech Republic, western Slovakia, Austria), except in the Tirol where Anabaptists were strong. Calvinism had a base in Austria and Slovakia, but it was strongest in Hungary and Transylvania, now part of Romania but then an independent country that was ethnically strongly Hungarian.

The issues were not just religious: Catholic versus Protestant. Rather, the religious issue was closely bound up with the emerging nationalisms of the time (German, Slovak, Magyar, Transylvanian), and especially with the Turkish threat emanating from southeastern Europe. The Turks had already captured the Balkans, southern Hungary, parts of Slovakia, and southeastern Austria; in 1583 they were at the gates of Vienna and potentially threatening all of Western Europe. In the midst of Protestantism's spread from the West to the East, Islam was also spreading from East to West. Vienna was the meeting place where Islam and Christendom clashed head-on. Hence, many of the wars ostensibly at this time between Protestants and Catholics were also conflicts involving local, regional, and national princes seeking to rally their forces and using religion to turn back the Turkish onslaught.

The countries/regions that are the most interesting to us here, because they were the most Calvinist, are Hungary and Transylvania. Hungary was a part of the Hapsburg empire, but for 150 years southern and central Hungary were a vassal state occupied by the Turks. The Turks were not interested in converting the Hungarians to Islam, however, only in extracting tribute and using it as a military base of operations.

Hence, the Turks put up no opposition to Hungary's conversion to Protestantism and even encouraged it as a way of dividing along religious lines the larger Austro-Hungarian empire based in Vienna. As a result, the Protestant Reformation, especially in its Calvinist manifestation, took strong root in Hungary. Calvin's writings became well known; the Hungarian pastors trained in Switzerland were particularly active; the Reformation spread quickly and, by the early seventeenth century, almost all the noble families had converted to the Calvinist form of Protestantism. They, in turn, converted their serfs to the new Reformist beliefs.

If anything, Transylvania, with a large Hungarian ethnic presence in its western areas, was even more Calvinist than Hungary. Though an Ottoman vassal state, it functioned for nearly a century-and-a-half as an independent country. Under the enlightened rule of Gábor Bethlen in the early seventeenth century, Transylvania secured its independence from both the Turks and the Austro-Hungarian empire. Bethlen stimulated agriculture, trade, and industry, opened new mines, encouraged the children even of serfs to acquire an education, and sent the country's best students to study in Protestant universities abroad. Protected on the north and east by the Carpathian Mountains, on the south by the Transylvania Alps, and to the west by their Ottoman overlords, Transylvania flourished for a time under Calvinist rule. Today, unfortunately, this area is one of the poorest and least developed areas in Romania, but there is still a considerable Calvinist presence; and in some of the mountainous hill towns, one still finds a form of Calvinism practiced that goes back to the early seventeenth century.

It is not just that Protestantism and Calvinism were identified with nationalism; in the underdeveloped east they were also associated with progress and modernity. Whereas the Catholic Church stood for feudalism, traditionalism, and the Middle Ages, Protestantism meant progress and development. Progress in agriculture, in science, in technology, in commerce—all these were associated with Protestantism, especially with the Calvinist branch. Calvinism meant enlightenment, the Renaissance, a middle class, rationalism, and, not least, greater prosperity. In East/Central Europe a clear division existed between the Catholic areas (poor, backward) and Protestant areas (moving ahead, developing, modernizing). As they converted, the Protestant areas of Eastern Europe seemed to be finally breaking out of their historic torpor and lack of progress, out of the Middle Ages and into the modern world.

But then came the Catholic Counter-Reformation, beginning with the Council of Trent (1545–1563) that determined to confront the Reformation head-on. The Counter-Reformation was strongest in Austria, but it was similarly effective throughout the vast Austro-Hungarian empire. From the Catholic point-of-view, the Counter-Reformation was eminently successful: it succeeded in exactly reversing the religious makeup of the Empire that had prevailed only a few decades earlier. Whereas by 1600 Austro-Hungary was 70 to 80 percent Protestant, by 1700 it had again become 80 percent Catholic. Protestants and Protestantism were on the run—often literally so.

The Catholic Church employed two techniques to recapture its flock and its territory from the Protestants. The first was renewal within the Catholic Church itself. To that end, the Church cleaned up its act, created new orders (such as the Jesuits, who served as the spearheads of the Counter-Reformation), renewed its long-neglected pastoral activities, rooted out corruption, reformed its theology, reformed the clergy, created new Catholic schools and social institutions, recruited new and better priests, and sought to resecure its position with its long-neglected flock. These reforms helped the Church to reestablish its position both with political leaders and the masses.

The other technique employed by the Church was repression, including torture. To accomplish this goal, the Church allied itself with secular authorities, arguing that religious unity under Catholic suzerainty would enable the Hapsburg monarchy better to resist Turkish and other outside challenges. Particularly during the rule of the Hapsburg Ferdinand II (1619–1637), who was also Holy Roman Emperor, the Catholic forces took the offensive. In the Battle of White Mountain (1620) the Catholic armies soundly defeated the Protestants, thus restoring Bohemia to Catholic rule.

In Austria, the center of the Hapsburg Empire, Ferdinand equated Protestantism with disloyalty and implemented a plan to impose religious restrictions throughout the Empire. He converted all the Hapsburg lands into a confessional state: Protestants were given six months to re-convert back to Catholicism or they would be expelled. These tactics were successful in the western parts of the empire (Czech Republic, Slovakia, Austria) but less so in the eastern parts (Hungary, Transylvania) where Protestantism, especially Calvinism, was stronger and was intimately tied up with Hungarian and Transylvanian nationalism and protected by Protestant princes.

The Peace of Westphalia (1648) not only resolved the Thirty Years' War between Protestants and Catholics in the German-speaking lands, but it also was, as every student of international relations knows, a milestone in the development of the doctrine of national sovereignty (recognizing, for instance, the existence and independence of The Netherlands) and of international law. One of the provisions of the treaty gave every prince the right to dictate the religion of the subjects within his territory. In the Austro-Hungarian Empire, that meant the heirs of Ferdinand II, Ferdinand III (1637–1657), and Leopold I (1658–1705) continued the pro-Catholic, anti-Protestant policies of their predecessor. If the reigns of all three of these powerful monarchs are combined, it means almost a full century of anti-Protestant activities until, by the early eighteenth century, Protestantism had been routed and almost completely eliminated from the Hapsburg hereditary lands. And because the Protestants were generally the best educated, most enlightened, and most progressive people in the Empire, their elimination also set back the economic, social, and political development of East/Central Europe by a full century and maybe two.

The repression forced upon Protestants was severe. They were subjected to forced conversions; their lands were seized; they were deprived of all public office; their churches were taken by the authorities; tens of thousands were forced to flee to other countries. Many, especially the pastors, were jailed and subjected to cruel torture: rot and vermin-infested cells, the plague, water torture techniques, the rack (which pulled limbs out of the body), burnings, screws under the fingernails, beatings, floggings, hangings, beheadings, etc. Torture techniques were widely used; in Bratislava in present-day Slovakia there is today a Museum of Torture that is a must visit for anyone interested in the history of Protestantism (or anyone interested in human rights and/or genocide) during this period.

There is even a Dutch connection here—but on the good side. In 1673–1674 an extraordinary judicial hearing was held in Bratislava. Over seven hundred Protestant pastors from all over the Empire, but mainly from Hungary, were ordered to stand trial. They were accused of slandering not only the Catholic Church and the Virgin Mary but the monarchy as well. The latter charge involved treason; the former, heresy. All were convicted. But then they were offered alternatives to the death sentence: conversion to Catholicism, resignation as pastors, or exile.

About a hundred refused these alternatives and accepted their fate as martyrs for Protestantism. They were then led on a death march to Italy where they were condemned to die as galley slaves. But in 1676 a Dutch admiral, Michael De Ruyter, liberated the twenty-four pastors who had survived. The published accounts of their trial and suffering were widely disseminated throughout Europe, arousing sympathy for the Hungarian Protestants and re-inforcing the anti-Catholicism already present in The Netherlands and other Protestant areas. Today, in Debrecen, western Hungary, there is a statue honoring Admiral De Ruyter; I have had my picture taken standing proudly in front of it.

For most of the rest of the eighteenth century, the position and condition of Protestants in the Empire remained precarious. Under Charles VI (1711–1740) and then Maria Theresa (1740--1780), both staunchly Catholic, Protestants were a persecuted minority, reduced to 10 to 20 percent of the population. They had often lost their lands, their homes, their pastors, their churches, and their right to work. The Protestant communities were confined to distant, marginal areas of the Empire: Shopron on the Hungarian-Austrian border (I spent a couple of days there once), Debrecen in western Hungary (the "capital" of Protestantism in Hungary), and Transylvania in eastern Romania where I have also visited.

But eventually Maria Theresa's successor, Joseph II (1780–1790), issued a Decree of Toleration in 1781 that enabled Protestants (as well as Jews and Orthodox Christians) to practice their religion more-or-less freely. But restrictions still remained. Those who have visited Budapest will be struck by the fact that both the Calvinist "Cathedral" (which I attended while living there) and the Jewish synagogue (one of the world's largest) are located just outside the old city walls because Joseph's decree prohibited them from building inside the city. Similarly in Vienna: the Protestant church that I attended there was permitted by Joseph to hold services, but it could not build a steeple on the church, have open windows, a door fronting on the street, or in any other way "advertise" that it was a Protestant church. In this way, the un-enlightened Hapsburgs (the eighteenth century was the age of the Enlightenment, after all) could give the appearance of being enlightened or tolerant, but not give any real freedom, let alone power, to the Protestants.

In the "long" nineteenth century (1789–1917), the position of the Protestant churches within the empire improved only slightly. Moreover, the fate of Protestantism was intimately bound up with rising Hungarian nationalism, as the Hungarians sought repeatedly to establish their independence from Austria, the Hapsburgs, and the Empire—all of which were heavily Catholic.

In my research work and meanderings around the far corners of Austria, Hungary, and the old Austro-Hungarian Empire in 2001–2002, I discovered a quite basic political, religious, and economic split in the Empire's soul that had its basis in these earlier times. On the one side were families like the Esterhásy (whose castle I visited) who were staunchly Catholic, staunchly pro-Hapsburg, anti-Enlightenment, anti-reform, absolutely reactionary, against Hungarian autonomy or independence, and strongly in favor of keeping their peasants uneducated and locked into a feudal landholding and economic system.[1] On the other side were families like the Széchenyis (whose castle I similarly visited) who were Protestant, anti-Hapsburg, rationalist, Enlightenment-oriented, progressive, favored freedom, democracy, and land reform—including for their own serfs—and also believed in autonomy or in-dependence for the various parts of the Empire. You can probably take a wild guess as to whom I favor in this contest. Suffice it to say that the Haps-burgs and their reactionary allies succeeded in keeping the Empire back-ward and semifeudal right through World War I (and even beyond, in the ru-ral areas), whereas the progressives were continuously frustrated. No wonder East/Central Europe was fated to lag way behind while Western Europe forged way ahead.

The fate of Protestantism hardly improved in the twentieth century. First came the Nazi occupation of Austria-Hungary which placed severe restric-tions on Protestant Church activities. Nazism and Fascism were totalitarian ideologies and that meant "total" control over all potentially independent organizations and associations, including the churches. And then, following the Nazi occupation, Eastern Europe was dominated and cowed by the Red (Soviet) Army and its puppet communist regimes. Under both systems, the Protestant churches suffered tremendously. Indeed, one is tempted to lump all three of these—Hapsburgs, Nazis, Communists—together and say all of them were bad for progress, democracy, and the human soul. By the time the Soviet yoke finally collapsed in 1989–1991, the Protestant churches in East-ern Europe were in pretty sad shape.

Personal Travels

In the spring and summer of 2001 I was living in Budapest, Hungary, as a Ful-bright research scholar. I had an affiliation with the Central European Uni-versity (CEU) founded by George Soros and was working on two major re-search projects: one, a study of EU/NATO enlargement into Eastern Europe, and the other, on comparative civil society and democratization in develop-ing nations, with one of the chapters devoted to Eastern Europe. Mine was a research scholarship as distinct from a teaching one; I spent most of my mornings at CEU doing research and writing but, with plenty of time on my hands, I devoted the afternoons to touring museums, interviewing, and learning more about Hungary.

I had, from my background and reading, a vague understanding that Hungary, like Geneva, The Netherlands, and France at one time (the Huguenots), had been a center of Calvinism. But I didn't know the history recounted above well, and I was not even sure if the Reformed tradition in Hungary was still alive, or kicking. Because at that time, I was already think-ing about my "Dutch Diaspora" project and the "fragments" thesis, and had already planned visits to South Africa and Indonesia (both former Dutch colonies) later in the year, I was determined to find out more about the Hungarian case.

The "Kalvin Church"

When I first arrived in Budapest, I started attending the main Evangelical Lutheran Church that was only three short blocks from my apartment. It was a beautiful, if a bit shabby and run down, church, and the people I met there were nice and welcoming; but since the service was all in Hungarian, the best part of the service for me was the music. The church had a wonderful organ, and I attended several evening Bach concerts there.

But one day, in studying my map of Budapest for a new area to explore on my daily walks, I discovered a Kalvin Square. Thinking it might be named after John Calvin, I went to see it. There I discovered, much to my surprise, not only a Hungarian Reformed (Calvinist) Church but also a statue of Calvin on the sidewalk in front of the church. The church was located on the far side of "the Ring," Vamhoz Street, the semicircular street that surrounds central Budapest, where the ancient, medieval city walls used to stand. In keeping with Emperor Joseph II's 1781 Decree of Toleration, the Calvinist Church (along with the Jewish Synagogue) had had to be built outside the city walls. I had a street person take a couple of pictures of me in front of the Calvin statue, thinking that was kind of campy and that I might be able to use them sometime.

Alongside the church is an alleyway and across the alley, a kind of dormitory residence used by the church. There I found a nice young man, a university student, who told me a little of the history of the church and how it had suffered under communism. He informed me that the Sunday service was at 10:00 A.M.; he also told me that this was the second largest Reformed Church in Hungary, the largest being out in Debrecen in Eastern Hungary, the Hungarian (like Grand Rapids) Calvinist "Zion." Although he didn't know much about church history in Hungary, he guided me to a Christian bookstore a couple of blocks away and told me that further down the street was a Reformed Church seminary.

I immediately walked down to the bookstore. There I found mostly religious tracts but also some books on the history of religion in Hungary, even some shorter booklets in English. Continuing down the street, I found the seminary—not a full campus with grassy lawns as you would find in the United States but a complex of buildings in an urban setting with a courtyard in back. The seminary contained classrooms, administrative offices, a dormitory for the students, and a small but fascinating museum on the history, struggles, and persecution of the Reformed Church in Hungary—wonderful for my research.

The building was mostly empty, a bit dingy, and the lighting dim; but I did find one young woman there who proved to be a seminary student. It's interesting, given the heated debate in other Reformed Churches about women exercising ministerial roles, that in Hungary about half the seminarians were women. She told me there were now only forty students in the seminary, that "no one wants to be a pastor any more." She told me that the seminary was having a hard time making ends meet (hence, the dim lights), that church attendance in Hungary was way down from past times, that vocations as well as church finances were in trouble. The church no longer received state support or, if it did, it was so little that it could not make ends meet. Yet she was dedicated to her training, committed to her religion, an all-around bright and nice person. If all Hungarian young people were like her, the country—and the world—would be a much better place.

When I attended the Kalvin Church the next Sunday, the girl's comments were confirmed. It is not at all a wealthy church. The sanctuary was only 20 percent full and almost all the attendees were elderly. There were few young people and almost no young families—clear signs of a dying church. To me, the service seemed old, old-fashioned, tired, and boring. It was like the Christian Reformed Church of Michigan used to be, sixty and more years ago: very stiff and formal. There was no special music; the hymns sung were from ancient hymn books; there appeared to be no special programs for children, young people, or other small groups. There were no greeters, no coffee hour, no hand of friendship. Once again, the contrast with my own Reformed Church in the United States, which is lively, vigorous, and with-it, was striking.

After the service I had the opportunity to speak with the minister and several of the elders. They all portrayed a church that had long been persecuted: first, by the Counter-Reformation; then, by the Hapsburgs; more recently, by the Nazis and then the Communists. Because Hungary is a poor country, the church could not be sustained by its members alone. But state support was meager and, under the influence of church-state separation issues emanating from abroad, might be cut off altogether. Yet I saw no sign that the Hungarian church was receiving assistance from other Reformed denominations in the United States or elsewhere. The overall picture was one of a fading church, like so many others in Europe, unable or unwilling to modernize on its own and gradually being overcome by the forces of poverty, secularism, and indifference.

I did continue during my time in Budapest to attend the church more-or-less regularly, however, out of a combined sense of loyalty, compassion, and solidarity. I'm sure I, as a "rich American," put more in the collection plate on Sundays than anyone else in the church, maybe more than the rest of the congregation combined. I also learned through my friends in the church that there was a Hungarian Reformed Church in Detroit, Michigan, among the Hungarian ethnic community there, but so far I have not been able to visit that church. Through my regular attendance at the Budapest Kalvin Church, I also learned that there were a couple of Americans of Hungarian descent temporarily living and working in the city who also attended and, through them, we were able to bridge the language and cultural barriers.

My best friend in the church was Zoltan Mester, a Hungarian by birth, forced abroad through his participation as a young person in the 1956 uprising against the Soviets, and now a U.S. citizen living in California where he has his own consulting company. He had a chemistry background and his consulting company dealt, profitably, with chemical damage to the environment. Zoltan was in Budapest to visit his aged mother and to attend an international conference on chemistry. He and I had lunch together; I gave him a tour of the Central European University; and we stayed in touch. Ours was an interesting relationship: two émigré families, mine and his, one Dutch and the other Hungarian, both of us coming out of quite distinctive Reformed traditions, both of our families finding their way to America, both succeeding in America's open and mobile society, and yet here we both were in Budapest attending the same Reformed church. Amazing!

Shopron

One of the things the Fulbright Program in Budapest did for us visiting Fulbrighters was to organize tours to different parts of the country. In my first weeks living here, the Program organized a bus tour to western Hungary, through some of the most historic parts of the country (the Hungarian nation was born here), out to Shopron on the Austrian border.

Shopron was founded in the thirteenth century. It is Hungary's most beautiful medieval town. Somehow, the Turks bypassed the city on their bloody and plundering march to Vienna. It is shaped like a horseshoe with a beautiful park and castle in the middle. Just outside of town is the place where the Iron Curtain first was breached in 1989 when groups of East German tourists were allowed through the barbed-wire fence into Austria and from there into what was then West Germany, without the Hungarian border guards mowing them down. It is a very pleasant city and, interesting for our purposes, a Protestant city—both Lutheran and Reformed—one of the few predominantly Protestant cities in all of Hungary.

We spent the night in Shopron at the Hotel Palatinus, had a wonderful dinner there, and then a late evening walking tour of the town, finally ending up in a downtown tavern, the Overbys, for a carafe of wine and conversation with my Fulbright colleagues. From them I learned more about the history of Hungarian Calvinism. First, that the Calvinists had been persecuted so long that many of them developed a siege mentality. Even today, because of that, many of them hide their religion from the outside world. Second, that 80 percent of the population had been Reformed, now it was about 20 percent and dwindling, mainly due no longer to persecution but to generational changes, rising secularism, and popular indifference. And third, that during the decade and even centuries of persecution, the Hungarian Calvinists had had to band together in walled cities like Shopron or Debrecen in the east which I would visit on another trip.

Along with our stay in Shopron, the most interesting part of our trip to western Hungary to me was our visit to the castles and estates of the Esterházy family, on the one hand, and the Széchenyi family, on the other. For, as indicated, these two great families came to symbolize the two main directions open to Hungary in the late eighteenth century and throughout the nineteenth century, and the reason Hungarian development, like that of Spain, failed to keep pace with development and modernization in the rest of Europe.

The Esterházys symbolized Catholic and reactionary Hungary. They were traditionalists, tied to the *ancien regime*, to the monarchy, to reaction, to the Counter-Reformation, to the Hapsburgs, to the elites and the existing social order, to the authoritarian, hierarchical world that existed before the French Revolution. They were against social change, against the Enlightenment, against progress and rationality, against Protestantism, and against modernity. They stood opposed to everything that most of the rest of us are for.

Whereas the Széchenyis were our kind of people. First of all, they were Protestants, Calvinists. They stood for reform, modernization, and education, even for their own peasants. They were progressives, of the Enlightenment. They opposed Catholic, Austrian, and Hapsburg hegemony, favoring autonomy, independence, and self-determination for Hungary. The Széchenyi clan wanted to lift Hungary up to European standards, to introduce rationalism and science; it was they who helped lead the Hungarian independence movements of the mid-nineteenth century that led to a greater sharing of power between Vienna and Budapest. It should be clear by now which side I am on in this debate.

But it is also clear that the division between these two paradigms, the Catholic, reactionary, imperial paradigm of the Esterházys and the Protestant, progressive, self-determination paradigm of the Széchenyis, tore Hungary apart during the nineteenth century. In fact, this division went back as far as the Hungarian Protestant Reformation of the sixteenth century, which means the split lasted for some four centuries—and more. This divide in the Hungarian soul and nation and the centuries-long and virtually constant division and civil war which it produced held Hungary back, prevented it from developing, and fated it to lag way behind the rest of Europe. And just about the time Hungary was finally breaking out of these vicious circles of poverty, civil war, and underdevelopment in the early twentieth century, along came two world wars and occupations, the Nazi regime and the Soviet occupation to retard development even more.

In thinking about the Hungarian experience in these regards, the parallel that I would draw is with Spain.[2] For here, too, we have an immensely talented and energetic people whose aspirations for modernity and progress were frustrated by a reactionary, backward-looking, Counter-Reformationary regime and elite that tore the country apart and produced civil war. It is probably no coincidence that both these non-progressive and stand-pat kingdoms, Spain and Austria-Hungary, were governed by branches of the Catholic Hapsburgs. In both cases, the reining Hapsburg royal families[3] held back change, frustrated development, and kept their kingdoms from taking their place among the developed, modern countries of Europe, instead confining them to Third World status. Here we have the principal reasons why these two great peripheral areas of Europe, South and East, not only remained peripheral but also lagged behind the core and modern area of Europe in Great Britain, The Netherlands, and Germany.[4]

Debrecen

Even before going to Debrecen in eastern Hungary, I'd heard a lot about it, mainly from some of my fellow Fulbrighters who had lived there. That it was the "capital" of the east, that it was the Protestant "Zion," that as a Calvinist mecca it was a kind of pilgrimage destination for many Dutch Calvinists. That in the tradition of the Protestant Széchenyis it was more progressive, nationalistic, business-oriented than the rest of Hungary. That it was clean, even spotless like a Dutch town. That it had not one but many Reformed or Calvinist churches. That it had a Calvinist high school, university, and seminary. That Dutch missionaries and theologians had often come to Debrecen in earlier times. Frankly, it sounded like Grand Rapids or maybe Pella, Iowa, or other Dutch, Calvinist enclaves.

I took the train out to Debrecen to spend the weekend. I wanted to go on the weekend so I could attend Sunday church services. It's about 200 kilometers or 125 miles from Budapest. It's located in the Hungarian "Great Plain," a flat, farming area just before you get to the Carpathian Mountains leading into Transylvania.

Alighting from the train, you have to walk the length of the main street to find the Protestant center. The first church I encounter is on that main street, Piac Utca. The door is open even on a Saturday so I go in. It seats about six hundred. The layout is unusual: the organ is in front where most churches have their pulpits; the pulpit is one-third back and on the side of the church, while a long balcony runs the complete length of the church on the other side. When I attend the 10:00 service in this church the next day, it's only about a quarter full. If this is Zion, I think to myself, it's got a ways to go.

The minister is very pleasant and welcomes me to his church. He speaks some broken English. As "souvenirs" he gives me a picture album of all the Reformed churches in the area, a history (in Hungarian) of Reformism in Hungary, and a bookmark with the church's picture. While the service is on (mostly elderly people again), the choir director looks to me like the most with-it person in the congregation; and I guess, correctly, that she speaks English. So after the service I introduce myself to her; and she, in turn, introduces me to her husband who's studying nuclear medicine. I assume that must be in Budapest but, no, Debrecen has its own medical school. Between the choir director and her husband, I learn a lot about Debrecen and the Reformed institutions here—all of which (churches, schools, seminary) seem to be having a hard time sustaining their membership, finances, and program.

The next stop was the great Calvinist Cathedral (the "Yellow Church") on the main Kalvin Square, a block farther down. This is the main Reformed Church of Debrecen, a large and imposing structure with twin towers. I'm so used to living in Catholic countries (Latin America, Iberia) that, when I find a Protestant and even Calvinist church on and dominating the main square, I'm a little disoriented. As far back as the twelfth century, there was a Catholic church on this spot; during the Reformation it was converted to Protestant use. The present structure dates to the early nineteenth century and is in the Imperial style with fancy latticework, a handsome inlaid pulpit, and hand-crafted pews. It is *the* principal Reformed church in all of Hungary and *the* center of the Hungarian Protestant Reformation. A visit here is a moving experience.

In 1849 the Hungarian Parliament, which had been forced to flee Budapest by invading Hapsburgian armies, convened in this church to depose the Hapsburgs and declare Hungarian independence. The declaration was read by Lajos Kossuth, the legendary independence leader, and most of the delegates came out of the progressive, nationalist, Hungarian Protestant movement—like my "friends," the Széchenyis. Protestantism, progressivism, and national independence—in Hungary they all go together and are identified with this church. It is out of this movement for independence that it became the Austro-Hungarian empire.

The Protestant "Cathedral" has the second largest organ in Hungary and is famous for its organ concerts. It's also famous for its bell tower (up the rickety stairs which I climbed—no Occupational Safety and Health Administration rules here) that pealed at the declaration of independence and can be heard even in neighboring towns. It's a very imposing church on the inside; because it's also a historical site, you pay (30 cents) to go in and another 30 cents to climb to the bell tower.

Around the corner from the Great Church is the Ferenz Deri Museum, a gem of a small museum containing much history and lore about the area. Nearby is the Reformed college and seminary which trains young people in theology and prepares them for the ministry but, as in the Budapest seminary I visited, the number of seminarians is down and the institution is having a hard time maintaining itself. Around the corner and down the side street is another Reformed church which I now recognize from the picture albums I was given; built of red brick, it looks remarkably like the Burton Heights Christian Reformed Church that I attended as a youth. Calvinist or Reformed churches are as thick here as in Grand Rapids!

But the most interesting part of the trip to Debrecen for me was discovering the famous statue of Dutch sea captain Michael De Ruyter in the park behind the Great Church. Remember, he's the admiral who, back in the seventeenth century, saved the Protestant pastors condemned by the Counter-Reformation from certain death as galley slaves. And there's the statues, on its pedestal, with a commemorative marker! People in the Great Church told me that "all" the Dutch tourists come here to have their pictures taken in front of the De Ruyter statue. I had mine taken, too, thinking it might be useful to include it in my book on "the Dutch Diaspora."

Debrecen is so obviously a Protestant town. Compared to other Hungarian cities, it's cleaner, more orderly, calmer, more traditional, honest. Unlike other Hungarian cities, there's no wastepaper or cigarette butts (or worse!) on the streets; people obey the traffic signals. There's no jay-walking or slovenliness. I don't want to overdo this, but Debrecen to me has the feel of a Weberian city: Protestant, self-reliant, individualistic, Calvinist, capitalistic. It chafed under communist rule just as it had for centuries under the Hapsburgs.

It's funny: even though I had never been to Debrecen before and can only barely understand and speak the language, I feel "at home" here in ways that I do not in other places, feel a brotherhood here; these good people are also my people. Somehow, though obviously not literally, I feel I have roots here. Going to Debrecen for me is like going on a pilgrimage.

However, there are major differences as well. Although my immigrant grandparents experienced hardship and privation, they were never persecuted for their religious beliefs as these poor Hungarian Protestants were. Another major difference is that Hungary was always so much poorer than either The Netherlands or Western Michigan. Their standard of living is about one-tenth that of The Netherlands or the United States. The poverty of Hungary is reflected not just in the country's underdevelopment but in the poverty, lack of infrastructure, and inadequate resources of its religious institutions as well.

Conclusion

The Hungarian research experience was invaluable for me. This was the first time I'd actually lived in the former communist East Europe. I learned a lot, had a marvelous time, made many good friends despite the language barrier, and made good progress in my research and writing on EU/NATO enlargement and comparative civil society.

My explorations and research on the Hungarian Reformed or Calvinist Church were really a sidelight to these other research projects. Nevertheless, I learned a lot about the Reformed tradition in Hungary that also gave me insights on Hungarian history, politics, and sociology.

First, I hadn't realized that Hungary as well as neighboring Transylvania (also ethnically Hungarian; if you continue the train ride east from Debrecen, you shortly arrive in Transylvania) were at one point 80 percent Protestant. That's an astounding percentage. But then it was all reversed, often bloodily, by the Counter-Reformation.

Second, very much unlike The Netherlands or my own experience growing up in Western Michigan, the history of the Reformed Church in Hungary is one of almost continuous persecution: the Counter-Reformation, the Hapsburgs, the Catholic Church, the Turks, the Nazis, the Communists. At times, because of the continuous persecution, the Hungarian church has barely survived; its history is one of continuous struggle against strong odds—something that I in my religious past or my cousins in The Netherlands never experienced. Even today in the tired and worn faces and stories of the congregants and the deteriorating condition of their churches and facilities, one can detect the discouragement that comes from this long history of persecution. There is a strong siege mentality.

Third, it is striking how in Hungary the Reformed Church was for so long associated with progress, rationalism, the Enlightenment, reform, the entrepreneurial spirit, and national independence. In modern-day Hungary that association is now fading, but in my travels and experiences in the various worlds the Dutch created (including The Netherlands itself) I have detected many of the same associations that I found in Hungary between progress, development, nationalism, and the Calvinist ethic.

In terms of the main themes of this book, Hungary is obviously not a Dutch enclave (although at different historical stages, we have seen, there were interesting connections between The Netherlands and Hungary), nor can it be considered a "fragment" of Dutch civilization and culture. But it is in a sense a fragment of Calvin's Geneva, and that also raises interesting issues.

Reading this chapter, it is clear that I identified with the Reformed Church of Hungary. I felt a certain pull here, a sense of common roots. There are many things in the Calvinist tradition of Hungary that I could identify with: the rationalism, the rigorous logic, the individualism and entrepreneurship, the sense of standing for progress and modernization. In many respects, despite the language and cultural barriers, I felt close to home here.

But there are big differences as well. The biggest and most obvious to me were: (1) the long history of persecution of the Hungarian Reformed Church which neither I nor my Dutch cousins ever really experienced, and (2) the low level of economic development of Hungary compared to The Netherlands or Western Michigan. Hungary is at about 10 percent of the per capita income of the United States or Holland. That makes it closer to the level of Suriname or South Africa. But while developmentally Hungary is closer to these other two, ethnically, sociologically, and in terms of its European location there are important differences as well.

All of which points to future, fascinating research projects. First, although Hungary was never a Dutch colony or a fragment of Dutch civilization, its history did run parallel to that of The Netherlands. Both countries converted to Protestantism in the sixteenth century; after that, they diverged. The Netherlands under its Calvinism prospered and became one of the world's leading nations, whereas in Hungary the Calvinists were persecuted and the country remained woefully underdeveloped. A wonderful study could be done comparing Holland and Hungary in these regards.

Second, it would be fascinating to compare Hungary's struggling Reformed church with similarly struggling or even disappearing Reformed churches in Curaçao, Suriname, South Africa, or Indonesia. There are obviously large sociological differences between all these countries. But what would be interesting is to study not how a church thrives among prosperity and affluence as in the United States or The Netherlands, but how a church in the Third World struggles to survive among poverty, hostility, and underdevelopment. That, too, would be a fascinating subject for research.

Notes

1. Music lovers will know that the composer Josef Haydn was similarly kept in semi-bondage by the Esterházys. Haydn was their court musician; he was obliged to compose new and original music *every day* by his masters. One can easily imagine a situation, not unlike that of a Charles Dickens novel, in which, if Haydn did not compose fast enough or to his masters' liking, he would not earn his meal for that day.

2. Howard J. Wiarda and Margaret MacLeish Mott, *Catholic Roots and Democratic Flowers: Politics in Spain and Portugal* (Westport, CT: Greenwood Press, 2000).

3. The Hapsburg monarchy in Spain died out in 1700; it was replaced by the equally authoritarian Bourbon dynasty. The Austrian Hapsburgs, healthier and less in-bred, continued to rule until 1918.

4. Howard J. Wiarda, ed., *European Politics in the Age of Globalization* (Fort Worth: Harcourt College Publishers, 2001), Introduction.

CHAPTER THIRTEEN

Conclusion: The Dutch Diaspora in Its One and Many Parts

This book is both a serious study of The Netherlands and its various colonies and "fragments" throughout the world, and as a personal voyage of discovery of my own roots, origins, and background. At one level, it is a scholarly analysis, from a comparative perspective, of how and why such former Dutch colonies and settlements as Indonesia, South Africa, Suriname, Curaçao, to say nothing of the United States, or parts thereof, went in the directions they did, developed as they did, or, alternatively, remained locked in place in the century in which they were founded. At another level, this is an effort to try to understand why the Dutch (me) are as they are, what unites as well as divides them in different parts of the world, what explains why the Dutch in Western Michigan (my ancestors) are so different from the Dutch in The Netherlands and in other historically Dutch enclaves such as South Africa, Indonesia, or New Amsterdam/New York.

Travels and Adventures

In an effort to trace my Dutch roots, as well as the various branches that grew from them, I have traveled and done research in all these areas. As indicated, I am a product of the Dutch community in Western Michigan where I grew up. As a small child, as well as later in life, we traveled to New York where my father taught me about the Dutch origins of New Amsterdam; en route we journeyed up and down the Hudson River (named for an explorer in The Netherlands' service), on both sides, and then across from Albany to Buffalo exploring the various Dutch-named cities along the route—Rensselaer, Schenectady, and others.

As a young (thirty-two) scholar living and writing a book about Portugal in 1972–1973, I traveled to Geneva for the first time and saw first-hand where John Calvin had preached, lived, and did his most important writing; and where I soon after discovered an entire Protestant and Calvinist network of churches, families, and social and political associations (civil society) that was especially intriguing because, although French-speaking, it was very similar to the one I grew up with in Grand Rapids.

Traveling to The Netherlands for the first time that same year was a similar eye-opener: I discovered that I had real, live relatives there, a family history and origins (since my immigrant grandfather had been an orphan, the discovery of a family and family history was a revelation), and a geography and location from which the Wiardas emerged. My perceptive wife Iêda on this first trip was amazed (or perhaps consternated) to discover other people there—indeed, an entire province, Friesland, full of them—who were similar to her husband: tall, thin, blond, ruddy-faced, stiff-necked, big-footed, hard-headed, stubborn. And even though most of the people we met were no longer Calvinist in their beliefs in any strict sense, they still had this powerful sense of calling, mission, accomplishment as well as guilt over failure that is distinctively Calvinist.

Over the next two decades we visited The Netherlands on several occasions but only as tourists. We also worked and lived in Geneva on several occasions, growing to love that city and elevating it to one of our favorite places. Even during this period, I had in the back of my mind that some day I would go back to Geneva or The Netherlands, or both, and do a research project on a subject that was still quite vague: something to do with Calvinism, my Dutch roots in Michigan and The Netherlands, or some combination of the two.

But it was not until an incredible sabbatical research leave year in 2001 that this project in its present form began to take shape. Indeed, I kind of stumbled into the project by accident without fully intending to do what I did. During the first six months of that year, I lived in Vienna, Austria, and Budapest, Hungary, working on a project on EU/NATO enlargement. But while living there, I discovered firsthand how extensive the Protestant Reformation, including its Calvinist branch, had been in the Austro-Hungarian empire, how it had been frustrated, turned back, and all but snuffed out by the Catholic Counter-Reformation, and how Protestantism and the Calvinist churches had struggled against oppression and long odds ever since that time.

In September of that same year, I was in Brazil and then South Africa working on a project on comparative civil society in Third World nations. As a one-time Brazil specialist, I already knew a lot about the Dutch in Northeast Brazil in the seventeenth century. What was really intriguing—and a new research terrain for me—was South Africa. I was interested not only in the transition to majority black rule but also in the efforts of the white Afrikaner community to maintain somehow their culture and society even though outnumbered and outvoted by a ratio of ten-to-one.

The culmination of this incredible travel year was a long trip to Asia in October and November. Once again my research project—the political legacy of Portuguese rule in Asia—had nothing to do with the Dutch or the Dutch legacy. But wherever I went in Asia to investigate the Portuguese—Japan, Formosa, China, Hong Kong/Macao, India, Indonesia—I discovered the Dutch had also been there, usually immediately subsequently and in greater force. I had, of course, known about the Dutch in Indonesia but not much about Dutch explorations and colonization in these other areas. Here was a vast new research terrain for my Dutch/Calvinism project.

Finally, to complete this project, I traveled in 2004 and 2005 to Curaçao and Suriname. This was the first time I had actually traveled to a place specifically for this project, not as a sidebar to some other project. But even here, fortuitous circumstances entered: in Curaçao I discovered that one of my former students, Amy De Wendt, from the Foreign Service Institute, was the assistant consul; in Suriname, I found out that another former student, this time from the National War College, Marcia Barnes, was ambassador. Both these persons opened doors for me and were extremely generous in giving me their time and the time of their staffs to help me better understand the societies in which they were serving. Meanwhile, to complete the research, we had made updating trips back to The Netherlands, Geneva, and my old home territory in Western Michigan.

The Hartz Thesis

In this book we have used as our take-off point what we have called "the Hartz thesis." In his 1957 book on *The Liberal Tradition in America*, Harvard Professor Louis Hartz had described the unique features of American democracy as an offshoot of Northwest Europe (England, The Netherlands) without a feudal past. Hartz focused on American political culture—the values and beliefs of its citizens—and particularly their faith in America's representative, democratic institutions, which he called "liberal." Hartz argued that there was widespread consensus in America on these fundamental beliefs, that almost all Americans—from Adlai Stevenson to John Foster Dulles (if writing today Hartz would say everyone from George W. Bush to John Kerry)—were liberals. And that in this consensus on liberalism, America was unique among nations, and certainly unique among the nations formed by European colonialism.

A few years after *The Liberal Tradition*, Hartz published an edited volume, *The Founding of New Societies*, employing multiple authors, which expanded on the earlier argument by looking at America in comparative perspective. In this volume Hartz examined a number of offshoots ("fragments," he called them) of European civilization—Australia, Canada, Latin America, South Africa, the United States—and argued that these societies, naturally enough, tended to reflect the societies from which they were born. Australia, Canada, and the United States were, in the main, offshoots of British civilization, while South Africa reflected its Dutch colonial past and Latin America was a reflection of the Iberian nations of Spain and Portugal.

But Hartz had in mind saying something stronger than merely that colonies tend to reflect their mother countries. First, Hartz was interested in the particular histories, religions, ideas, and political sociologies—what we would today call their "political culture"—that the mother countries bequeathed to their colonies. He was especially interested, from his earlier *The Liberal Tradition*, in the underlying values, beliefs, and political ideas that the distinct colonists imbibed and carried with them from the mother countries. While also interested in, and by no means belittling them as unimportant, such factors as class structure, institutions, and the economic determinants of change, Hartz chose to focus on broadly defined political-culture variables. That has also been the main focus of this book.

Second, Hartz argued that his model of mother country-fragment relations had predictive value. He differentiated not only among colonial powers and their colonies but also in terms of the time period of their colonization efforts. He argued that the colony both reflected the values and institutions of the mother country and the values and institutions of the time period in which it was colonized. Thus, Latin America reflected the Spain and Portugal of the (pre-modern, still semi-feudal and semi-medieval) fifteenth and sixteenth centuries; South Africa reflected the Dutch Calvinist ideas of the seventeenth century; in contrast, the United States reflected English republican ideas of the seventeenth century; while Australia reflected the more radical and populist ideas of the French Revolution as they reverberated in England at the turn of the nineteenth century.

But then Hartz went a step farther. Not only did the colonies reflect the ideas and organizing principles of the mother countries, he said, but those

original ideas remained locked in place. While the mother countries continued to evolve in accord with broader European currents, the colonies they
had settled remained fixated on their original principles, struggling to preserve them even while the rest of the world passed them by. Thus, Latin
America remained locked into its sixteenth-century, quasi-medieval, semi-
feudal model; South Africa sought at all costs to preserve seventeenth-century Dutch Calvinism; the United States continued to adhere to sometimes
outmoded political principles from the eighteenth century; and Australia retained its radical, populist traditions even on into the age of large-scale bu-
reaucratization and organization. Hence, while the mother countries continued to change and modernize, the colonies they had founded clung to
often-outmoded ideas, practices, and institutions long after they had outlived
their relevance or usefulness.

One final element of the Hartz thesis commands our attention. Hartz was
particularly interested in the impact of colonization on native lands and peoples and the interaction—the warp and woof—of European ideas as they met
up with indigenous elements. That meant Indians in Latin America, blacks
in South Africa, much smaller numbers of Indians in North America, and
aborigines in Australia. Were these groups assimilated and integrated into
Western ways and to what extent; alternatively, did native peoples and their
practices affect how the Western ideas and institutions functioned far from
their European origins? In this way, Hartz built a dynamic, even dialectical,
factor into his thesis: how European ideas underwent modification as they
came in contact and interacted with native ways of doing things.

I have long been interested in the Hartz thesis, not least because I myself
am a product of one of the European fragments—in my case, a small Dutch
community set down in an isolated, far distant, mid-nineteenth-century
American soil. And as I have traveled around the world and encountered
other Dutch fragments—Curaçao, Suriname, South Africa, and Indonesia,
for instance—the Hartz thesis has stayed with me. Because my own experience, in part, reinforces Hartz's conclusions: South Africa exhibits strong aspects of its seventeenth-century, Dutch Calvinist past; my own background
in Western Michigan reflects the conservative, Calvinist Secession movement of mid-nineteenth-century Holland; Indonesia and Suriname are products of a particular kind of Dutch plantation society; while Curaçao and New
Amsterdam reflect their Dutch commercial backgrounds.

But in my travels and research, I recognized right away that the Hartz thesis needed to be modified, if not rejected, in certain particulars. I discovered
that the relations between colonies and mother country, the evolution of the
colonies themselves, their interrelations, and the dynamics of the mother

country, too—in this case focused only on The Netherlands—was much more complicated and varied than Hartz had portrayed. In some instances, the colonies actually surpassed the mother country; there were in the former colonies quite distinct forms of relations with native peoples; and the dynamics between Holland and its present or former fragments were infinitely complex. Hence, the idea for this writing project which is aimed not at reaching final conclusions, but at mapping the intellectual and research terrain and at suggesting research topics for future scholars. Both with regard to the Dutch and their colonies as well as other former colonial powers and their also quite variegated "fragments."

Research Findings and Conjectures

I grew up in Grand Rapids, Michigan, in the bosom of the Dutch (Christian) Reformed Church. The Dutch community in Western Michigan is very conservative, heavily (80 percent) Republican, and perhaps as or more religious than any other Dutch community in the world.

The origins of the Dutch community in Grand Rapids, often referred to by its members as "Zion," lie in the Secession movement in The Netherlands of the 1830s, and then the exodus of these conservative, breakaway (from the established state church) Calvinist Christians to the New World of America in the 1850s. There they faced extreme hardship and very difficult living conditions in an inhospitable, frontier community close by Lake Michigan. But the community, here as in Pella, Iowa; Sheboygan, Wisconsin; and Lynden, Washington, not only survived but eventually thrived and prospered in the American environment.

Today that community, especially in Western Michigan, is wealthy, strong, and conservative. While retaining much of its nineteenth-century and Kuyperian Dutch Calvinism, it has also been thoroughly modernized and Americanized. Its members are highly educated professionals or, as businessmen, own banks, car dealerships, and a myriad of family-based manufacturing plants—even while still refusing to open for business on Sunday. It is a prosperous, clean (in the Dutch way), peaceful, virtually crime-free community. In these ways, it conforms closely to the Hartz "fragments" thesis.

Yet in many ways the Dutch community in Michigan is no longer a mere fragment. Instead, it has surpassed the former mother country in many ways. It has a life and culture (American as well as Dutch Calvinist) of its own. It is successfully adapting to black, Hispanic, Korean, and other non-Dutch members—multiculturalism—in its midst. It is richer and more prosperous on a per capita basis than The Netherlands itself, and in many of its social programs, its concept of an "ownership society," and its outreach activities, it is more progressive than the "Old Country."

And, whereas religion seems to be a dying force in The Netherlands, in Western Michigan it is alive, vibrant, and, with its special music, dynamic leadership, and programs for youth, women, minorities, everyone, much more energetic than anything I have seen in the churches of Holland. In these and other ways the Dutch in Western Michigan on the road to progress may have passed the former mother country by. In this connection it was particularly striking to me that, when the Reformed churches of South Africa or Indonesia look for guidance, spiritual direction, or just fraternal brotherhood, they now look to Western Michigan and no longer to The Netherlands. The Western Michigan "former" fragment is now in the process of replacing the mother country as the leading center of Dutch and Calvinist culture in the world.

The East Coast or "Upper Hudson" Dutch in America, including New Amsterdam, are much closer to The Netherlands' Dutch and in striking contrast to the Western Michigan Dutch. They have been in America longer, since the seventeenth century, are so thoroughly assimilated and Americanized that they are nearly indistinguishable from other Americans, and have largely forgotten or abandoned their older, rock-ribbed Calvinism. Many of the East Coast Dutch no longer self-identify as Dutch and they have little ethnic solidarity; unlike the Western Michigan Dutch, they vote liberal and Democrat in the majority. When they attend church at all, their churches are more like establishment churches (Congregationalists, Presbyterians, even Anglican); they are poorly attended and with few programs. The East Coast Dutch have become, far more so than their Western Michigan counterparts, part of the great American melting pot, thoroughly integrated into American ways, and without strong ties any longer to The Netherlands or to Dutch Calvinism. There's not much of a specifically Dutch "fragment" here.

The mother country has been, to us, a disappointment. Viewed as "progressive" and exceedingly tolerant in the European context, to us it seems, with its heavy drug culture, euthanasia, socialized medicine, legalized prostitution, full frontal nudity on public television, such advanced social programs that they make a work-free life possible, and now legally recognized gay marriage, a country that has lost its way. Though prosperous and successful by most indices, The Netherlands over a thirty-four-year period beginning in the 1960s, seems to be a country that has abandoned its roots, its religion, its soul, and its historic work ethic.

The Netherlands is today a country shaken to its roots by the failure of its tolerance, assimilation, and socialization policies to absorb the large Muslim population (about 10 percent) in its midst. Instead of becoming "Good Dutchmen," many among the Muslim population have turned to radical Islam, and have rejected the hard-work ethos of Holland; and some have turned to extremism and terrorism. These events, particularly the killing of Dutch filmmaker Theo Van Gogh (a distant cousin of the artist) by an Islamic fanatic, have shaken The Netherlands to its very foundations.

So today the Dutch are engaged in a frantic process of self-examination that is examining all the basics of national life. The new introspection is unlikely to produce a revival of Dutch religion (although The Netherlands, especially in rural areas, is more church-going than a brief visit to Amsterdam would suggest and beneath the "anything goes" surface a majority of the Dutch people have held onto their disciplined Dutch values). But it may stimulate the Dutch to go back, reexamine, and re-identify with the culture of the past, including to some extent their Calvinist religious values and work ethic, which do, after all, remain the values of the majority.

Elsewhere in the Americas, the Dutch influence has largely faded. In Recife in Northeast Brazil, the Dutch conquest of 1624–1654 is now mainly of historical interest, something for the tourists, a way to stimulate Brazilian nationalism and, in some quarters, a certain nostalgia for what might have been if Brazil had remained a Dutch instead of a Portuguese colony. Suriname, though independent since 1975, has been able to continue milking Dutch guilt over racism, colonialism, and imperialism in the form of massive subsidies to this impoverished nation. The Dutch government is trying to rid itself of these commitments but, with one-third the Suriname population now living in Holland and strong family ties there, it is not certain the Dutch will be able to disassociate themselves from this legacy so quickly. However, the Dutch colony in Suriname is now very small; there is little Dutch presence left; and certainly I found very little lasting influence of either Dutch Calvinism or the Dutch work ethic. Meanwhile, America and the English language are gradually supplanting the Dutch influence.

The Dutch islands in the Caribbean—Aruba, Bonaire, Curaçao, St. Eustatius, Saba, half of St. Maarten—are a different story. They mainly are "Caribbean" in their racial and ethnic makeup, but they remain a part of metropolitan Holland. Their laws are Dutch, as we have recently learned from the case of missing American teenager Natalie Holloway; many of their administrative practices are Dutch; and, though largely self-governing, their governments are appointed by the Dutch monarchy. Educationally, in part culturally, in part politically, and in terms of their business and commerce, the islands are still strongly oriented toward Holland. There is a small Dutch community here and a struggling Dutch Reformed Church, but as in Suriname, both the Dutch population and the Dutch Calvinist Church are shrinking. Meanwhile, there, too, as the Dutch influence fades, the English language, American tourists, and American ways of doing things are slowly replacing the older Dutch influences.

Our travels next took us around East and Southeast Asia. In our research, we were in search of the legacy of Portuguese rule, but we mainly found the Dutch. Dejima Island in Nagasaki harbor was chiefly an important Dutch commercial entrepot in the seventeenth century (it is only of historical interest now) and, other than some Dutch words in the Japanese language, there is no real Dutch influence in modern-day Japan. There are small Dutch enclaves ("white tribes") in Macao/Hong Kong, India, Sri Lanka, and Malacca, but these are isolated and have no major and lasting impact on the culture, society, and future politics of these communities. Nor is the Dutch Calvinist religion of significance in any of these places, even among the few Dutch-descendant people who still live there.

Indonesia is another story. This was a major and highly valued Dutch colony. It was, like Suriname, a prized, but exploitive, plantation economy. But the Dutch left Indonesia in 1950 and Suriname a quarter of a century later so that, allowing for a single generation of difference, their histories are parallel. In Indonesia the Dutch language is now spoken only by a small, quite elderly minority; the Dutch cultural influence is similarly fading; and the Dutch Reformed Church is strong mainly among immigrant or separatist groups: the Chinese minority or the Protestant Moluccans. The old Dutch quarter near the port area is rundown; there is little Dutch architecture left; and even the famed Batavia Café has fallen on hard times.

There are still some enclaves of Dutch farmers and businessmen left, but they have no influence on the larger Indonesian culture, let alone its politics. There are Dutch tourists around for nostalgic reasons as well as the beaches; KLM Airlines still flies into Jakarta; and the Dutch embassy is still one of the larger ones. But the United States, Japan, China, and Australia are the main players at present in Indonesia; and once the present, still Dutch-speaking generation passes from the scene, the overall Dutch influence here will be almost nil. If we give Suriname twenty-five more years and, assuming the Dutch are by then successful in reducing their aid, Suriname will bear a close resemblance to Indonesia: little and fading Dutch influence. Both colonies, in addition, because of earlier colonialism, harbor bitter and strongly anti-Dutch attitudes.

South Africa is still another story. And like Grand Rapids, Suriname, or Indonesia, it is a wonderful test case for Hartz's fragments thesis. For here we have a small, Dutch, Calvinist community set down in the mid-seventeenth century in the wilds and wilderness at the tip of Southern Africa. Slowly that community spread out eastward and northward into even more isolated areas cut off from the main currents (the Enlightenment, the scientific and industrial revolutions, the movement toward limited self-government) of Western civilization. In these wilderness areas, the Dutch trekkers were attacked by disease and wild animals; they also ran up against the far more numerous black tribes of Southern Africa.

Living in not-so-splendid isolation for so long, the Dutch in South Africa learned independence and self-reliance. They were also cut off from the mother country and gradually developed their own language, Afrikaans, a derivative of Dutch, and culture. Their Calvinist religious beliefs continued to reflect the rigid, old-fashioned, seventeenth-century era in which the colony was founded.

When the British seized and colonized the Cape Colony in the nineteenth century, and the Dutch government failed to come to their defense, either then or in the Boer War at the turn of the twentieth century, the Dutch colonists were even more isolated and cut off from the mother country. Absorbing German Protestant and French Huguenot elements, the Dutch in South Africa became the Afrikaners—no longer Dutch. In 1911 the Union of South Africa was formed, independent from both Great Britain and The Netherlands.

Unhappily and unfortunately, the Calvinism of the Afrikaners was used to justify the oppressive apartheid system. Apartheid resulted in South Africa— and Calvinism itself—being cast as a pariah, isolated and condemned by the community of nations. It came close to producing civil war between blacks and whites. While internally the apartheid regime and its Calvinism had begun to undergo modernization and liberalization in the 1970s and 1980s, internationally it was strongly criticized—and in The Netherlands itself, which, after all, gave origin to this culture, the Afrikaners and their language were despised. Among thoughtful persons, this divorce between mother country and former colony was a terrible tragedy.

Today we have black majority rule in South Africa. Though economically still powerful, the "white tribe" of Afrikaners has been marginalized politically. Their churches, their language, their religion, their culture, even their lands and properties, are all under attack; Afrikaner civil society is similarly falling apart. Many Afrikaner young people, seeing no future for themselves in South Africa, would love to emigrate; but The Netherlands doesn't want them and in the United States any large-scale immigration of white South Africans is politically not feasible. So what kind of a "fragment" is this where the colony goes its own way for several centuries; the mother country no longer wants anything to do with it; and the Calvinism of the Afrikaners—and maybe Calvinism more generally—is cast out from the community of acceptable religious beliefs?

I said from the beginning that the chapters on Geneva and Hungary/Transylvania would be different from the others in this book. Neither of these is really a fragment of Dutch culture and civilization as are the other colonies and former colonies visited here. Geneva, after all, was the initial incubator of Calvinism; from there the Protestant beliefs spread to Holland and the Low Countries, not the other way around. But Geneva was for a long time a Calvinist bastion in an otherwise Roman Catholic area, and even today the religious, ethnic, and "tribal" politics of Geneva are indelibly shaped by this earlier religious history. One would need to be an anthropologist and sociologist, which I am not, to understand Genevan religious politics beneath the still summary presentation that I have provided.

Hungary comes closer to fitting the "fragments" thesis because of the many Dutch, Swiss, and German pastors who brought the Protestant Reformation to Central Europe. But mainly, Hungarian Protestantism was an indigenous phenomenon, popularized by Hungarian pastors, and closely tied in with Hungarian nationalism. The Counter-Reformation, and later Nazism and Communism, came close to eliminating the Hungarian Reformed Church. It is a weak church, not at all wealthy, and now facing the common European problems of rising secularism, indifference toward religion, generational changes, withdrawal of state funding, and shrinking congregations. It is nothing short of a miracle that the Hungarian Reformed denomination has survived all these onslaughts and still continues as a viable, if not exactly vibrant, church. A good approach here is not to think of Hungary as a "fragment" but as a national experience comparable to that of The Netherlands itself.

Wrapping Up

A number of common themes emerge from this exploration of the "Dutch Diaspora" and the fragments of Dutch culture and civilization in various parts of the world. One of these is the decline of religion in general under the impact of secularizing and modernizing trends, and of Calvinism, in particular. All over the world, in the various Dutch and Reformed enclaves explored here, the decline of religion is underway. Calvinism, particularly, because of its unpopular doctrine of predestination, its identification with apartheid, and its assumed hard and rock-ribbed conservatism, is under special attack. Western Michigan, of all the areas visited, remains the most religious, but even here the inroads of secularism, indifference, and alternative life styles are being felt.

Another common thread, related to the first, is the decline of Dutch culture, including language, in the various areas visited. What in Grand Rapids we call "Dutchiness" is in decline; in other areas it is in full retreat. By this we mean not just the Dutch language but also Dutch cooking, traditional Dutch ways of behaving (stubborn, hard-headed), the place of the Bible within the home, family prayers, obligations to keep the Sabbath holy (Sunday closing laws), prohibitions against gambling, drinking, and dancing—a whole collection of behaviors and expectations that grew out of the Dutch-Calvinist culture. Part of this decline is due to the passing of time and generations, part to Americanization (in the case of the East Coast and Western Michigan Dutch), part again to secularization, and part to rising pluralism, multiculturalism, globalization, and the erasure of old ethnic loyalties and behavior. Obviously, these trends affect many ethnic groups and not just the Dutch.

The result of these and other trends is that the previously distinct Dutch fragments throughout the world are becoming increasingly less "Dutch," less distinguishable and less distinct. The Dutch influence is increasingly less dynamic and vigorous and more a matter of purely historical interest. Dejima Island in Japan and Recife in Brazil are the most obvious cases, where the Dutch influence has been completely lost and is now remembered or captured only in museum displays. The East Coast Dutch in the United States have followed a similar trajectory, now so Americanized and assimilated that they have been completely absorbed into the American culture and their unique Dutch background all but completely forgotten. In Indonesia and Suriname similar processes are underway: once the present generation departs, almost no one will speak the Dutch language anymore; the Dutch Reformed religion will have been all but completely abandoned; Dutch architecture, Dutch foods, and Dutch culture will be gone. As a historian and one interested in Dutch civilization in all its dimensions, I lament the fading or passing of this tradition and its institutions, but I also understand the forces forever changing and undermining it.

There are three, maybe four, variations on this theme. First, the Dutch islands in the Caribbean, so long as they remain administrative units within the kingdom of The Netherlands, will retain Dutch law, courts, bureaucracy, etc., even though they are primarily Caribbean in culture and ethnicity. Second, South Africa, because of its peculiar history, still uses the Afrikaner (a derivative of Dutch) language—or at least some segments of the population do—and the Reformed Church is still a powerful cultural as well as religious force in the white community. Third, there is Western Michigan which, among all the fragments, is still closest to the Dutch Calvinist tradition and seeks vigorously to maintain it, perhaps now acquiring leadership among the various, scattered Dutch communities in the world. Finally, there is The Netherlands itself, which below the surface is more Calvinist than it would like to admit and which may experience, under fear of Islamic fundamentalist terrorism, a rebirth of interest in those ingredients that make the country uniquely Dutch.

While the influence of Dutch culture, the Dutch language, and the Dutch Reformed religion is certainly in decline at present all over the world, we may yet see a revival of interest in these themes—if only for historical interest, but maybe more than that. In my travels I have been surprised by the sheer numbers of Dutch tourists I have seen—in Dejima, Jakarta, Debrecen, Paramaribo, Cape Town, Curaçao, New York, and even Grand Rapids. In Curaçao—the wave of the future?—there is now even a Dutch-owned hotel, the Kurá Hulanda, that doubles as an anthropological museum, art gallery, and cultural experience designed to give Dutch tourists a certain flavor of the history (including especially in this museum the slave trade) of the islands. These Dutch tourists, like myself, are interested in both their roots and the various overseas branches of their culture; and in an era of "identity politics," rising interest in genealogy, and preoccupation with our roots and origins, we may yet see a revival of interest in, and a certain cultural flowering of, the Dutch diaspora. The various Dutch "fragments" throughout the globe may yet be rediscovered, as I have tried to do in this book.

This journey throughout the Dutch world has certainly been a learning experience for me. In the course of my travels, I have learned a great deal about the Dutch, Dutch culture, and my own roots. But there is still much to do. This effort has been part history, part social science, and part travelogue, but I am the first to acknowledge that I have just scratched the surface of a very large topic. We need far more in-depth studies of these various fragments, their relations with the mother country, how they are changing internally, and how The Netherlands is itself undergoing transformation. And, while we included here a comparative chapter on the Reformed Church in Hungary, why not other comparative studies of Calvinism and its fate in France, Belgium, Italy, and Germany? There is much yet to do, and it is a fascinating subject area; I commend a whole new generation of scholars to undertake the studies suggested here and everyone with Dutch background to "play tourist" as I have done and go out and explore your roots, origins, and branches in various parts of the world. Good travels!

Suggested Reading List

Boxer, C.R. 1973. *The Dutch in Brazil, 1624–1654*, by C. R. Boxer, Hamden, CT: Archon Books.

De Jong, L. 2002. *The Collapse of a Colonial Society: The Dutch in Indonesia During the Second World War*. Leiden : KITLV Press.

Goodfriend, Joyce D., ed. 2005. *Revisiting New Netherland: Perspectives on Early Dutch America*. Leiden, The Netherlands; Boston: Brill.

Goslinga, Cornelis Ch. 1990. *The Dutch in the Caribbean and in Surinam, 1791–1942*. Assen, Netherlands: Van Gorcum.

Gouda, Frances. 1995. *Dutch Culture Overseas: Colonial Practice in the Netherlands Indies, 1900–1942*. Amsterdam: Amsterdam University Press.

Hiss, Philip Hanson. 1943. *Netherlands America: The Dutch Territories in the West*. New York: Duell, Sloan and Pearce, 1943.

Hoefte, Rosemarijn, and Johanna Kardux, eds. 1994. *Connecting Cultures: The Netherlands in Five Centuries of Transatlantic Exchange*. Amsterdam: VU University Press.

Jacobs, Jaap. 2005. *New Netherland: A Dutch Colony in Seventeenth-Century America*. Leiden, the Netherlands; Boston: Brill.

Klatter-Folmer, Jetske, and Sjaak Kroon, eds. 1997. *Dutch Overseas: Studies in Maintenance and Loss of Dutch as an Immigrant Language*. Tilburg: Tilburg University Press.

Knight, G. Roger. 2000. *Narratives of Colonialism: Sugar, Java, and the Dutch*. Huntington, NY: Nova Science Publishers.

Kuperus, Tracy. 1999. *State, Civil Society, and Apartheid in South Africa: An Examination of Dutch Reformed Church-State Relations*. New York: St. Martin's Press.

Nooter, Eric, and Patricia U. Bonomi, eds. 1988. *Colonial Dutch Studies: An Interdisciplinary Approach*. New York: New York University Press.

Oostindie, Gert. 2005. *Paradise Overseas: The Dutch Caribbean: Colonialism and Its Transatlantic Legacies*. Oxford: Macmillan Caribbean.

Rink, Oliver. 1986. *Holland on the Hudson: An Economic and Social History of Dutch New York*. Ithaca, NY: Cornell University Press.

Schama, Simon. *The Embarrassment of Riches: An Interpretation of Dutch Culture in the Golden Age*. New York: Knopf, 1987.

Shorto, Russell. 2004. *The Island at the Center of the World: The Epic Story of Dutch Manhattan, the Forgotten Colony That Shaped America*. New York: Doubleday.

Stellingwerff, Johan, and Robert P. Swierenga, eds. 2004. *Iowa Letters: Dutch Immigrants on the American Frontier*. Grand Rapids, MI: Wiliam B. Eerdmans.

ten Harmsel, Larry. 2004. *Dutch in Michigan*. East Lansing: Michigan State University Press.

Theal, George McCall. 1969. *History of South Africa Under the Administration of the Dutch East India Company, 1652 to 1795*. New York: Negro Universities Press.

van Goor, Jurrien; with the assistance of Foskelien van Goor. Hilversum. 2004. *Prelude to Colonialism: The Dutch in Asia*. Hilverjum: Uitgeverij Verloren.

Index

About the Author

Howard J. Wiarda is the Dean Rusk Professor of International Relations and Head of the Department of International Affairs at the University of Georgia. He is also senior associate of the Center for Strategic and International Studies in Washington, D.C. Professor Wiarda is the author or editor of over sixty books and is recognized as one of the country's leading scholars on international—relations, comparative politics, and foreign policy. Of Dutch background—his grandparents emigrated from The Netherlands to the Dutch settlement in Western Michigan in the 1880s; he has visited and done research in all the Dutch enclaves described in this book: Brazil, Curaçao, Indonesia, South Africa, Suriname, New Amsterdam, and The Netherlands itself.